THE BIG BOOK OF
TEA COZIES

THE BIG BOOK OF
TEA COZIES

THE GUILD OF MASTER CRAFTSMAN
PUBLICATIONS

First published 2015 by
Guild of Master Craftsman Publications Ltd
Castle Place, 166 High Street
Lewes, East Sussex BN7 1XU

ISBN: 978-1-86108-961-8

A catalogue record for this book is available from the
British Library.

Publisher: Jonathan Bailey
Production Manager: Jim Bulley
Senior Project Editor: Sara Harper
Managing Art Editor: Gilda Pacitti
Designer: Ginny Zeal

Set in Gill Sans
Colour origination by GMC Reprographics
Printed and bound in China

Note
If you cannot find the yarn specified, you can use a
substitute of the same weight. Contact your yarn
supplier for advice.

Why we love tea cozies

SHARING A POT OF TEA IS A GESTURE OF FRIENDSHIP.
It is an opportunity to share exciting news, to have a reviving brew
at the end of the day, and it is the ideal way to welcome a visitor. Yet, as
we rush about, we so often only have time to dunk a teabag straight into
a mug and gulp down a few mouthfuls before hurrying out of the door.
The teapot is left forlorn, gathering dust at the back of the cupboard.

We think it's time to dust off the teapot, dress it up with a stylish cozy
and use it for its intended purpose. Why not invite your friends round
for a really delicious treat? What could be better than enjoying a lavish
spread of cakes alongside the iconic centrepiece: a steaming hot teapot
dressed for the occasion.

This bumper book of tea cozies brings you 75 eye-catching designs from
the finest yarn-craft authors, divided into five sections for quick reference.
Whether you want to dress up your teapot with hearts and flowers, knit
something timeless and classy, use up your yarn stash, remind yourself of
the great outdoors or just fancy something outrageously over the top,
you'll find all the inspiration you need in this book.

Contents

Simply Stylish

Geometric

38

39

40

41

42

43

44

45

46

47

48

49

50

51

52

53

55

54

56

57

59

58

60

Hearts & Flowers

Dress up your teapot and keep your brew piping hot with one of these gorgeous cozies.
You'll find plenty of inspiration to knit a cozy suitable for a lazy summer afternoon teatime treat,
a springtime special occasion or just to bring a splash of colour to a cold winter's day.

This beautiful cozy with its elaborate poppy flowers will bring a feeling of instant luxury to the most spartan of tea tables. The lining gives it extra insulation to keep your tea piping hot while you indulge.

Black poppy

Materials

Wendy Supreme Luxury Cotton DK, 100% mercerized cotton (219yd/201m per 100g ball):
2 balls in 1949 Poppy Red (A)
King Cole Bamboo Cotton DK, 50% bamboo viscose, 50% cotton (252yd/230m per 100g ball):
1 ball in 534 Black (B)
A pair each of 4.5mm (UK7:US7) and 3.75mm (UK9:US5) needles
4mm (UK8:USG/6) crochet hook

Spare needle or stitch holder
Small amount of wadding or wool tops for stuffing
Tapestry needle

Tension

19 sts and 23 rows to 4in (10cm) square over main pattern using Wendy Supreme Luxury Cotton DK yarn double and 4.5mm needles. Use larger or smaller needles if necessary to obtain the correct tension.

Pattern notes

The main body of the tea cozy and the lining are made with the yarn held double.

Body and lining (make 2)

With 4.5mm needles and yarn A held double, cast on 37 sts.

Row 1: P1, *k1 tbl, p1; rep from * to last st, p1.

Row 2: Knit.

These 2 rows form pattern.

Rep rows 1–2 18 more times ending with row 2 and RS facing for next row.

Transfer these sts to a spare needle or stitch holder.

Work second side of cozy the same, then place both pieces side by side and work joining row.

Joining row: Work 36 sts in pattern across first piece then purl last st and first st on second piece tog, cont in patt to end of row (73 sts).

Shape top

Row 1: P1, *skpo; rep from * to end (37 sts).

Row 2: Knit.

Rep these two rows three times more

until 6 sts rem. Break yarn leaving a long tail, thread tail through these sts and fasten off securely.

Work the lining of tea cozy in the same way.

Poppy bases (make 7)

With 4mm hook and B, and leaving a long tail, make 39ch.

Row 1: 1tr into 6th ch from hook, *1ch, miss 2ch, (1tr, 2ch, 1tr) into next ch; rep from * to end.

Row 2: 3ch (counts as 1tr), (1tr, 2ch, 2tr) into first ch sp, *1ch, (2tr, 2ch, 2tr) into next 2ch sp; rep from * to end of row.

Row 3: 3ch (counts as 1tr), 5tr into first 2ch sp, (1dc into next 1ch sp, 6tr into next 2ch sp) twice, (1dc into next 1ch sp, 8tr into next 2ch sp) four times, (1dc into next 1ch sp, 10tr into next 2ch sp) five times.

Fasten off and sew in small end.

Starting at centre with long tail, form poppy by coiling straight edge loosely around centre, catching down as you go. Do not cut yarn; leave at back of flower.

Poppy centres (make 7)

With 3.75mm needles and A, cast on 10 sts.

Row 1: Purl.

Row 2: Inc into every st (20 sts).

Work 7 rows in st st.

Next row: K2tog across row (10 sts). Leave a long tail and break yarn. Using a tapestry needle, run tail through all sts before sliding them off the needle, pull to gather tight and fasten securely. Sew up seam, stuff and then make a gathering stitch around base to close. Sew into centre of poppy base. With long tail of black yarn, come up where centre joins base then go down through hole in middle of centre. Repeat this seven more times equally round centre. Fasten off and weave in ends.

Making up

Join the side seams of the tea cozy and lining, leaving an opening for the handle and the spout.
Attach three poppies to each side of the tea cozy evenly and one in the centre at the top.
Finally, place the lining into the tea cozy with WS facing and slip stitch around the handle and spout openings and around the hem. Weave in all ends.

Tip
It will be easier to arrange and attach the decorations to the tea cozy if you place it over a teapot first.

The design of this elegant tea cozy is easy to tackle even if you are a beginner to crochet. You simply make the basic cozy and embroider the heart pattern onto it in cross stitch afterwards.

Cross stitch

Materials

Rico Design Essentials Cotton DK, 100% cotton (142yd/130m per 50g ball):
1 ball in 051 Nature (A)
Small amount of red embroidery thread or 4-ply cotton yarn (B)
3.5mm (UK9:USE/4) crochet hook
Stitch markers
Tapestry needle
2 x ½in (12.5mm) buttons
Sewing needle and thread

Tension

20 sts and 26 rows to 4in (10cm) square over dc using 3.5mm hook. Use a larger or smaller hook if necessary to obtain the correct tension.

THE BIG BOOK OF TEA COZIES

Tea cozy

Row 1: With 3.5mm hook and A, make 50ch.

Row 2 (WS): 1dc in 2nd ch from hook, 1dc into each ch to end, turn (49 sts).

Row 2 forms the pattern. Work a further 99 rows. Fasten off and weave in ends.

Buttonholes

Fold the work in half and, with a stitch marker, mark each end of the row. With WS facing, join yarn to the end stitch, 10ch, sl st back into row end. Rep on the other side to create buttonhole loops. Fasten off and weave in ends.

Cross-stitch pattern

The crocheted fabric forms the grid on which you will cross stitch. The corners of each 'square' are located on either side of a double crochet, horizontally, and over two rows of double crochet, vertically. Using the chart as a guide, work in cross stitch using B on both sides of the cozy.

Making up

With right sides together, push the buttonhole loops through to between the right sides of the crochet. Slip stitch both sides of the cozy together. Fasten off and weave in ends. Sew a button either side of the cozy eight rows below the buttonhole loops. Put the button through the buttonholes.

Cross-stitch chart

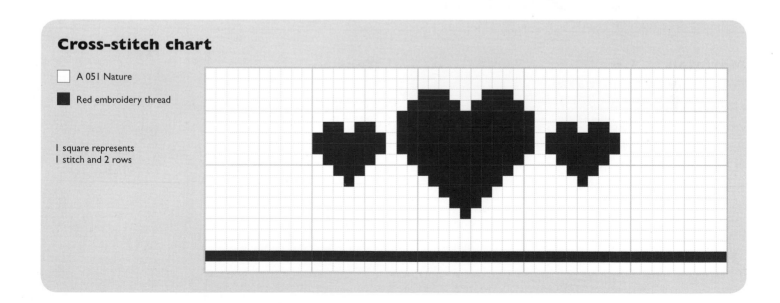

☐ A 051 Nature

■ Red embroidery thread

1 square represents
1 stitch and 2 rows

By using fresh spring colours, this crocheted tea cozy evokes a sea of bluebells in a woodland meadow. Make sure to space the bluebells when attaching them so as to create a natural effect.

Bluebells

Materials

Rowan Pure Wool DK, 100% wool
(137yd/125m per 50g ball):
2 balls in 019 Avocado (A)
Rowan Amy Butler Belle Organic DK, 50% cotton, 50% wool
(131yd/120m per 50g ball):
2 balls in 002 Cornflower (B)
3.5mm (UK9:USE/4) and 4mm (UK8:USG/6) crochet hooks
Tapestry needle

Tension

9 sts and 10½ rounds to 4in (10cm) square over treble st using 4mm hook. Use larger or smaller hook to obtain correct tension.

Special abbreviations

1cl: 1 cluster.
(Yarn round hook, insert hook into the 1ch, from behind the previous cluster, into the back of the stitch and out through the front of the work, draw loop through) 3 times, yarn round hook, draw through all loops on hook, 1ch.

Tr2inc: 2tr into next stitch (to increase).

Dc2inc: 2dc into next stitch (to increase).

Main part

With 4mm hook and A, wind yarn round finger a couple of times to form a ring.

Round 1: Into ring work 1dc, 2ch (to count as first tr), 17tr, sl st to top of 2ch. Pull tight on short end to close ring (18 sts).

Round 2: 3ch (to count as first tr), 1tr, tr2inc, *(yarn round hook, insert hook through top of next stitch, draw loop through) 3 times, yarn round hook, draw through all loops on hook, 1ch, (tr2inc) twice; rep from * 5 times, (yarn round hook, insert hook through top of next stitch, draw loop through) 3 times, yarn round hook, draw through all loops on hook, 1ch, sl st to third of 3ch (6 clusters and 24 tr).

Round 3: 3ch (to count as first tr), (tr2inc) twice, 1tr, *1cl, 1tr, (tr2inc) twice, 1tr; rep from * 5 times, 1cl, sl st to third of 3ch.

Round 4: 3ch (counts as first tr), 1tr, (tr2inc) twice, 2tr, *1cl, 2tr, (tr2inc) twice, 2tr; rep from * 5 times, 1cl, sl st to third of 3ch.

Round 5: 3ch (counts as first tr), 2tr, (tr2inc) twice, 3tr, *1cl, 3tr, (tr2inc) twice, 3tr; rep from * 5 times, 1cl. Sl st into third of 3ch (50 sts and 6 clusters).

Rounds 6–7: 3ch (to count as first tr), 9tr, *1cl, 10tr; rep from * 5 times, 1cl. Sl st into third of 3ch.

Divide for side openings

The following is worked in rows:

Row 8: Sl st across the next 6tr, 3ch (to count as first tr), 1tr in next 4tr, (1cl, 10tr) twice, 1cl, 5tr. Fasten off leaving the ends to be caught up and crocheted over, or woven in at the end.

Rows 9–10: With RS facing, rejoin yarn to the beginning of the last row. 3ch (to count as first tr), 1tr in next 4tr, (1cl, 10tr) twice, 1cl, 5tr. Fasten off.

Row 11 (inc): With RS facing, rejoin yarn to the beginning of the last row. 3ch (to count as first tr), 1tr, tr2inc, 2tr, *1cl, 4tr, (tr2inc) twice, 4tr; rep from * once more, 1cl, 2tr, tr2inc, 2tr. Fasten off.

Rows 12–15: With RS facing, rejoin yarn to beginning of the last row. 3ch (to count as first tr), 5tr, (1cl, 12tr) twice, 1cl, 6tr. Fasten off.

Complete other side

Turn the work over. Repeat rows 8–15 to match first side, omitting sl sts across the 6tr at the beginning of row 8.

Lower edge

The following is continued in rounds:

Round 16: With RS facing, rejoin yarn to beginning of last row. 3ch (to count as first tr), 5tr, *1cl, 12tr*; rep from * to * once more, 1cl, 6tr. Continuing onto the other side of work, 1tr into third of 3ch to join, 1tr into next 5tr; rep from * to * twice, 1cl, 6tr, sl st to third of 3ch on first side to join.

Rounds 17–18: 3ch (to count as first tr), 5tr, (1cl, 12tr) 5 times, 1cl, 6tr, sl st to third of 3ch. Fasten off and weave in ends.

Bluebells (make 30)

With 3.5mm hook and B, leaving a long length of yarn at the beginning of the work, make 4ch and join with a sl st to the first ch to form a ring.

Round 1: 1ch (does not count as a stitch), 5dc into ring.

Round 2: (Dc2inc) 5 times (10 sts).

Rounds 3–7: 10dc.

Shape petals

Round 8: *(1tr, 2dtr, 1tr) in next st, sl st in next st; rep from * 4 more times (5 petals).

Fasten off and weave in short end.

Leaf (make 24)

With 3.5mm hook and A, leaving a long length of yarn at the beginning of the work, make 20ch.

Work 1dc into the second ch from hook, *1dc in next ch, 1htr in next 3ch, 1tr in next 9ch, 1htr in next 3ch, 1dc in next ch*, 2dc in end ch; rep from * to * down reverse side of foundation ch, 1dc in next ch, sl st to first dc, fasten off. Weave in short end.

Making up

Using the tapestry needle and the long length of yarn left at the beginning of the bluebell, stitch it in place on the left side of the first cluster at the top of the cozy. Miss two clusters and sew the next bluebell to the right side of the next cluster. Stitch three more bluebells in the same way so they cascade down each side of the stem. There should be five flowers to each stem. Sew the leaves in between the bluebells, four to a stem, so they hang in the opposite direction to the flower above. The leaves will curl naturally.

Loop

With 3.5mm hook and A, make 12ch and join with a sl st to form a ring, make 1ch.
Into ring work 20 dc, sl st to first dc, fasten off and attach to the top of the cozy.

Bluebells

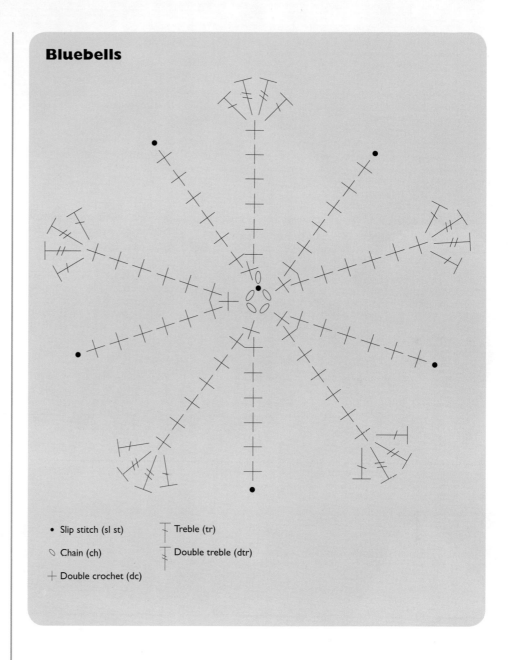

- • Slip stitch (sl st)
- ⬭ Chain (ch)
- ✚ Double crochet (dc)
- ⊤ Treble (tr)
- ⊤ Double treble (dtr)

A traditional Fair Isle pattern is used for this cozy. The yarn gives the surface a soft, blurred effect, with embroidered French knots for added texture. Using the Fair Isle stranded technique will add warmth to your cozy.

Fair Isle hearts

Materials

Rowan Alpaca Cotton, 72% alpaca, 28% cotton (148yd/135m per 50g ball):
1 ball in 400 Rice (A)
1 ball in 407 Smoked Salmon (B)
1 ball in 405 Storm (C)
1 ball in 411 Dark Damson (D)
A pair of 5mm (UK6:US8) needles
Embroidery needle
Darning needle

Tension

21sts and 20 rows to 4in (10cm) square over Fair Isle st st using 5mm needles. Use larger or smaller needles to obtain correct tension.

Pattern notes

The tea cozy is worked using the Fair Isle method (see page 352) and the intarsia method (see page 353), where separate balls of yarn are used for each block of colour. Read chart from right to left on right-side rows and from left to right on wrong-side rows.

Sides (make 2)

With 5mm needles and A, cast on 50 sts.

Row 1: K2, *p2, k2; rep from * to end.

Row 2: P2, *k2, p2; rep from * to end.

These 2 rows set rib. Repeat these 2 rows once more, then continue as follows.

Row 1: K1A, rep 16 sts row 1 of chart 3 times, k1A.

Row 2: K1A, rep 16 sts of row 2 of chart 3 times, k1A.

Keeping k1 st at each end of row, using the Fair Isle technique continue to follow chart until 39 rows have been completed.

Next row: Purl.

Eyelet row: Using A only, K2, *yf, k2tog, k3; rep from * to last 3 sts, yf, k2tog, k1.

Using A and starting with row 2 of rib border, work 4 rows in rib.

Next row: Join in C, and work 1 row in rib.

Cast off in rib using C.

Press according to ball band instructions.

Embroidery

With the embroidery needle and D, embroider French knots (see page 361) at the centre of the C diamonds.

Making up

Sew side seams, leaving gaps for the handle and spout.

Tie

Cut two strands each of A, B and C measuring 30in (75cm).
Make into a plait, knot at each end.
Thread through eyelets and tie at front.

Tip

Adding more embroidery or wooden beads can add texture and interest to the Fair Isle.

Fair Isle hearts chart
(16 sts x 39 rows)

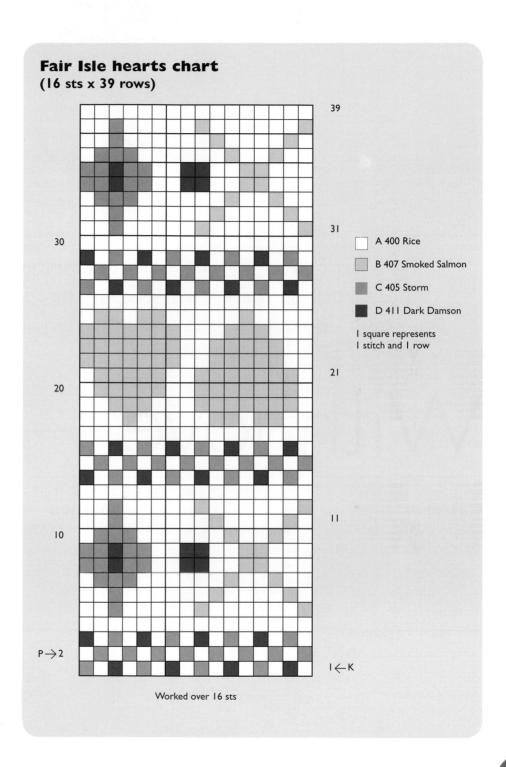

☐ A 400 Rice

▨ B 407 Smoked Salmon

▨ C 405 Storm

■ D 411 Dark Damson

1 square represents
1 stitch and 1 row

Worked over 16 sts

The heart on this design is worked separately and attached using blanket stitch, so there is no need for complicated colour changes. The yarn is held double so the resulting fabric is thick and fast to knit.

With love

Materials

Patons Fairytale Colour 4 Me DK, 100% wool (98yd/90m per 50g ball):

2 balls in 04962 Pale Pink (A)

Oddment of deep pink DK yarn for the heart (B)

A pair each of 4mm (UK8:US6) and 5mm (UK6:US8) needles

Stitch holder or spare needle

Tiny amount of washable polyester toy stuffing

Dressmaking pins

Tapestry needle

Tension

12 sts and 18 rows to 4in (10cm) square over st st using 5mm needles and yarn held double. Use larger or smaller needles if necessary to obtain the correct tension.

Tip

If you are worried about working the heart shape, decorate the cozy using a simple square in a contrasting colour or use a purchased motif.

Sides

Side 1

With 5mm needles and two strands of A, cast on 28 sts and work 4 rows in g-st.

Next row: Inc1, k across row until last st, inc1 (30 sts).

Work a further 7 rows in g-st.

Next row: Knit across.

Next row: K2, p to last 2 sts, k2.

Rep last 2 rows eight times. Work should measure 5in (12.5cm). Adjust length here if necessary.

Break off yarn and set stitches aside on a stitch holder or spare needle.

Side 2

Work as for side 1, but do not break off yarn.

Join sides

Knit across 30 sts of side 1, then knit across 30 sts of side 2 (60 sts).

Next row: Purl all sts.

Next row: (K4, skpo) to end (50 sts).

Next row: Purl.

Next row: (K3, skpo) to end (40 sts).

Next row: Purl.

Next row: (K2, skpo) to end (30 sts).

Next row: Purl all sts.

Next row: (K1, skpo) to end (20 sts).

Next row: Purl.

Next row: (Skpo) to end (10 sts).

Work 6 rows of st st on these 10 sts for spike.

Next row: (Skpo) to end (5 sts).

Next row: Purl.

Break off yarn, thread end through stitches and fasten off securely, leaving a long end for sewing up.

Heart motif

With 4mm needles and B, cast on 2 sts.

Row 1: Inc in first st, k1 (3 sts).

Row 2: Inc in first st, k2 (4 sts).

Row 3: Inc in first st, k3 (5 sts).

Cont in this way until there are 14 sts on needle.

Work 8 rows in g-st.

Next row: K2tog, k to last 2 sts, k2tog (12 sts).

Next row: Knit.

Next row: K2tog, k2, k2tog. Turn work, leaving last 6 sts on a stitch holder or spare length of yarn.

Next row: K4.

Next row: K2tog, k2.

Next row: K2tog, k1.

Cast off last 2 sts. Rejoin yarn to 6 sts set aside and complete in same way.

Making up

Join the garter-stitch sections at the bottom side edges of the cozy. Join the top side edges of the cozy to the start of the two-stitch garter-stitch border. Using the point of a knitting needle, insert a small amount of stuffing into the spike.

Catch the stitch in place from the inside, ensuring that no stitches show on the right side. Pin the heart motif in place and attach using blanket stitch (see page 360) and a length of matching yarn. Weave in all ends.

This fun and quirky cozy will bring a ray of sunshine and warmth to even the greyest winter's day. The vibrant sunflower design is decorated on top with wooden beads to represent seeds.

Sunny delight

Materials

Patons Washed Haze Aran, 50% cotton, 50% acrylic
(approx. 101yd/92m per 50g ball):
2 balls in Faded Green (A)
Patons DK Fab, 100% acrylic
(approx. 299yd/274m per 100g ball):
1 ball in 02305 Canary (B)
1 ball in 02357 Chocolate (C)
24 x ³⁄₁₆in (5mm) wooden beads
A pair of 4.5mm (UK7:US7) needles
4mm (UK8:USG/6) crochet hook

Tapestry needle
Sewing needle and thread

Tension

18 sts and 24 rows to 4in (10cm) square over st st using 4.5mm needles. Use larger or smaller needles to obtain correct tension.

Sunflower motif

Working with 2 strands of yarn throughout, make ring and work 6dc into ring, sl st into 1st st.

2nd round: Work 1dc into 1st dc, 2dc into next st, 1dc into next st until round worked, sl st into 1st st.

3rd round: Work 2dc into each st, sl st into 1st st.

4th round: As 2nd.

5th round (joining petals): Hold petal with RS facing, right side of sunflower middle, dc through petal and middle – 3dc to each petal. Space petals evenly round middle and sl st to first st.

Main piece (make 2)

With 4.5mm needles and A, cast on 43 sts.

1st row: *Pl, k1 tbl, rep from * ending on pl.

2nd row: Knit.

Work these two rows for 30 rows (adjustable) ending on a knit row. Leave sts on holder and work second side. With RS facing, knit across all sts from both sides.

Knit 1 row.

K2tog along next row (43 sts).

Next row: Knit.

Next row: K2tog 21 times, k1 (22 sts).

Next row: K2tog 11 times.

Next row: Knit.

Next row: K2tog 5 times, k1.

Next row: Knit.

Cut yarn and thread through sts, pull tight and stitch seams, leaving openings for spout and handle.

Petals (make 12)

With 4mm crochet hook and 2 strands of B, make 12 ch. Turn and dc into 2nd ch from hook, dc into each foundation chain, 9dc. Work 2 more dc into last ch space and dc into each ch on other side of foundation chain. Work 2 more dc into last space and dc into each st to end. Work 2 more dc into last st and dc into each st of previous round. Fasten off.

Making up

Sew beads into two circles on middle of sunflower motif and either sew the completed sunflower onto green tea cozy or crochet to top with dc all round middle, underneath petals to top of tea cozy (i.e., where shaping began). Neaten any remaining loose ends.

Folk motifs in warm bright colours form the design of this cheerful cozy, while embroidered flowers are scattered around the main motif and border. Use a smooth yarn to enhance the stitch definition in this pattern.

Folk flowers

Materials

Sublime Extra Fine Merino Wool DK, 100% extra fine merino (127yd/116m per 50g ball):
1 ball in 17 Redcurrant (A)
1 ball in 19 Waterleaf (B)
Sublime Cashmere Merino Silk DK, 75% extra fine merino, 20% silk, 5% cashmere (127yd/116m per 50g ball):
1 ball in 250 Pineapple (C)
1 ball in 03 Vanilla (D)
1 ball in 166 Pashmina (E)

A pair each of 3.75mm (UK9:US5) and 4mm (UK8:US6) needles
4mm (UK8:USG/6) crochet hook
Tapestry needle
Embroidery needle

Tension

22 sts and 28 rows to 4in (10cm) square over st st using 4mm needles. Use larger or smaller needles to obtain correct tension.

Pattern notes

The tea cozy is worked using the Fair Isle method (see page 352) and the intarsia method (see page 353), where separate balls of yarn are used for each block of colour. Read the chart from right to left on right-side rows and from left to right on wrong-side rows.

Sides (make 2)

With 3.75mm needles and A, cast on 47 sts using thumb method.
Knit 3 rows.
Purl 1 row.
Change to 4mm needles.
With RS facing for next row, beginning with a knit row and working in st st throughout, work 2 rows D, 2 rows A, 2 rows D and 4 rows A.

With RS facing, work the following:
Row 1: K19A, k9D, k19A.
Row 2: P19A, p9C, p19A.
These 2 rows set the position of the chart. Continue from row 3 of chart until row 32 has been completed.
With A only work 4 rows in st st.
With RS facing, work eyelet row as foll: yrn, k3; rep from * to last 3 sts, k3.

Beg with a purl row, cont in st st as follows:

Work 3 rows A, 2 rows D, 2 rows A, 2 rows D and 1 row A.

Change to 3.75mm needles and working with A only, cont as foll:

Next row: *P1, k1; rep from * to last st, p1.

Next row: *K1, p1; rep from * to last st, k1.

These 2 rows set rib.

Change to E.

Picot cast-off row: Cast off 4 sts in rib, *slip remaining st on the right-hand needle onto left-hand needle, cast on 2 sts, cast off 2 sts knitwise and 6 sts in rib; rep from * to end.

Embroidery

Embroider flowers using French knots (see page 361) for centres around main motif and on border.

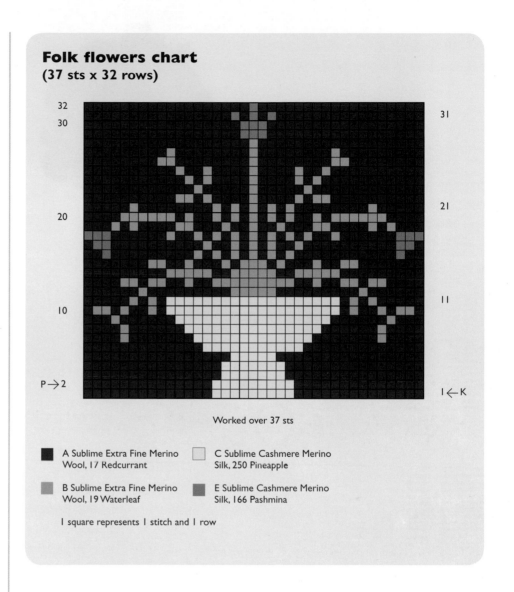

Folk flowers chart
(37 sts x 32 rows)

32
30
31
20
21
10
11
P→2
1←K

Worked over 37 sts

- ■ A Sublime Extra Fine Merino Wool, 17 Redcurrant
- ■ B Sublime Extra Fine Merino Wool, 19 Waterleaf
- □ C Sublime Cashmere Merino Silk, 250 Pineapple
- ■ E Sublime Cashmere Merino Silk, 166 Pashmina

1 square represents 1 stitch and 1 row

Making up

Press as given on ball band.
Sew up sides of cozy leaving a gap of 3½in (9cm) for spout and 4in (10cm) for handle.

Make a plait or crochet a length of chain using A, B and E together. Thread it through the eyelets at the top of the cozy beginning and ending at the spout end, pull it tight to fit teapot and tie into a bow.

This gorgeous pattern, with its profusion of tea roses, creates a very special and luxurious cozy that is sure to become a treasured item. The lining ensures that you'll have a well-insulated teapot.

Tea roses

Materials

Wendy Supreme Luxury Cotton DK, 100% mercerized cotton (219yd/201m per 100g ball):
2 balls in 1851 Cream (A)
Woolyknit DK Classics, 100% merino wool (106yd/96m per 50g ball):
12 balls in Red (B)
1 ball in Forest (C)
A pair of 4.5mm (UK7:US7) needles
Spare needle or stitch holder
Tapestry needle

Tension

19 sts and 23 rows to 4in (10cm) square over main pattern using Wendy Supreme Luxury Cotton DK yarn double and 4.5mm needles. Use larger or smaller needles if necessary to obtain the correct tension.

Pattern notes

Note that body and lining of cozy are made with yarn A held double. The flowers and leaves are knitted and then placed in a net bag, washing bag or pillowcase and lightly felted in a washing machine at 100–120°F (40–50°C), depending on your machine. Test a sample first to achieve the best results. If the pieces don't come out felted enough the first time, put them back in, maybe at a higher temperature. However, do not over-felt as the petals will fuse together.

Body and lining (make 2)

With 4.5mm needles and double strand of A, cast on 37 sts.

Row 1: P1, *k1 tbl, p1; rep from * to last st, p1.

Row 2: Knit.

These 2 rows form the pattern.

Rep rows 1 and 2, 18 more times, ending with row 2 and RS facing for next row. Transfer these sts to a spare needle or stitch holder.

Work second side of cozy the same, then place both side by side and work joining row.

Joining row: Work 36 sts in pattern across first piece then purl last st and first st on second piece together, cont in patt to end of row (73 sts).

Shape top

Row 1: P1, *skpo; rep from * to end (37 sts).

Row 2: Knit.

Rep these 2 rows three times more until 6 sts rem. Break yarn, leaving a long tail; thread tail through these sts and fasten off securely.

Work the lining of tea cozy in the same way.

Tea roses (make 37)

With 4.5mm needles and B, leave a long tail and cast on 6 sts.

Small petals

Row 1: Purl.

Row 2: Inc, k5 (7 sts).

Row 3: K1, p4, inc, p1 (8 sts).

Row 4: Inc, k7 (9 sts).

Work 4 rows in st st.

Row 9: K1, p5, p2tog, p1 (8 sts).

Row 10: K1, skpo, k5 (7 sts).

Row 11: K1, p3, p2tog, p1 (6 sts).

Rep rows 2–11 another three times (4 petals). Do not break yarn.

Medium petals

Carrying on from small petals:

Row 1: Inc, k5 (7 sts).

Row 2: K1, p4, inc, p1 (8 sts).

Row 3: Inc, k7 (9 sts).

Row 4: K1, p6, inc, p1 (10 sts).

Row 5: Inc, k9 (11 sts).

Work 4 rows in st st.

Row 10: K1, p7, p2tog, p1 (10 sts).

Row 11: K1, skpo, k7 (9 sts).

Row 12: K1, p5, p2tog, p1 (8 sts).

Row 13: K1, skpo, k5 (7 sts).

Row 14: K1, p3, p2tog, p1 (6 sts).

Rep rows 1–14 twice more (3 petals). Do not break off yarn.

Large petals

Carrying on from medium petals:

Row 1: Inc, k5 (7 sts).
Row 2: K1, p4, inc, p1 (8 sts).
Row 3: Inc, k7 (9 sts).
Row 4: K1, p6, inc, p1 (10 sts).
Row 5: Inc, k9 (11 sts).
Row 6: K1, p8, inc, p1 (12 sts).
Row 7: Inc, k11 (13 sts).
Work 8 rows in st st.
Row 16: K1, p9, p2tog, p1 (12 sts).
Row 17: K1, skpo, k9 (11 sts).
Row 18: K1, p7, p2tog, p1 (10 sts).
Row 19: K1, skpo, k7 (9 sts).
Row 20: K1, p5, p2tog, p1 (8 sts).
Row 21: K1, skpo, k5 (7 sts).
Row 22: K1, p3, p2tog, p1 (6 sts).
Rep rows 1–22 once more (2 petals).
Next row: Work 4 more rows, dec
1 st every row as above until 2 sts rem.
Fasten off.

Using the long end of yarn, starting at centre with the small petals and with the purl side facing outwards, form rose by coiling straight edge around itself. This should form a flat base that you catch together with a tapestry needle as you go. Pull out the centre petals slightly; the outer petals will curve outwards naturally.

Sew in ends, then place in a net bag and felt in a washing machine at 100–120°F (40–50°C).

Leaves (make 6)

With 4.5mm needles and C, cast on 3 sts.

Row 1 (RS): Knit.
Row 2: Inc twice, k1 (5 sts).
Row 3: K2, yf, sl1 p-wise, yb, k2.
Row 4: K1, inc twice, k2 (7 sts).
Row 5 and every odd row: K to centre st, yf, sl1 p-wise, yb, k to end.
Row 6: K2, inc twice, k3 (9 sts).
Row 8: K3, inc twice, k4 (11 sts).
Row 10: K4, inc twice, k5 (13 sts).
Row 12: K5, inc twice, K6 (15 sts).
Row 14: K6, inc twice, k7 (17 sts).
Work 7 rows in st st.
Row 22: K1, skpo, k11, k2tog, k1 (15 sts).
Row 24: K1, skpo, k9, k2tog, k1 (13 sts).
Row 26: K1, skpo, k7, k2tog, k1 (11 sts).
Row 28: K1, skpo, k5, k2tog, k1 (9 sts).
Row 30: K1, skpo, k3, k2tog, k1 (7 sts).
Row 32: K1, skpo, k1, k2tog, k1 (5 sts).
Row 34: K1, sl2, k1, p2sso, K1 (3 sts).
Row 36: K3tog, fasten off.
Sew in ends, place in a net bag and felt in washing machine at 100–120°F (40–50°C).

Making up

Join side seams of tea cozy and lining, leaving an opening for the handle and for the spout.
Attach the leaves around the top of the tea cozy with cast-on edges together in centre.
Starting at the base of the hem, arrange and attach roses to each side of the cozy as shown here:

Place the final rose in the centre of the leaves at the top and sew in place.
Finally, place the lining into the tea cozy with wrong sides facing and slip stitch (see page 355) around the handle and spout openings and around the hem.
Weave in all ends.

This ultra-simple design incorporates a heartfelt sentiment. You can personalize the cozy and show someone special how much you care by substituting their initial for the 'T'.

I love Tea

Materials

Rowan Handknit DK, 100% cotton (93yd/85m per 50g ball):
1 ball in 205 Linen (A)
Oddments of same yarn in 252 Black (B) and 215 Rosso (C)
A pair of 4.5mm (UK7:US7) needles
Tapestry needle

Tension

20 sts and 28 rows to 4in (10cm) square over st st using 4.5mm needles. Use larger or smaller needles to obtain correct tension.

Body (worked in one piece until end of rib)

Using A, cast on 82 sts and work 8 rows in g-st for lower edge.

Row 1: K41, turn leaving rem sts on holder. Work on these 41 sts for first side.

Row 2: k2, p to last 2 sts, k2.

Rows 3–8: Work in st st, keeping a 2-st g-st border at the end of every row.

Rows 9–22: Work motif from chart, placing it centrally. Transfer sts from holder to needle, then place sts from first side on holder. Work 21 rows in st st, keeping a 2-st g-st border at the end of every row.

Next row: P40, k1. Transfer 41 sts from holder to needle; k1, p40 on these sts.

Next RS row: K1,* (k6, k2tog); rep from * to last st, k1.

Next and alt rows (WS): P all sts.

Next RS row: K1,* (k5, k2tog); rep from * to last st, k1.

Next RS row: K1,* (k4, k2tog); rep from * to last st, k1.

Next RS row: K1,* (k3, k2tog); rep from * to last st, k1.

Next RS row: K1,* (k2, k2tog); rep from * to last st, k1.

Next RS row: K1,* (k1, k2tog); rep from * to last st, k1.

Next RS row: K1, *(k2tog); rep from * to last st, k1.

Loop yarn through rem st and pull tight.

Bobble

Using C, cast on 3 sts.

Row 1: Inc in first st, k1, inc in last st (5sts).

Row 2: P2 into first st, p1, p2 into next st, p1, p2 into next st (8sts).

Next row: K2tog, k1, k2tog, k1, k2tog (5sts).

Next row: P2tog, p1, p2tog (3sts). Cast off.

Tie knot through last st and use running stitch to go round the edge of knitted circle. Pull tight to form bobble.

Making up

Join top and bottom seam. Sew in ends.

I love tea chart
(27 sts x 15 rows)

Each square = 1 st and 1 row Read RS rows from R to L and WS rows from L to R

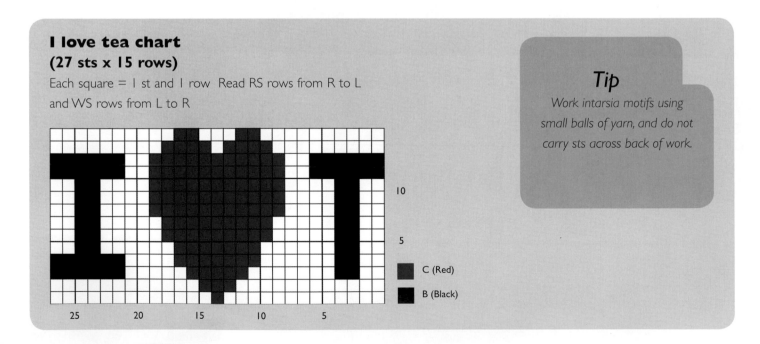

C (Red)

B (Black)

> ### Tip
> *Work intarsia motifs using small balls of yarn, and do not carry sts across back of work.*

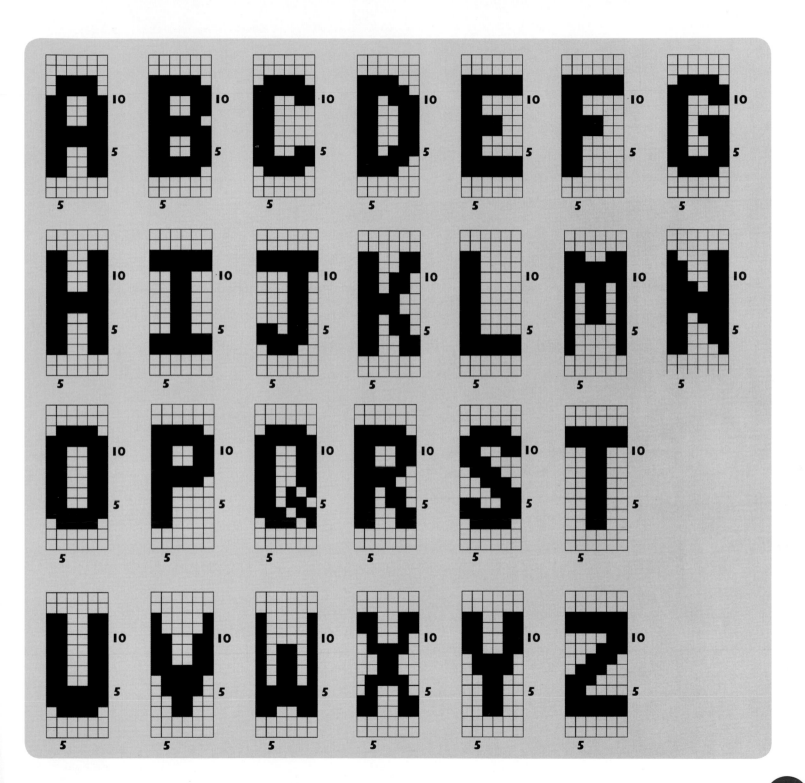

The body of this cozy knits up quickly in mega-chunky yarn, and it is lined for extra warmth. The flower design may look complicated, but is worked by simply casting on and casting off stitches.

Gerbera

Materials

Any mega-chunky wool or wool-mix yarn in denim blue (A): 2 x 50g balls or 1 x 100g ball
Oddment of DK yarn in bright pink for petals (B)
Oddment of 4-ply yarn in white for flower centre (C)
1 x 50g ball DK yarn in cream for lining (D)
A pair each of 6mm (UK4:US10), 4mm (UK8:US6) and 3.25mm (UK10:US3) needles
Spare needle or stitch holder
Dressmaking pins

Tapestry needle
Length of narrow pink ribbon for tie

Tension

Cozy: 11 sts to 4in (10cm) over st st using 6mm needles. Only the width is crucial. Use larger or smaller needles if necessary to obtain the correct tension.
Lining: 20 sts to 4in (10cm) over st st using 4mm needles. Only the width is crucial.

Tip

Using the cable cast-on method (see page 346) for this design creates a good firm edge with a twisted rope effect.

Sides

Side 1

With 6mm needles and A, cast on 27 sts and work 3½in (9cm) in st st, slipping the first st of every row to produce a tidy edge. Adjust length at this point if necessary. Break yarn and set aside sts on a spare needle or stitch holder.

Side 2

Work as side 1 from * to *. Do not break yarn. Knit across sts on needle, then knit across set-aside sts of side 1 (54 sts).

Next row: Purl.

Next row: (K7, k2tog) across row (48 sts).

Next row: Purl.

Next row: (K6, k2tog) across row (42 sts).

Cont as set, decreasing on every alt row until 18 sts rem.

Next row: Purl.

Next row (eyelets): K2, (yf, k2tog) to end.

Next row: Purl.

Next row: Inc in every st (36 sts). Beg with a knit row, work 6 rows of rev st st on these 36 sts. Cast off loosely.

Flower petals

With 4mm needles and B, cast on 11 sts, then cast them off immediately, *using loop left on needle, cast on 11 sts and cast them off immediately; rep from * 18 times. Break off yarn leaving a long thread, run through base of each petal in turn and draw up. Fan out petals, pin to front of work and sew in place.

Flower centre

With 3.25mm needles and C, and leaving a long end, cast on 6 sts.

Next row: Inc in each st (12 sts).

Next row: K to end.

Next row: (K1, inc in next st) to end (18 sts).

Next row: Knit.

Break off yarn and thread through all sts. Run long end through sts at cast-on end, join into a circle, pull tight and secure. Pull the length of yarn threaded through the sts into a circle and secure. Sew in place in centre of the petals.

Lining (make 2)

With 4mm needles and D, cast on 48 sts using cable cast-on and work 3in (7.5cm) in st st, ending on a purl row.

Next row: (K10, k2tog) across row (44 sts).

Next row: Purl across.

Next row: (K9, k2tog) across row (40 sts).

Next row: Purl across.

Cont as set until 12 sts rem. Cast off.

Making up

Join the lower side edges of the work for approx. ¾in (2cm). Join the top side edges for approx. 4in (10cm). Join the top and bottom side edges of the lining sections. Turn the work inside out and catch the lining neatly in place just inside the edges of the cozy. Turn the work right side out, thread the ribbon through the eyelets and tie in a bow, allowing the top section to roll over. Weave in all ends.

What better way to capture the essence of an English teatime in an English country garden than with a profusion of blooming roses? This gorgeous cozy will ensure your teapot takes pride of place on your table.

Rosy posy

Materials
Rowan Pure Wool DK, 100% wool
(137yd/125m per 50g ball):
6 balls in 026 Hyacinth (A)
Rowan Cashsoft DK, 57% merino, 33% microfibre,
10% cashmere (126yd/115m per 50g ball):
1 ball in 533 Gothic Green (B)
A pair each of 3.25mm (UK10:US3) and 4mm
(UK8:US6) needles
Darning needle

Tension
22 sts and 30 rows to 4in (10cm) square over st st using 4mm needles. Use larger or smaller needles to obtain correct tension.

Special abbreviations
Kfbf: Knit into the front, back and front again of the next stitch.
Kfb: Knit into the front and back of the next stitch.

Main part (make 2)

With 3.25mm needles and A, cast on 49 sts.

Knit 3 rows.

Change to 4mm needles and working in g-st, cont until work measures 3½in (9cm), ending with a WS row.

Begin shaping

Next row (RS) (dec): K1, k2tog, (k13, k2tog) 3 times, k1 (45 sts).

Knit 5 rows.

Next row (RS) (dec): K1, k2tog, k12, k2tog, k11, k2tog, k12, k2tog, k1 (41 sts).

Knit 5 rows.

Next row (RS) (dec): K1, k2tog, k10, k2tog, k11, k2tog, k10, k2tog, k1 (37 sts).

Knit 5 rows.

Next row (RS) (dec): K1, k2tog, (k9, k2tog) 3 times, k1 (33 sts).

Knit 5 rows.

Next row (RS) (dec): K1, k2tog, k8, k2tog, k7, k2tog, k8, k2tog, k1 (29 sts).

Knit 5 rows.

Next row (RS) (dec): K1, k2tog, k6, k2tog, k7, k2tog, k6, k2tog, k1 (25 sts).

Knit 5 rows.

Next row (RS) (dec): (K1, k2tog) 8 times, k1 (17 sts).

Next row (WS) (dec): K1, (k2tog) 3 times, k3tog, (k2tog) 3 times, k1 (9 sts).

Next row (RS) (dec): K1, (k2tog) 4 times (5 sts).

Thread yarn through remaining stitches, draw up and fasten off.

Make 1 more piece the same.

Rose (make 15)

With 4mm needles and A, cast on 4 sts.

Small petal

Row 1 (RS): Kfbf, k3 (6 sts).

Row 2 and every alternate row: K1, p to end.

Row 3: Kfbf, k5 (8 sts).

Row 5: Kfbf, k7 (10 sts).

Rows 7–9: Knit.

Row 11 (dec): Sl1, k2tog, psso, k7 (8 sts).

Row 13 (dec): Sl1, k2tog, psso, k5 (6 sts).

Medium petal

Row 15: As row 3 (8 sts).

Row 17: As row 5 (10 sts).

Row 19: Kfbf, k9 (12 sts).

Rows 21–25: Knit.

Row 27 (dec): Sl1, k2tog, psso, k9 (10 sts).

Rows 29–31: As rows 11–13.

Row 32: K1, p to end.

Rep rows 15–32 four more times.

Large petal

*Work from rows 15–19.

Next row: K1, p to end.

Next row (inc): Kfbf, k11 (14 sts).

Next row: K1, p to end.

Next row (inc): Kfbf, k13 (16 sts).

Work 9 rows in st st, ending with a wrong-side row.

Next row (dec): Sl1, k2tog, psso, k to end.

Next row: K1, p to end.

Rep last 2 rows until 6 sts remain*.

Rep from * to * twice more.

Next row (dec): Sl1, k2tog, psso, k3 (4 sts).

Next row: K1, p to end.

Next row (dec): Sl1, k2tog, psso, k1 (2 sts).

Next row: P2tog, fasten off.

Leaf (make 17)

With 4mm needles and B, cast on 3 sts.

Row 1: Kfb into first st, k1, kfb into last st (5 sts).

Row 2: Knit.

Repeat these 2 rows until there are 11 sts.

Knit 4 rows.

Next row: K2tog, k to last 2 sts, k2tog (9 sts).

Next row: Knit.

Repeat last 2 rows until there are 3 sts.

Next row: Sl1, K2tog, psso, fasten off.

Making up

Join the side seams of the main part, leaving an opening each side 1½in (4cm) from the lower edge and 3½in (9cm) from the top for the handle and spout. With WS of work facing out, wind the rose up from the cast-on sts, sewing in place at the straight edge as you go, ensuring that it is not too tightly wound. Gather the outside of the base and work a few stitches through the centre of the flower to pull it in. Shape the finished piece, curling the petals out, which the knitting will do naturally. Sew the roses onto the main part in a row of 4 across the bottom of each side, 3 in a line above and 1 on the top. Stitch a leaf to the base of each flower with 3 leaves around the single rose on the top.

The hearts on this stylish cozy are created using the intarsia colourwork technique. The yarn is an aran weight to give the cozy some substance and help keep your tea deliciously hot.

Love hearts

Materials

Rowan Pure Wool Aran, 100% wool
(186yd/170m per 100g ball):
1 ball in 670 Ivory (A)
1 ball in 679 Ember (B)
A pair each of 5mm (UK6:US8) and 4mm (UK8:US6) needles
Tapestry needle

Tension

18 sts and 24 rows to 4in (10cm) square over st st using 5mm needles. Use larger or smaller needles if necessary to obtain the correct tension.

Sides (make 2)

With 5mm needles and B, cast on 43 sts.

Knit 3 rows.

Join in A and work 2 rows in st st.

Starting with row 1 of chart, follow until completed, shaping as shown on chart.

Cast off.

Hearts (make 5)

With 4mm needles and B, cast on 2 sts.

Row 1: Inc in both sts (4 sts).

Row 2 (and every foll alt row): Knit.

Row 3: K1, M1, k2, M1, k1 (6 sts).

Row 5: K1, M1, k4, M1, k1 (8 sts).

Knit 3 rows.

Row 9: K2tog, k4, k2tog (6 sts).

Row 10: K1, k2tog, turn, cast off.

Join yarn to rem sts, k2tog, k1.

Cast off, leaving a length of yarn to sew to cozy.

Making up

Sew up side seams, leaving openings for the handle and the spout. Sew up the top seam.

Sew three of the hearts on top of the cozy, pulling through the yarn to secure.

Tie

Using three strands of B, 20in (50cm) long, make a plait. Secure to the top under the hearts, and then sew the remaining two hearts onto the ends of the plait. Weave in all ends.

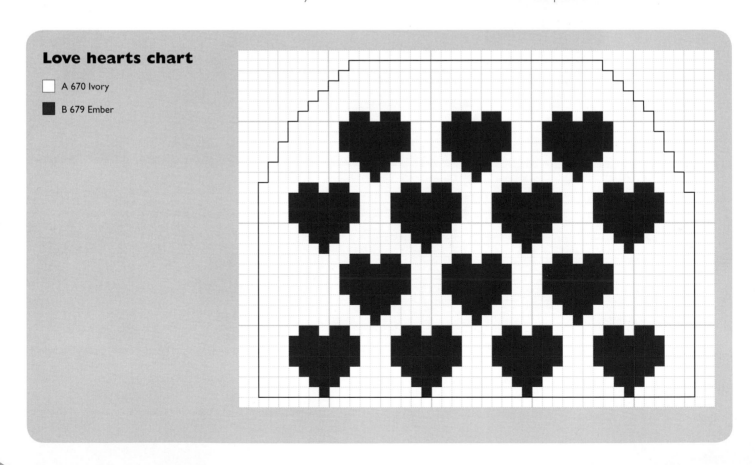

Love hearts chart

☐ A 670 Ivory

■ B 679 Ember

Bring the freshness of springtime to your tea table with this elegant cozy. Large 3D leaves form the body of the cozy while woodland-inspired primroses sit on the top and remind us of gentle country walks.

Primroses

Materials

Debbie Bliss Cashmerino Aran, 55% merino wool, 33% acrylic, 12% cashmere (98yd/90m per 50g ball):

2 balls in 202 Blue (A)

Sublime Extra Fine Merino Wool DK, 100% extra fine merino (127yd/116m per 50g ball):

1 ball in 19 Green (B)

1 ball in 203 Yellow (C)

A pair each of 5mm (UK6:US8), 4.5mm (UK7:US7) and 3.75mm (UK9:US5) needles

3mm (UK11:USC/2 or D/3) crochet hook

Darning needle

Tension

18 sts and 24 rows to 4in (10cm) square over st st using 5mm needles. Use larger or smaller needles to obtain correct tension.

Special abbreviations

M1: Pick up the horizontal yarn between the st just worked and the next st and knit into the back of it.

Skpo: Slip one st, knit next st and pass the slipped st over.

S2kpo: Slip two sts as if to knit two sts together, knit one st and pass the slipped sts over (2 sts decreased).

Wyif: With yarn in front.

Pattern notes

When working this pattern it is important to note that the stitch count will alter from row to row.

Sides (make 2)

With 4.5mm needles and A, cast on 41 sts.

Knit 3 rows.

Change to 5mm needles.

Purl 1 row.

Knit 1 row.

Now commence leaf pattern as follows:

Row 1 (RS): P4, *m1, yf, k1, yf, m1, p7; rep from * to end, finishing last repeat with p4 (61 sts).

Row 2: K4, *p5, k7; rep from * to end finishing last repeat with k4.

Row 3: P4, *k2, yf, k1, yf, k2, p7; rep from * to end, finishing last repeat with p4 (71 sts).

Row 4: K4, *p7, k7; rep from * to end, finishing last repeat with k4.

Row 5: P4, *k2tog, k1 yf, k1, yf, k1, skpo, p7; rep from * to end, finishing last repeat with p4.

Row 6: As row 4.

Row 7: P4, *k2tog, k3, skpo, p7; rep from * to end, finishing last repeat with p4 (61 sts).

Row 8: K4, *p5, k7, rep from * to end, finishing last repeat with k4.

Row 9: P4, *k2tog, k1, skpo, p7; rep from * to end, finishing last repeat with p4 (51 sts).

Row 10: K4, *p3, k7; rep from * to end, finishing last repeat with k4.

Row 11: P4, *s2kpo, p7; rep from * to end, finishing last repeat with p4 (41 sts).

Row 12: Knit.

Row 13: Purl.

Row 14: Knit.

Rows 15 to 28: Repeat rows 1 to 14, but instead of working p4 and k4 at the beginning and end of each row, work p8 and k8.

With row 28 of the leaf pattern completed and RS facing for next row, take the decreases being made into the pattern and work the following:

Decrease row: P1, p2tog, p1, *m1, yf, k1, yf, m1, p1, p2tog, p1, p2tog, p1; rep from * ending last repeat with p1, p2tog, p1 (51sts).

Next row: K3, *p5, k5; rep from * to end, finishing last repeat with k3.

Next row: P3, *k2, yf, k1, yf, k2, p5; rep from * to end, finishing last repeat with p3.

Next row: K3, *p7, k5; rep from * to end, finishing last repeat with k3.

Next row: P3, *k2tog, k1, yf, k1, yf, k1, skpo, p5; rep from * to end, finishing last repeat with p3.

Next row: K3, *p7, k5; rep from * to end, finishing last repeat with k3.

Decrease row: P3, *k2tog, k3, skpo, p1, p2tog, p2; rep from * ending last repeat with p3 (47 sts).

Next row: K3, *p5, k4; rep from * to end, finishing last repeat with k3.

Next row: P3, *k2tog, k1, skpo, p4; rep from * to end, finishing last repeat with p3.

Next row: K3, *p3, k4; rep from * to end, finishing last repeat with k3 (27 sts).

Decrease row: K2tog to last st, k1 (14 sts).

Purl 1 row.

Decrease row: K2tog to lend (7sts).

Leaving a length of yarn, thread through remaining sts and pull tight to secure.

Primrose flowers (make 3)

Stem

With 3mm hook and B, make a slip ring as follows:

Make a loop by wrapping yarn around forefinger, take loop off finger but still hold it between thumb and forefinger, insert hook through loop, yrh (1 loop on hook), draw through ring, yrh, draw through loop.

Now work 5dc into ring, pull the loose end firmly to close ring then sl st into first dc of round, do not turn.

Round 1: 1ch, 1dc into each dc of round, sl st into first dc of round, do not turn.

Round 2: As round 1.

Round 3: 1ch, 2dc into each dc of round, sl st into first dc of round (10dc).

Fasten off.

These rounds form a small tube.

With C and 3mm hook work into the back loops of the stem (the inner edge) on the last round worked as follows:

Petals

Row 1: Sl st into the first dc of round, 1dc into same place, 2dc into next dc, turn.

Row 2: 1ch, 1dc into each dc, turn.

Row 3: 1ch, 3dc into same place as 1ch, 1dc into next dc, 3dc into last dc, turn.

Row 4: 3ch, 1tr into next 2dc, sl st into next dc, 1tr into next 2dc, 3ch, sl st into top of tch of previous row. Fasten off.

Rejoin yarn to next dc on stem, work 1dc into this place, 2dc into next dc, turn. Now work from row 2 of first petal and complete as set. Repeat this 3 times more to form 5 petals in total.

Note: *To make it easier, sew in ends as you go along.*

Cut a small length of B, thread this around the top of the stem where the petals join, pull tight and secure.

Leaves (make 3)

Note: *The cast-on row is the outer edge of leaf.*

With 3.75mm needles and B, cast on 5 sts.

Foundation row (WS): Knit.

Row 1: K2, m1, wyif, sl1 purlwise, yb, m1, k2 (7 sts).

Row 2 and every foll alt row: Knit.

Row 3: K3, m1, wyif, sl1 purlwise, yb, m1, k3 (9 sts).

Row 5: K4, m1, wyif, sl1 purlwise, yb, m1, k4 (11 sts).

Row 7: K5, m1, wyif, sl1 purlwise, yb, m1, k5 (13 sts).

Rows 9, 11, 13 and 15: K6, wyif, sl1 purlwise, yb, k to end.

Row 17: K2tog, k to centre st, wyif, sl1 purlwise, yb, to last 2 sts, skpo (11 sts).

Row 19: K to centre st, wyif, sl1 purlwise, yb, k to end.

Rows 21 and 23: As row 17 (7 sts).

Row 25: As row 19.

Row 26: Knit.

Cast off knitwise.

Making up

Sew up sides of tea cozy leaving a gap of 3½in (9cm) for spout and 4in (10cm) for handle.

Place leaves around the centre top of the cozy, sew in place. Place the flowers centrally on top of the leaves to form a small posy and sew in place.

This cheerful design in garter stitch stretches to give a really snug fit, and the yarn is used double for extra warmth. The combination of fresh spring green and vibrant purple will brighten up any tea table.

Devon violets

Materials

Wendy Merino Bliss DK, 100% merino wool
(126yd/116m per 50g ball):
1 ball in 2359 Light Green (A)
Patons Fairytale Dreamtime 4 ply, 100% wool
(186yd/170m per 100g ball):
1 ball in 2942 Purple (B)
Oddment of yellow DK or 4 ply for flower centres
Oddment of dark green 4 ply for leaves
A pair each of 5.5mm (UK5:US9) and 4mm (UK8:US6) needles
4mm (UK8:USG/6) crochet hook for flowers
Darning needle

Tension

15 sts and 30 rows to 4in (10cm) square over g-st using 5.5mm needles and yarn double. Use larger or smaller needles if necessary to obtain the correct tension.

Special abbreviations

M1: Pick up loop between stitch just worked and next stitch and knit into the back of it to form an extra stitch.

Pattern notes

Yarn A is used double throughout.

Side 1

**With 4mm needles and A double, cast on 30 sts.
Work 4 rows in st st.
Picot row: K2, (yf, k2tog, K1) to last st, k1.
Work a further 4 rows in st st.
Change to 5.5mm needles and work 3½in (9cm) in g-st, ending with RS facing for next row**.
Break off yarn and leave sts on a spare needle.

Side 2

Work as side 1 from ** to **.

Join for top

Next row: Knit across all sts, then knit across sts of side 1 (60 sts).
Work 3 rows in g-st.

Shape top

Row 1: (K4, k2tog) to end (50 sts).
Next and every foll alt row: Knit.
Row 3: (K3, k2tog) to end (40 sts).
Row 5: (K2, k2tog) to end (30 sts).

Row 7: (K1, k2tog) to end (20 sts).
Row 9: (K2tog) to end (10 sts).
Row 10: Knit.
Next row: Work into front and back of every st (20 sts).
Work 7 rows in g-st.
Cast off.

Flowers (make 10–12)

With 4mm hook, make a loose loop of yellow yarn. Work 10 dc into the loop and sl st to join. Draw up loop tightly and knot ends of yarn securely. Change to B.
Petal row: (1dc, 1htr, 2tr, 1htr, 1dc) into first dc, 1dc into second dc; rep to end, sl st to join. Fasten off (5 petals made).

Leaves (make 6)

With 4mm needles and oddment of green, cast on 3 sts.
Row 1: Knit.
Row 2: Knit.
Row 3: K1, m1, k1, m1, k1 (5 sts).
Row 4: K2, p1, k2.
Row 5: K2, m1, k1, m1, k2 (7 sts).
Row 6: K3, p1, k3.
Row 7: K3, m1, k1, m1, k3 (9 sts).
Row 8: K4, p1, k4.
Row 9: K4, m1, k1, m1, k4 (11 sts).
Row 10: K5, p1, k5.
Row 11: K5, m1, k1, m1, k5 (13 sts).
Row 12: K6, p1, k6.
Row 13: Knit.

Row 14: As row 12.
Row 15: Knit.
Row 16: As row 12.
Row 17: Knit.
Row 18: As row 12.
Row 19 (dec): Skpo, knit to last 2 sts, k2tog (11 sts).
Row 20: K5, p1, k5.
Row 21: Skpo, knit to last 2 sts, k2tog (9 sts).
Row 20: K4, p1, k4.
Cont to dec in this way until 3 sts rem.
Work 4 rows in g-st.
Cast off, leaving a long end for sewing on leaf.

Making up

Press picot edge lightly, avoiding main garter-stitch section. Join picot section and first 2 rows of garter stitch. Fold back hem and catch stitch loosely in place on WS of work. Join sides of work from the top edge down, leaving a gap of approx. 2in (5cm) for the spout and handle. Adjust by trying on pot if possible. Allow the last few rows of the top edge to roll over and catch stitch invisibly in place. Pin flowers and leaves to top and sew neatly in place.

This gorgeous knitted fruit-topped design will bring back memories
of lazy summer afternoon cream teas, even if you're just grabbing
a quick cuppa and a biscuit in the depths of winter.

Strawberries & cream

Materials

Blue Sky Alpacas Organic Worsted (Aran) Cotton, 100% cotton
(150yd/137m per 100g ball):

1 ball in 80 Bone (A)

Rowan Handknit DK, 100% cotton (92yd/85m per 50g ball):

Small amount of 215 Red (B)

Small amount in 090 Green (C)

A pair each of 4.5mm (UK7:US7) and 3.25mm
(UK10:US3) needles

Small quantity of stuffing (kapok or an old pair of tights)

Tapestry needle

Tension

Not crucial as fabric is very stretchy.

Special abbreviations

Make bobble (MB): (Pl, kl, pl, kl, pl) into the same st
(5sts), then pass 2nd, 3rd, 4th and 5th sts (one at a time)
over the first st.

Sides (make 2)

With 4.5mm needles and A, cast on 43 sts and work in pattern.

Bobble rib pattern

Rows 1 and 5 (RS): *P1, k1; rep from * to last st, p1.

Rows 2, 4, 6 and 8 (WS): *K1, p1; rep from * to last st., k1.

Row 3 (1st bobble row): *P1, k1, MB; rep from * to last st, k1.

Row 7 (2nd bobble row): P1, *MB, p1, k1; rep from * to end.

These 8 rows form the patt.

Rep rows 1–8 once.

Now work in p1, k1 rib until work measures 6in (15cm) from cast-on row, ending with a WS row.

Note: *Adjust height here if necessary to suit the height of your teapot.*

Shape top

Row 1 (RS): P1, *skpo, p2tog; rep from * to last 2 sts, k2tog (22 sts).

Next row (WS): *P1, k1; rep from * to end.

Next row: P1, *skpo; p2tog; rep from * to last st, k1 (12 sts).

Next row: *P1, k1; rep from * to end.

Next row: (K2tog) 6 times.

Leave rem 6 sts on a stitch holder or spare needle, leaving a tail about 8in (20cm) long.

Complete second side to match the first, leaving final 6 sts on the needle.

Joining the sides

Working in k1, p1 rib, work across 6 sts left from second side, then pick up and work across 6 sts from holder, joining tail ends of yarn with a knot in centre of row (12 sts).

Work across these sts in k1, p1 rib for a further 7 rows.

Cast off in rib.

Strawberries (make 3)

With 3.25mm needles and B, cast on 10 sts.

Row 1: Knit.

Row 2: Purl.

Row 3: *K1, (p1, k1) into next st; rep from * to end (15 sts).

Row 4: Purl.

Row 5: *K1, (p1, k1) into next st; rep from * to last st, k1 (22 sts).

Row 6: Purl.

Row 7: *K3 B, join in C and k1, (k4 B, k1 C) 3 times, twisting yarns tog between cols to avoid holes, k3 B.

Row 8: *P2 B, p3 C; rep from * to last 2 sts, p2 B. Cut red yarn, leaving a tail about 8in (20cm) long.

Row 9: Using C, knit all sts.

Row 10: (P2tog) 11 times, (11sts).

Row 11: (K2tog) to last st, k1 (6sts).

Row 12: (P2tog) 3 times (3 sts).

Work 4 rows in st st over rem 3 sts. Cast off, leaving a tail about 8in (20cm) long.

Making up

Fold strawberry in half with right sides out. Using the green tail, join along stem edge and green part from the outside. Join the red part of the berry to about halfway, using the red tail. Fill with stuffing, then complete the seam and fasten off, pulling the strawberry to a point as you work.

Fold cozy in half, right sides facing. Use long ends to join across top of cast-off edge and side seams, leaving room for the spout and handle. Sew in ends. Sew the strawberries onto the top of the cozy, using the photograph for reference.

Simply Stylish

Check out these designs for timeless style. Whether you wish to knit a cozy to match your decor, recreate the atmosphere of an old-fashioned afternoon tea dance, or set a sophisticated mood, you'll find plenty of options to choose from.

Delicately smocked and decorated with pearly beads and silk ribbon, this stylish cozy would be perfect for a genteel afternoon tea party complete with fancy cakes and refined company.

Beaded beauty

Materials

Lang Baby Cotton Bambini, 100% cotton, or other 4-ply yarn (168yd/154m per 50g ball):

1 ball in 0001 White

A pair of 3.25mm (UK10:US3) needles

1yd (90cm) narrow ribbon

Approx. 44–48 large beads (used for bottom trim, see picture)

Approx. 100 small beads (used for main smocking trim, see picture)

Sewing needle and thread

Darning needle

Tension

24 sts and 32 rows to 4in (10cm) square over st st using 3.25mm needles. Use larger or smaller needles to obtain correct tension.

Smocked knitting

Knit the basic pattern in the usual way, in this case a 3 purl and 1 knit rib with additional knit stitches to show where ribs will be stitched together. Beads sit on top of each smocking stitch.

Sides (make 2)

With 3.25mm needles, cast on 69 sts.
Row 1: (RS) k1, (p3, k1) to end.
Row 2: P1 (k3, p1) to end.
Rows 3 & 4: As rows 1 & 2.
Row 5: As row 1.
Row 6: P1, (k3, p5) to last 4 sts, k3, p1.
Row 7: As row 1.

Row 8: As row 2.
Row 9: As row 1.
Row 10: P5, (k3, p5) to end.
Rep rows 1–10 until 50 rows have been worked.

Shape top

Row 1: K1, p2, k2tog, (p2, k2tog) to end.
Row 2: K3, p1, (k2, p1) to end.
Row 3: K1, (p1, yf, k2tog) to end.
Row 4: P1, k2 to end.
Row 5: P2 k1 to end.
Row 6–11: As rows 4 & 5, 3 times.
Cast off loosely in pattern.

Making up

Press lightly under a dry cloth using a cool iron. Sew pieces together, leaving an opening for spout and handle. Thread ribbon through eyelet row at top and tie in a bow.

To smock tea cozy

At rows 6 and 10 the pattern is set up to facilitate easy smocking.

1 Bring the darning needle up to the front of the work to the left of the rib st. Stitch into the knit st at the left across the front into the knit st at the right.

2 Pull the ribs together by tightening the st.

3 Add beads onto thread and repeat sewing.

4 Smocked fabric becomes heavy, firm and about 25 per cent narrower after it has been stitched so knit an extra-large tension swatch to account for this (if using finer wool, extra stitches will be needed). Lining optional.

The stitch used for this design produces a textured
fabric that looks just like a plump blackberry, but you could
substitute red yarn if you prefer raspberries!

Purple berry

Materials

Twilley's Freedom Spirit, 100% wool
(131yd/120m per 50g ball):
2 balls in 518 Purple Mix (used double throughout)
A pair each of 4.5mm (UK7:US7) and 5mm
(UK6:US8) needles
Darning needle

Tension

16 sts and 18 rows to 4in (10cm) over st st using
5mm needles. Use larger or smaller needles to obtain
correct tension.

Special abbreviations

Sl5wyif: Slip 5 sts with yarn held in front of work.
Skpo: Slip 1 st, k1, pass slipped st over.

Sides (make 2)

With 4.5mm needles and a strand of yarn from each ball, cast on 39 sts and work 4 rows in g-st. Change to 5mm needles and work in pattern for 40 rows (2 reps).

Buttterfly stitch pattern

Rows 1, 3, 5, 7 and 9 (RS): K2, *(sl5wyif, k5); rep from * to end, sl5wyif, k2.

Rows 2, 4, 6 and 8: K1, p to last st, p1.

Row 10 (RS): K1, p3, *(insert right needle up through the loose strands at the front of work and transfer them to the left needle, p the next st so the strands slip over the top and are held by it, p9); rep from * across row, ending last rep p4.

Rows 11, 13, 15, 17 and 19: K7, *(sl5wyif, k5); rep from *to last 2 sts, k2.

Rows 12, 14, 16 and 18: K1, p to last st, k1.

Row 20: K1, p8, *(insert right needle up through loose strands at front of work and transfer to left needle, p the next st so the strands slip over the top and are held by it, p9); rep from * ending last rep p8, k1.

Break off yarn and place sts on holder. Work the second side to match but do not break off yarn.

Joining the sides

Row 1: K2, *(sl5wyif, skpo, k1, k2tog); rep from * to last 7 sts, sl5wyif, sl1, k tog 1 st from needle and 1 st from holder, k1, cont from * to last 7 sts, sl5wyif, k2tog (64 sts).

Row 2: Purl.

Row 3: K2, (sl5wyif, k3); rep to last 6 sts, sl5wyif, k1 (64 sts).

Row 4: Purl.

Row 5: Skpo, *(sl5wyif, sl1, k2tog, psso); rep from * to last 6 sts, sl5wyif, k1 (49 sts).

Row 6: Purl all sts.

Row 7: K1, *(sl5wyif, k1) to end (49 sts).

Row 8: P3, *(insert RH needle up through loose strands at front of work and transfer them to LH needle, purl next st so they slip over the top and are held by it, p5); rep from * ending last rep p3.

Row 9: K1, *(skpo, k1, k2tog, k1) to end (33 sts).

Row 10: Purl.

Row 11: *(K1, skpo) to end (22 sts).

Row 12: Purl.

Row 13: (K2tog) to end (11 sts).

Row 14: Purl.

Row 15: Inc in each st to end (22 sts). Work 5 rows st st.
Cast off.

Making up

Sew in ends of yarn. Join from the bottom of the cozy (spout side) about ¾in (2cm). Join down from the top, letting the reverse st st roll over and leaving a gap of about 3in (7.5cm) for the spout.

> ### Tip
> Do not strand the yarn too loosely across the front of the work when slipping the 5 sts, or the fabric will not pull in when they are gathered together on the next row.

There's no right or wrong side to this cozy – the textured stitch produces a reversible fabric with embossed diamonds on one side and cabled diamonds on the other, so simply turn inside out for a different look.

Double diamonds

Materials
Sirdar Country Style DK, 40% nylon, 30% wool, 305 acrylic (170yd/155m per 50g ball):
2 balls in 423 Dusty Pink
A pair each of 3.25mm (UK10:US3) and 4mm (UK8:US6) needles

Tension
11 sts and 15 rows to 10cm square over st st using 4mm needles. Use larger or smaller needles to obtain correct tension.

Special abbreviations
Inc: Increase by working into front then back of stitch.
M1p: Increase by picking up the loop between the stitch just knitted and the next stitch, and purling into the back of it.
P2tog tbl: Purl 2 sts together through the back of the loops.

Sides (make 2)

With 3.25mm needles and the thumb method, cast on 41 sts and work 5 rows in k1, p1 rib.

Next row: *Rib 3, inc in next st; rep from * to last st, k1 (51 sts).

Change to 4mm needles and foll the 20-row diamond patt, noting that all incs are made purlwise (m1p).

Diamond pattern

Row 1: K8, (p3, k1, p3, k11) twice, p3, k4.

Row 2: K3, (p1, m1p, k3, p2tog, p7, p2tog tbl, k3, m1p) twice, p1, m1p, k3, p2tog, p3, K3.

Row 3: K7, (p3, k3, p3, k9) twice, p3, k5.

Row 4: K3, p2, (m1p, k3, p2tog, p5, p2tog tbl, k3, m1p, p3) twice, m1p, k3, p2tog, p2, k3.

Row 5: K6, (p3, k5, p3, k7) twice, p3, k6.

Row 6: K3, p3, (m1p, k3, p2tog, p3, p2tog tbl, k3, m1p, p5) twice, m1p, k3, p2tog, p1, k3.

Row 7: K5, (p3, k7, p3, k5) twice, p3, k7.

Row 8: K3, p4, (m1p, k3, p2tog, p1, p2tog tbl, k3, m1p, p7) twice, m1p, k3, p2tog, k3.

Row 9: K4, (p3, k9, p3, k3) twice, p3, k8.

Row 10: K3, p5, (m1p, k3, p3tog, k3, m1p, p9) twice, m1p, k3, p2tog, k2.

Row 11: K3, (p3, k11, p3, k1) twice, p3, k9.

Row 12: K3, p4, (p2tog tbl, k3, m1p, p1, m1p, k3, p2tog, p7) twice, p2togtbl, k3, m1p, k3.

Row 13: K4, (p3, k9, p3, k3) twice, p3, k8.

Row 14: K3, p3, (p2tog tbl, k3, m1p, p3, m1p, k3, p2tog, p5) twice, p2togtbl, k3, m1p, p1, k3.

Row 15: K5, (p3, k7, p3, k5) twice, p3, k7.

Row 16: K3, p2, (p2tog tbl, k3, m1p, p5, m1, k3, p2tog, p3) twice, p2togtbl, k3, m1p, p2, k3.

Row 17: K6, (p3, k5, p3, k7) twice, p3, k6.

Row 18: K3, p1, (p2tog tbl, k3, m1p, p7, m1p, k3, p2tog, p1) twice, p2togtbl, k3, m1p, p3, k3.

Row 19: K7, (p3, k3, p3, k9) twice, p3, k5.

Row 20: K3, p2tog tbl, (k3, m1p, p9, m1p, k3, p3tog) twice, k3, m1p, p4, k3. Work 30 rows in this diamond patt. Change to 3.25mm needles and work 20 further rows in patt.

Decrease for top

Work in g-st throughout.

Next row: K1, *k2tog, rep from * to end (26 sts).

Knit 4 rows.

Next row: *k2tog, rep from * to end (13 sts).

Knit 4 rows.

Next row: *k1, k2tog, rep from * to end (9 sts).

Knit 3 rows.

Cast off loosely using a 4mm needle.

Making up

Join seam for 1¼in (3cm) at the lower edge and 2½in (6cm) at the top for the handle seam. Join 1in (2.5cm) at the lower edge and 4in (10cm) at the top for spout seam. These measurements are approx.imate: try the cozy on the pot and adjust as necessary before fastening off.

Sometimes you really do want no fuss, no frills and no decorations. This simple design in chunky yarn is an ideal bazaar item or would make a great gift for anyone who prefers the minimalist look.

No frills

Materials
Any chunky yarn or DK yarn (used double):
Approx. 1 ball in red
A pair of 5mm (UK6:US8) needles
Darning needle

Tension
15 sts and 20 rows to 4in (10cm) square over st st on 5mm needles. Use larger or smaller needles to obtain correct tension.

Sides (make 2)

With 5mm needles, cast on 31 sts and work 4 rows in g-st.

Now work in st st with a 2-st g-st border thus:

Row 1: K across.

Row 2: K2, p to last 2 sts, k2.

Rep these 2 rows 8 times more (18 rows in total).

Break off yarn and leave sts on a spare needle.

Complete second side to match but do not break off yarn.

Next row: K30, then k2tog using last st from this needle and first st from spare needle, k across rem sts on spare needle (61 sts).

Purl 1 row.

Shape top

Next row: *(k8, skpo); rep from * to last st, k1.

Next and alt rows: P all sts.

Next row: *(k7, skpo); rep from * to last st, k1.

Cont as set until the row *(k1, skpo); rep from * to last st has been worked.

Knit one row.

Cast off.

Making up

Join garter stitch lower border. Join handle side from the top down to just above where the 2-st g-st border begins, leaving a hole for the knob of the teapot. Sew in ends of yarn.

Spoil yourself with this delicate cabled design. The luxurious alpaca and merino-mix yarn is gorgeous to look at, sumptuously soft, strong and warm, and is perfectly complemented by the toning velvet ribbon.

Simply soft

Materials

UK Alpaca Luxury Knit DK, 80% baby alpaca, 20% merino (122yd/112m per 50g ball):

2 balls in 03 Fawn

A pair of 3.75mm (UK9:US5) needles

Cable needle

Darning needle

1yd (90cm) narrow velvet ribbon

Tension

23 sts and 32 rows to 4in (10cm) over st st using 3.75mm needles. Use larger or smaller needles to obtain correct tension.

Sides (make 2)

With 3.75mm needles, cast on 72 sts and knit 4 rows.

Cable pattern

Row 1: K1, *(k2, p2); rep from * to last 3 sts, k3.

Row 2: K1, P2 *(k2, p2): rep from * to last st, k1.

Row 3: (cable row): K3, *(p2, C6B); rep from * to last 5 sts, p2, k3.

Row 4: As Row 2.

Rows 5 & 7: As Row 1.

Rows 6 & 8: As Row 2.

These 8 rows form the patt. Rep until work measures 6in (15cm), ending with a cable row.

Note: *If your teapot is taller or shorter than a standard model, adjust the length here by working more or fewer rows.*

Shape top

First dec row: (WS) K1, p2, k2, p2tog, *(p2, p2tog, k2, p2tog); rep from * to last 5 sts; k2, p2tog, k1 (55 sts).

Second dec row: K2, *(p2tog, k4); rep from * to last 5 sts, p2tog, k3 (46 sts).

First eyelet row: (WS): K1, p2, *(yo, p2tog, p3); rep from * to last 5 sts, p2tog, yrn, p2tog, k1.

Beg with a knit row, work 8 rows st st.

Picot edging

Next row (RS): K1, *(k2tog, yo); rep. from * to last st, k1.

Beg with a purl row, work 8 rows st st.

Second eyelet row (WS): K1, p2, *(yo, p2tog, p3); rep from * to last 5 sts, p2tog, yo k1.

Beg with a knit row, work 4 rows st st. Cast off.

Making up

Press the tops of both sides of the cozy from the eyelet rows up. With right sides together, join side seams from the top down to 1in (2.5cm) below the first eyelet row. With work still inside out, fold top section down along picot edging row, so the picot edge is at the top. Sew cast-off edges to the wrong side of work, then turn work to the right side. Thread ribbon through eyelets and draw up into a bow. Try cozy on the pot for size and measure seams below the handle and spout, then join from the wrong side.

> ### Tip
> *When attaching the edgings, place a spare needle through both sets of eyelets. This will keep them aligned and hold the work flat, making it easier to thread the ribbon through later.*

This textured wool-mix cozy knitted in a versatile bulky yarn will cover your teapot in restrained charm, and the shaggy pompom and pretty buttons add interesting details.

Peruvian pompom

Materials

Sirdar Peru Naturals, 64% wool, 31% acrylic, 5% alpaca (98yd/90m per 50g skein):

1 skein in 0555 Pico (A)

1 skein in 0550 Andean White (B)

A pair of 6mm (UK4:US10) bamboo needles

5mm (UK10:USD/3) crochet hook

3 x buttons

Sewing needle and thread

Tapestry needle

Tension

18 sts x 36 rows to 4in (10cm) square over patt using 6mm needles (yarns used double throughout). Use larger or smaller needles to obtain correct tension.

Special abbreviations

Sl1p: Slip 1 st purlwise (with yarn in front of work).

Pattern notes

Use yarns double. You can divide each ball into two smaller balls before you start. Wind the strands together on one ball before you begin to knit.

Sides (make 2)

With 6mm needles and two strands of A, cast on 38 sts and work in patt thus:

Pattern

Row 1: Using A, *(k1, sl1p), rep from * to end.
Row 2: Using B, *(sl1p, k1), rep from * to end.
Row 3: Using B, *(sl1p, k1); rep from * to end.
Row 4: Using A, *(k1, sl1p); rep from * to end.
These four rows form the pattern.
Rep patt for a further 32 rows.

Decrease for top

Row 37: Ssk, *(k1, sl1p); rep from * to last 2 sts, k2tog (36 sts).
Row 38: Ssk, k1, *(sl1p, k1); rep from * to last 3 sts, sl1p, k2tog (34 sts).
Row 39: Ssk, *(sl1p, k1); rep from * to last 2 sts, k2tog (32 sts).
Row 40: Ssk, sl1p, *(k1, sl1p); rep from * to last 3 sts, k1. K2tog (30 sts).
Rows 41–49 inclusive: Cont in patt with no decs.
Row 50: Ssk, *(sl1p, k1); rep from * to last 2 sts, k2tog.

Row 51: Ssk, k1, *(sl1p, k1); rep from * to last 3 sts, sl1p, k2tog (26 sts).
Row 52: Ssk, *(k1, sl1p); rep from * to last 2 sts, k2tog (24 sts).
Row 53: Ssk, sl1p, *(k1, sl1p); rep from * to last 3 sts, sl1p, k2tog (22 sts).
Row 54: Ssk, *(sl1p, k1); rep from * to last 2 sts, k2tog (20 sts).
Row 55: Ssk, k1, *(sl1p, k1); rep from * to last 3 sts, sl1, k2tog (18 sts).
Row 56: Ssk. *(k1, sl1p); rep from * to last 2 sts, k2tog (16 sts).
Row 57: Ssk, sl1p, *(k1, sl1p); rep from * to last 3 sts, k1, k2tog (14 sts).
Row 58: Ssk, *(sl1p, k1); rep from * to last 2 sts, k2tog (12 sts).
Row 59: K1, *(sl1p, k1); rep from * to last st, sl1p.
Row 60: Sl1p, *(k1, sl1p) to last st, k1.
Row 61: Sl1p, *(k1, sl1p); rep from * to last st, k1.
Row 62: K1, *(sl1p, k1); rep from * to last st, sl1p.
Row 63: K1, *(sl1p, k1); rep from * to last st, k1.
Cast off using A.

Making up

Join sides on the spout edge, leaving a gap for the spout. Join all the way to the top, across the cast-off edges and about ⅜in (1cm) down handle side.

Crocheted border

Beg at lower edge on one side, work a dc border round handle side to neaten edges, dec by working 3 sts tog at the top to stop it splaying out. Make 14-ch button loops above the handle, in the centre of the handle and at the lower edge. After each chain loop, work 1 dc back into the same st and cont in dc. Work dc round spout side, dec at top and lower edge as before.

Attach buttons. Sew in yarn ends. Make a fairly loose pompom (see page 363) using both yarns and attach to the top of the cozy.

This lacy pattern worked with yarn used double produces a lovely textured design, and the lining adds even more warmth to keep your tea piping hot. Using a contrasting shade for the lining adds extra interest.

Chunky lace

Materials

Jamieson & Smith Shetland Aran, 100% wool
(98yd/90m per 50g ball):
2 balls in BSS 1 Blue
Any fine DK yarn:
1 ball in pink for lining
A pair each of 6mm (UK4:US10) and 4mm
(UK8:US6) needles
Darning needle

Tension

17 sts and 17 rows to 4in (10cm) square over patt using 6mm needles and yarn double for main part.
20 sts to 4in (10cm) over st st using 4mm needles for lining.
Use larger or smaller needles to obtain correct tension.

Pattern notes

The lace pattern is a little tricky so you will need to pay close attention to your work, noting especially the variation at the end of row 12.

Side 1

**With 6mm needles and yarn double, cast on 29 sts and work in single rib thus:

Row 1: (K1, p1) to last st, k1.

Row 2: (P1, k1) to last st, p1.

Rep rows 1 and 2 once.

Row 5: Inc in first st, rib across to last st, inc in last st (31 sts).

Now work in pattern with a 2-st g-st border thus:

Pattern

Row 1 (WS): K2, p3, *k3, p3; rep from * to last 2 sts, k2.

Row 2: K5, *p2tog, yrn, p1, k3; rep from * to last 2 sts, k2.

Row 3: As row 1.

Row 4: K5, *p1, yrn, p2tog, k3; rep from * to last 2 sts, k2.

Row 5: As row 1.

Row 6: K3, k2tog, *(p1, yrn) twice, p1, sl1, k2tog, psso; rep from * to last 5 sts, skpo, k3.

Row 7: K5, *p3, k3; rep from * to last 2 sts, k2.

Row 8: K2, p1, yrn, p2tog, *k3, p1, yrn, p2tog; rep from * to last 2 sts, k2.

Row 9: As row 7.

Row 10: K2, p2tog, yrn, p1, *k3, p2tog, yrn, p1; rep from * to last 2 sts, k2.

Row 11: As row 7.

Row 12: K2, p2, yrn, p1, *sl1, k2tog, psso, (p1, yrn) twice, p1; rep from * to last 8 sts, sl1, k2tog, psso, p1, yrn, p2, k2.

These 12 rows form pattern.

Rep 12 rows of patt once, ending with WS facing for next row**. Break off yarn and leave sts on a spare needle.

Side 2

Work as for side 1 from ** to ** but do not break off yarn.

Join for top

Row 1 (WS): K2, p3, *k3, p3; rep from * to last 2 sts, k2tog; now work across sts of first side thus: k2, *(p3, k3); rep from * to last 5 sts, p3, k2 (61 sts).

Row 2 (RS): P2, *(k3, p3); rep from * to last 5 sts, k3, p2.

Row 3 (WS): K2, *(p3, k3); rep from * to last 5 sts, p3, k2.

Row 4 (RS): P2, *(k3, p3); rep from * to last 5 sts, k3, p2.

Row 5 (WS): K2, *(p3, k3); rep from * to last 5 sts, p3, k2.

Row 6: P2, *sl1, k2tog, psso, p3; rep from * to last 5 sts, sl1, k2tog, psso, p2 (41 sts).

Row 7: K2, *p1, k3; rep from * to last 3 sts, p1, k2.

Row 8: P2tog, *k1, p3tog; rep from * to last 3 sts, k1, p2tog (21 sts).

Row 9: (P2tog) 10 times, p1 (11 sts).

Row 10 (inc): K1, knit twice into each of next 9 sts, k1 (20 sts).

Work 8 rows in rev st st on these 20 sts.

Break off yarn and thread through sts. Fasten off securely.

Lining

With 4mm needles and fine DK yarn, cast on 42 sts and work 2 rows in g-st. Work in st st with a 2-st g-st border until work measures 4½in (11.5cm). Make another piece the same but do not break off yarn.

Join for top

Knit across sts of second side, then across sts on first side (84 sts).

Purl 1 row.

Next row: (K4, k2tog) across row (70 sts).

Next row: Purl.

Next row: (K3, k2tog) across row (56 sts).

Next row: Purl.

Next row: (K2, k2tog) across row (42 sts).

Next row: Purl.

Next row: (K1, k2tog) across row (28 sts).

Next row: Purl.

Next row: K2tog across row (14 sts). Cast off.

Making up

Outer cozy

Join sides of work from lower edge for just under 1in (2.5cm). Join from top of cozy downwards, leaving a gap each side of approx. 2¾in (7cm) for spout and handle and allowing rev st st top edge to roll over. Catch stitch top roll in place.

Lining

Join first two rows of lower edge of lining. Join from the top down, leaving a hole for the spout. Place inside main cozy, making sure wrong sides of work are together. Catch stitch in place at lower edge and just inside 2-stitch garter stitch border on handle and spout holes, making sure stitches do not show on right side.

Keep your cuppa steaming with this striking tea cozy knitted in sizzling hot pinks and purples. With the natural warmth of merino wool, this design has a feeling of richness and indulgence.

Colourful cables

Materials

Louisa Harding Kashmir Aran, 55% merino, 35% microfibre, 10% cashmere (99yd/91m per 50g ball): 2 balls in 10 (A)
Debbie Bliss Merino Chunky, 100% merino (71yd/65m per 50g ball): 2 balls in 14072 (B)
Debbie Bliss Merino Aran, 55% wool, 33% acrylic, 12% cashmere (100yd/90m per 50g ball): 1 ball in each of 325001 (C), 325606 (D), 325702 (E)
A pair each of 3.25mm (UK10: US3), 4mm (UK8:US6) and 5mm (UK6:US8) needles
Cable needle
Darning needle

Tension

18 sts and 25 rows to 4in (10cm) square over st st using 5mm needles. Use larger or smaller needles to obtain correct tension.

Special abbreviations

(CB): Slip next 3 sts onto a cable needle and leave at the back, knit the next 3 sts, then knit the 3 off the cable needle. Follow cols as in pattern.

Pattern notes

This pattern may look complicated but is easy to do if you make sure that each stitch is knitted the same colour as previously, even when twisted with the cable. That is the colours swap sides after each cable twist. Use the intarsia method (see page 353) of knitting with small balls or long lengths of wool for each section.

Outer cozy (make 2)

Using 3.25mm needles and A, cast on 66 sts and knit 4 rows.

Break off A, change to 4mm needles and using the intarsia method of knitting, join in the colours as shown on the cable chart. Work from colour and cable chart repeating the 12 rows twice more. Then repeat cable row 3.

Next row: (Dec row) Change to A and 3.25mm needles and *p2tog along the row (33sts).

Next row: Knit.

Next row: Purl.

Eyelet row: K2 * yo, k2tog, k2, rep from * to last 3 sts, yo, k2tog, k1. Starting with a purl row, work 3 rows st st.

Break off A and join in colours as striped rib chart, knitting all sts on first row.

Next row: Knit all the B sts and purl the rest to form a single rib.

Rib the next 6 rows in cols as set.

Change to A and knit 4 rows.
Cast off.

Lining (make 2)

Using A and 4mm needles, cast on 45 sts and knit 4 rows.

Change to 5mm needles and st st. Shape the sides by dec at each end of 7th and every foll 6th row to 33 sts. Cont in st st until length matches the front to the dec row.

Change to 3.25mm needles and work 2 rows st st.

Eyelet row: K2 * yo, k2tog, k2, rep from * to last 3 sts, yo, k2tog, K1. Starting with a purl row, work 3 rows st st.

Change to 4mm needles.

Joining in short length of B, knit as follows: 2A, * 1B, (leave yarn at front) 3A, rep to last 2 sts 2A.

1st row: Keeping cols as set, p2A, * put RH needle, k-wise through next st, cross A over B, k st with B, p3A, rep to last 2 sts, p2A.

2nd row: K2A, * put RH needle through next st p-wise, cross A over B, p st using B, K3A, rep to last 2 sts, k2A. Rep these 2 rows twice more and first once.

Knit 4 rows g-st in A.

Making up

Press cable sections over a towel. Press lining sections. Join side seams of the outside cover, leaving room for the spout and handle. Join side seams of the lining in the same way. Slip stitch the lining inside the cover. Make a cord or crochet chain approx. 18in (46cm) long. Thread through eyelet holes. Make and attach tassels (see page 364) to either end and tie in a bow.

Striped rib chart
(33 sts x 7 rows)

Read RS rows from R to L and WS rows from L to R.

Work in st st. Each square = I st and I row.

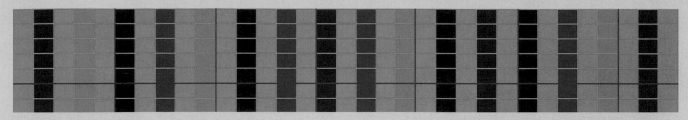

■ A ■ D

■ B ■ E

■ C

Cable pattern chart
(12-row repeat)

Read RS rows from R to L and WS rows from L to R.

Work in st st. Each square = I st and I row.

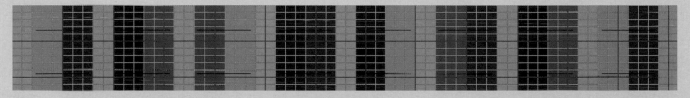

■ A

■ C   } Knit on RS (odd rows).

■ D   } Purl on WS (even rows).

■ E

■ B   Purl on RS and knit on WS.

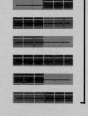

Cable positions (CB)

Slip next 3 sts onto cable needle and leave at back.

Knit next 3 sts, then knit the 3 off the cable needle.

This show-stopping tea cozy covered in beads was inspired by the opulent ballrooms and afternoon tea dances of bygone times. It will certainly make a glittering addition to any tea table.

Glitter ball

Materials

James C Brett's Marble Chunky, 100% acrylic
(220m/240yd per 100g):
1 x 100g ball in MC3 Turquoise Mix (A)
James C Brett's Aran Denim, 80% acrylic, 20% wool
(700yd/640m per 400g):
1 x 400g ball in Turquoise Green (B)
A pair of 6.5mm (UK3:US10.5) needles
Beads or buttons for decoration
(You could use beads from old necklaces that can be bought
cheaply in charity shops.)
Sewing needle and thread
Darning needle

Tension

14 sts and 20 rows to 4in (10cm) square over st st using 6mm needles. Use larger or smaller needles to obtain correct tension.

Linings (make 2)

With 6.5 mm needles and 3 strands of B held together, cast on 31 sts. Work in st st for 12 rows.

Shaping rows

Row 1: K1, *k2tog, k8, rep from * to end (28 sts).
Rows 2–4: St st.
Row 5: K1, *k2tog, k7, rep from * to end (25 sts).
Rows 6–8: St st.
Row 9: K1, *k2tog, k6, rep from * to end (22 sts).
Row 10: Purl.
Row 11: K1, *k2tog, k5, rep from * to end (19 sts).
Row 12: Purl.
Row 13: K1, *k2tog, k4, rep from * to end (16 sts).
Rows 14–16: St st.
Row 17: K1, *k2tog, k3, rep from * to end (13 sts).
Row 18: Purl.
Row 19: K1, *k2tog, k2, rep from * to end (10 sts).
Row 20: *P1, p2tog; rep from * to last st, p1 (7 sts).
Row 21: K1 (k2tog) 3 times (4 sts).
Row 22: P1, work into the front and back of the next 2 sts, p1 (6 sts).
Row 23: Knit into the front and back of every st (12 sts).
Row 24: Purl.
Cast off.

Fronts (make 2)

With 6.5mm needles, 2 strands of A and 1 strand of B, cast on 38 sts. Work in double rib (k2, p2 etc) for 12 rows.

Shaping rows

Row 1: *K2, p2tog, k2, p2, rep from * to last 6 sts, k2, p2tog, k2 (33 sts).
Row 2: *P2, k1, p2, k2, rep from * to last 5 sts, p2, k1, p2.
Row 3: *K2, p1, k2, p2, rep from * to last 5 sts, k2, p1, k2.
Row 4: *P2, k1, p2, k2, rep from * to last 5 sts, p2, k1, p2.
Row 5: *K2, p1, k2, p2tog, rep from * to last 5 sts, k2, p1, k2 (29 sts).
Row 6: *P2, k1, rep from * to last 2 sts, p2.
Row 7: *K2, p1, rep from * to last 2 sts, k2.
Row 8: *P2, k1, rep from * to last 2 sts, p2.
Row 9: *K2tog, p1, rep from * to last 2 sts, k2tog, (19 sts).
Row 10: *P1, k1, rep from * to last st, p1.
Row 11: *K1, p1, rep from * to last st, k1.
Row 12: *P1, k1, rep from * to last st, p1.
Row 13: *K1, p1, rep from * to last st, k1.
Row 14: *P1, k1, rep from * to last st, p1.
Row 15: *K1, p1, rep from * to last st, k1.
Row 16: *P1, k1, rep from * to last st, p1.
Row 17: *K1, p1, rep from * to last st, k1.
Row 18: *P1, k1, rep from * to last st, p1.
Row 19: *K2tog, rep from * to last st, k1 (10 sts).
Row 20: *P1, p2tog, rep from * to last st, p1 (7 sts).
Row 21: K1 (k2tog) 3 times (4 sts).
Row 22: P1, work into the front and back of the next 2 sts, p1 (6 sts).
Row 23: Knit into the front and back of every stitch (12 sts).
Row 24: Purl.
Cast off.

Making up

Sew beads down the furrows made by the rib. Then sew each front to a lining with the right sides facing outwards. Sew the two pieces together at top and bottom of the sides, leaving holes for the spout and the handle.

The inspiration for this elegant cozy is a staple of every woman's wardrobe. This new take on a classic design incorporates the fashion designer Coco Chanel's love of texture and a stylish trademark camellia.

Little black dress

Materials

Sirdar Hayfield Bonus DK, 100% acrylic (306yd/280m per 100g) ball: 1 x 100g in 965 Black (A)
Palette DK, 100% wool (348yd/320m per 100g ball): 1 x 100g in 23730 Cream (B)
20 x 5mm and 8 x 4mm cream-coloured pearls
1yd (90cm) of 1in (2.5cm) wide cream ribbon
A pair each of 4mm (UK8:US6) and 3.25mm (UK10:US3) bamboo needles
A pair of 3.75mm (UK9:US5) double-pointed needles
Sewing needle and thread; tapestry needle
Dressmaker's pins
Clear nail varnish

Tension

22 sts and 28 rows to 4in (10cm) square measured over moss stitch on 4mm needles. Use larger or smaller needles if necessary to obtain the correct tension.

Special abbreviations

P1tbs/P1tfs: Purl through the back of the (next) st, then purl through the front of this st to increase 'invisibly'.
PB: Place bead (see instructions).

Pattern notes

Placing beads: take bead to where it is to be placed, as close to next st as possible. Slip this st onto right needle, place bead, take yarn back and knit the next st. Ensure the bead is positioned over the slipped st, and keep the tension medium to tight to prevent it from working through to the back.

Sides (make 2)

Thread 20 x 5mm pearl beads onto a strand of A, using sewing cotton and a sewing needle to assist.
Using 4mm needles and the thumb method, cast on 42 sts. Push the beads along the yarn until they are needed.

Row 1: P to end.
Row 2: K to end.
Row 3: P to end.

Row 4 (picot row): K2 *(yrn, k2tog), rep from * to last 2 sts, yrn, k2 (43 sts).
Row 5: P to end.
Row 6: K to end.
Row 7: P to end.
Change to B, keeping tension tight if using Palette DK.
Row 8: K to end.
Row 9: K to end. Change to A.
Row 10: K to end.
Row 11: P to end.
Row 12 (bead row): K3, PB on the next st, *(k3, PB); rep from* to last 3 sts, k3.
Row 13: P to end.
Change to B.
Row 14: K to end.
Row 15: K to end.
Change to A.
Row 16: K to end.

Row 17: P1, k1 to end.
Row 18: K1, p1 to end.
Rows 17 and 18 form the moss stitch patt. Rep these two rows until the moss stitch segment measures 6in (15cm), ending on a wrong side row.

Eyelet section

Row 1: (RS): K to end.
Row 2: P to end.
Row 3 (eyelet row): K4 *(yrn, k2tog, k3); rep from *to last 4 sts, yrn, k4 (44 sts).
Row 4: P to end.
Row 5: K to end.

Moss stitch section

Row 1: P1, k1 to end.
Row 2: K1, p1 to end.
These two rows form the moss stitch pattern; rep for a further 18 rows until this new moss stitch segment measures 2in (5cm), ending with a RS row.
Cast off.

Camellia

Note: *Working the dec 1 st in from the edge gives the flower its characteristic curved petal. Leave long tails at the beg and end for assembly and stitching.*
Using 3.25mm needles, thumb method and B, cast on 2 sts.
Row 1: K2.
Row 2: P1, p1tbs, p1tfs (3 sts).
Row 3: K to end.

Row 4: P1, p1tbs, p1tfs, purl to end (4 sts).
Row 5: K to end.
Row 6: P1, p1tbs, p1tfs, purl to end (5 sts).
Row 7: K to end.
Row 8: P1, p1tbs, p1tfs, purl to end (6 sts).
Row 9: K to end.
Row 10: P1, p1tbs, p1tfs, purl to end (7 sts).
Row 11: K to end.
Row 12: P1, p1tbs, p1tfs, purl to end (8 sts).
Row 13: K to end.
Row 14: P to end.
Row 15: K to end.
Row 16: P to end.
Row 17: K to end.
Row 18: P1, p2tog, p5, purl to end (7 sts).
Row 19: K to end.
Row 20: P1, p2tog, p4, purl to end (6 sts).
Row 21: K to end.
Row 22: P1, p2tog, p3, purl to end (5 sts).
Row 23: K5 to end.
Row 24: P1, p2tog, p2, purl to end (4 sts).
Row 25: K to end.
Row 26: P1, p2tog, p1, purl to end (3 sts).
Row 27: K to end.
Row 28: P1, p2tog (2 sts).

Row 29: K2 to end.
Rep rows 2–29 three times more (4 petals in all).
Cast off, leaving two long tails.

Stamen

Using 3.75mm double-pointed needles, cast on 6 sts. Knit a row, but do not turn. With yarn at back, push sts along needle and knit them again. Rep until work measures approx. 1½in (4cm). Cut yarn, leaving a long tail. Thread tail on a tapestry needle. Thread through rem sts and draw together very gently to keep the top stitches tidy. Draw the darning needle down through the middle of these stitches and unthread. Neaten and fasten off cast-off row.

Making up
Camellia

With the work on its side, thread through the first row of sts along the end opposite curved petals, gathering and overlapping as necessary to produce flower effect. Fasten off but do not cut yarn. Using cast-on tail, work along the same row in the opposite direction to pull the flower centre even closer together. Fasten off but do not cut yarn. Place stamen in centre of flower, bend to the left and secure to the first petal on left using one of the tail threads; do not cut thread. Split one of the tail threads, and thread one of the sections on a regular needle. Manoeuvre to lower left side of the right petal thus: attach a 4mm bead; rep until 8 beads form a semi-circle at the bottom of the stamen. Fasten off and cut. Take rem tail back and forth two or three times across the centre back of flower to form a short loop. Neaten loop using buttonhole stitch and fasten off.

Cozy

Join sides using mattress stitch, leaving gaps for handle and spout. Leave a gap in each seam of eyelet row to form two extra eyelets. Fasten off. Thread ribbon through, beg at centre eyelet on right side. Draw up and form a bow. Loop the right-hand ribbon and thread through loop on back of flower. Turn cozy upside-down and finish tying bow so the ribbon tails face the bottom of cozy. Trim ribbon and coat ends with clear nail varnish to prevent fraying.

Tip
Make sure the ribbon matches the cream yarn exactly, as any variation will make the yarn look 'dirty'.

Pure wool yarn is used double to give this design extra warmth to keep your tea hot for longer. The pattern hugs the pot snugly and is easier than it looks once you have mastered the cable technique.

Ginger spice

Materials

Patons Merino Wool DK, 100% wool
(142yd/130m per 50g ball):
2 balls in 00027 Ginger
1 pair of 5mm (UK6:US8) needles
Cable needle or double-pointed needle
Darning needle

Tension

13 sts and 20 rows to 4in (10cm) square over st st using 5mm needles and yarn double. Use larger or smaller needles to obtain correct tension.

Special abbreviations

BC (back cross): Sl 2 sts to cable needle and hold at back of work; k2, then p2 from cable needle.
FC (front cross): Sl 2 sts to cable needle and hold at front of work; p2, then k2 from cable needle.

Pattern notes

The stitch count of this pattern increases on rows 3 and 9 so will vary from the original number of stitches cast on.

Sides (make 2)

With 5mm needles and yarn held double, cast on 32 sts and work in pattern thus:

Pattern

Row 1 (RS): K1, p3, k4, *(p6, k4); rep from * to last 4 sts, p3, k1.

Row 2: K4, p4, *(k6, p4); rep from * to last 4 sts, k4.

Row 3: K1, p1, *(BC, insert needle under yarn running between st just worked and the next st and (k1, p1) into it, FC, p2); rep from * to last 2 sts, p1, k1 (38 sts).

Row 4: K2, *(p2, k2); rep from * to end.

Row 5: K1, p1, *(k2, p2); rep from * to last 4 sts, k2, p1, k1.

Row 6: K2, *(p2, k2); rep from * to end.

Row 7: K2, *(skpo, p6, k2tog, k2); rep from * to end (32 sts).

Row 8: K1, p2, k6, *(p4, k6); rep from * to last 3 sts, p2, k1.

Row 9: K1, insert needle under yarn running between st just worked and the next st and k1 into it, *(FC, p2, BC, insert needle under yarn running

between st just worked and the next st and (k1, p1) into it; rep from * but end last rep FC, p2, BC, k1 into running yarn, k1 (38 sts).

Row 10: K1, p1, *(k2, p2); rep from * to last 4 sts, k2, p1, k1.

Row 11: K2, *(p2, k2); rep from * to end.

Row 12: K1, p1, *(k2, p2); rep from * to last 4 sts, K2, p1, k1.

Row 13: K1, p3, *(k2tog, k2; skpo, p6); rep from * but end last rep k2tog, k2, skpo, p3, k1 (32 sts).

Rows 2–13 now form the pattern. Rep them until work measures approx. 5in (12.5cm) ending after row 4 of patt.

Note: *There will be 38 sts on the needle after row 4.*

Break off yarn. Work another piece the same way but do not break off yarn.

Join for top

Next row (RS): Working across sts of second side, K1, p1, *k2, p2; rep from * to last 4 sts, k2, p2tog, move to first 2 sts of side 1 and p2tog, then working across rem sts of second side, k1, p1, *k2, p2; rep from * to last 4 sts, k2, p1, k1 (74 sts).

Next row: Work as for row 6 of patt.

Next row (RS): Work as for row 7 of patt (62 sts).

Next row: Work as for row 8 of patt.

Next row (dec): K3, *(p2tog) 3 times, k4; rep from * to last 9 sts,

(p2tog) 3 times, k3 (44 sts).

Next row: P1, p2tog, *k3, (p2tog) twice; rep from * to last 6 sts, k3, p2tog, p1 (32 sts).

Next row: *K2tog, p3; rep from * to last 2 sts, k2tog (25 sts).

Next row: *P1, sl1, k2tog, psso; rep from * to last st, p1 (13 sts).

Knit 1 row.

Cast off.

Making up

Do not press. Join the first few rows of the lower edge at both sides. Join from top edge down, leaving a gap of approx. 4in (10cm) for the spout and handle. There will be a 'hole' in the top of the work to accommodate the knob of the pot.

Vibrant turquoise yarn adds a modern twist with a traditional feel to this tasteful design. The pure wool yarn and cables produce a thick fabric that provides excellent insulation for your pot.

Turquoise cables

Materials

Patons Fairytale Colour 4 Me DK, 100% wool (98yd/90m per 50g ball):
2 balls in 4957 Aqua
A pair each of 3.75mm (UK9:US5) and 4mm (UK8:US6) needles
A pair of 3.75mm or 4mm double-pointed needles
2 small buttons (optional)
Darning needle

Tension

30 sts and 32 rows to approx. 4in (10cm) over cable pattern using 4mm needles. Use larger or smaller needles to obtain correct tension.

Special abbreviations

C6F: Place next 3 sts on a double-pointed needle and leave at front of work. Knit next 3 sts, place the cable needle in working position, then slide the sts it holds towards the point and knit. Return to main work and continue along row.

Pattern notes

Do not press the finished work, as it will flatten the cables.

Side 1

Using 3.75mm needles, cast on 60 sts and work 6 rows in g-st.

Increase row: K12, *inc by working into front and back of next st, k12; rep from * to end (64 sts).

Change to 4mm needles and cont in pattern:

Pattern

Row 1: Knit.

Row 2: K1, *p6, k2; rep from * to last 7 sts, p6, k1.

Row 3 (cable row): K1, *C6F, k2; rep from * to last 7 sts, C6F, k1.

Row 4: K1, *p6, k2; rep from * to last 7 sts, p6, k1.

Row 5: Knit.

Row 6: K1, *p6, k2; rep from * to last 7 sts, p6, k1.

Cont in patt until work measures approx. 5in (12.5cm), ending with RS facing for next row. Adjust height of sides here if required. Break off yarn and leave sts on spare needle.

Side 2

Using 3.75mm needles, cast on 60 sts. Work as for side 1 but do not break off yarn.

Join for top

Next row: K2tog, k across all sts of side 2, then k across sts of side 1 to last 2 sts, k2tog (126 sts).

Next row: Knit.

Next row: (K5, k2tog) to end (108 sts).

Next row: Knit.

Next row: (K4, k2tog) to end (90 sts).

Next row: Knit.

Next row: (K3, k2tog) to end (72 sts).

Next row: Knit.

Next row: (K2, k2tog) to end (54 sts).

Next row: Knit.

Next row: (K1, k2tog) to end (36 sts).

Next row: Knit.

Next row: (K2tog) to end (18 sts).

Next row: Knit.

Next row (eyelets): K1, (yf, k2tog, k1) to last 2 sts, yf, k2tog.

Next row: Knit.

Next row: Knit into front and back of each st (36 sts).

Work 9 rows in g-st.

Cast off loosely.

I-cord

With dpns, cast on 3 sts. Do not turn work.

Working row: Knit across sts on needle. Pull yarn tightly across back of work but do not turn. Slide sts from left to right ready for next row. Rep working row until I-cord is long enough to thread through eyelets and tie in a bow.

Making up

Join lower edge of work for approx. 1in (2.5cm). Join from top edge of work, leaving a gap of approx.. 2½in (7cm) for spout and handle on each side and allowing garter stitch 'funnel' to roll over. Adjust spout and handle holes by trying on pot if possible. Thread I-cord through eyelets, gather loosely and tie in a bow. Attach a small button to each end of I-cord if desired.

The cup and saucer perched on top of this design will be a real talking point at tea time, and the tea cozy is lined for extra insulation. It's the ideal accessory for traditional blue and white pottery.

Cornish ware

Materials
Sirdar Supersoft Aran, 100% acrylic
(258yd/236m per 100g ball):
1 ball in 870 Denim (A)
Any Aran-weight yarn, approx. 30g in white (B)
A 4.5mm (UK7:US7) circular needle, approx. 16in (40cm) long
A pair of 4.5mm (UK7:US7) needles
Set of 5 x 4.5mm (UK7:US7) needles
Pipe cleaner or short length of fine wire to stiffen cup handle
Darning needle

Tension
19.5 sts and 28 rows to 4in (10cm) over st st using 4.5mm needles. Use larger or smaller needles to obtain correct tension.

Special abbreviations
MB: Make bobble (see instructions).

Body (worked in one piece)

With 4.5mm circular needle and A, cast on 100 sts and work in rounds.

Rounds 1–5: *(K1B, p1A); rep from * to end to form striped rib.

Rounds 6–7: Knit, using A.

Round 8: MB in 2nd and every foll 4th st to end (25 bobbles).

Make bobble

Into next st: k1, k1tbl, k1, k1tbl, k1, turn.

Next row: K5, turn.

Next row: K5, turn.

Next row: (K2tog) twice, k1, turn.

Next row: K3tog tbl.

Round 9: Knit, using A.

Rounds 10–13: Knit, using B.

Divide for handle and spout

The sides are now worked separately using st st and straight needles.

Next row: Using A, k50, leave rem sts on spare length of yarn.

Work a further 23 rows in stripe patt (4 rows A, 4 rows B), carrying yarn not in use up side of work.

Break off yarn, rejoin to other side and complete to match.

Join for top

Begin working using the circular needle, changing to the double-pointed needles when necessary.

Next round: With circular needle and A. work across both sides (100 sts).

Work 3 rows in A.

Shape top

Round 1: Using B, work to end.

Round 2: (k8, k2tog) to end (90 sts).

Round 3 and alt rounds: Knit.

Round 4: (k7, k2tog) to end (80 sts).

Cont as set until the row '(k3, k3tog) to end' has been worked (40 sts).

Break off B and cont in A only.

Saucer

Round 1: Purl.

Rounds 2 and 3: Knit.

Round 4: (k2tog, yo) to end.

Round 5: Knit, working all yo sts.

Round 6 and 7: Knit.

Round 8: Purl.

Round 9 and alt rounds: Knit.

Round 10: (k2, k2tog) to end (30 sts).

Round 12: (k1, k2tog) to end (20 sts).

Round 14: K2tog to end (10 sts).

Round 16: K2tog to end (5 sts).

Break off yarn and thread end through these 5 sts. Pull up tightly and secure.

Teacup

Using A and leaving a tail approx. 6in (15cm) long, cast on 24 sts and work 4 rows of striped rib as for sides.

Break off B and cont in A only.

Work 2 rows in st st.

Next row: Knit, MB as before in sts 2, 5, 8, 11, 14, 17, 20 and 23.

Work 3 rows in st st.

Cast off.

Lining

With 4.5mm circular needle and A, cast on 96 sts and work 8 rows in the round.

Change to straight needles and work 24 rows st st on first 48 sts only.

Complete second side to match.

Next round: Resume working all the round and knit 6 rows across all sts.

Top shaping

Round 1: (k6, k2tog) to end (84 sts).
Round 2 and alt rounds: Knit.
Round 3: (k5, k2tog) to end (72 sts).
Round 5: (k4, k2tog) to end (60 sts).
Round 7: (k3, k2tog,) to end (48 sts).
Round 9: (k2, k2tog,) to end (36 sts).
Round 11: (k2tog) to end (18 sts).
Cast off.

Making up

Sew in ends. Join side seam of teacup.
With RS of work facing, place the two
purl rows of the saucer tog and stitch
through carefully so the yo sts form a
picot edge. Turn cozy inside out and
place lining inside, WS tog. Pin the two
pieces together at spout and handle
openings. Sew lower edge of lining in
place just above ribbing and at top
saucer edge. Join lining and main piece
at spout and handle openings. Turn
work RS out and, working from the
inside of the cup, attach securely to
top of cozy.
To make the handle, cover a short
length of pipe cleaner in blanket stitch
(see page 350) and attach to the side
of the cup.

This simple yet sophisticated design will appeal to the young professional tea-lover with minimalist tastes but who likes to make time in their hectic lifestyle for a leisurely tea break.

Contemporary cool

Materials

RYC Cashsoft Aran, 10% cashmere, 57% merino wool, 33% acrylic (87m/95yd per 50g ball):
1 ball in Charcoal (A)
3 balls in Blue (B)
1 ball in Cream (C)
(These amounts include the teapot stand)
A pair of 4.5mm (UK7:US7) needles

Tension

19 sts x 25 rows measure 4in (10cm) square over st st using 4.5mm needles. Use larger or smaller needles to obtain correct tension.

First half

With 4.5mm needles and A, cast on 49 sts in A and work 6 rows g-st. Break off A and join in B. Using B, begin with a knit row, work st st for 4 rows, knitting the first 2 and last 2 sts on every purl row. Join on the second ball of B and also C and work in patt twisting yarn when changing colours.

Row 1: K22 B, k5C, k22B (second ball).

Row 2: B, k2, p20, p5C, p20 B, k2 (first ball).

Rows 3 & 5: As row 1.

Rows 4 & 6: As row 2.

Row 7: Knit in B (first ball).

Row 8: First ball of B K2, purl to last 2 sts, k2.

Repeat rows 1–8 twice more.

Continue with first ball of B and work 2 rows st st, knitting the first 2 and last 2 sts on purl row.

Begin decreasing

Dec row: K10, (k2tog) twice, k21, (k2tog) twice, k10 (45 sts).

Next row: K2, purl to last 2 sts, k2.

Dec row: K9, (k2tog) twice, k19, (k2tog) twice, k9 (41 sts).

Next row: K2, purl to last 2 sts, k2.

Shape top

Dec row: K8, (k2tog) twice, k17, (k2tog) twice, k8 (37 sts).

Next row and 6 foll alt rows: Purl.

Dec row: K7, (k2tog) twice, k15, (k2tog) twice, k7 (33 sts).

Dec row: K6, (k2tog) twice, k13, (k2tog) twice, k6 (29 sts).

Dec row: K5, (k2tog) twice, k11, (k2tog) twice, k5 (25 sts).

Dec row: K4, (k2tog) twice, k9, (k2tog) twice, k4 (21 sts).

Dec row: K3, (k2tog) twice, k7, (k2tog) twice, k3 (17 sts).

Dec row: K2, (k2tog) twice, k5, (k2tog) twice, k2 (13 sts).

Dec row: K1, (k2tog) twice, k3, (k2tog) twice, k1 (9 sts).

Break yarn and set aside.

Second half

Work as for first half, do not break yarn.

Join pieces

With wrong sides of work facing, purl across sts of second half and then with the same yarn continue purling across sts of first half (18 sts).

Dec row: (K2tog) to end (9 sts).

Beg with a purl row, work 6 rows st st, ending on a knit row.

Cast off k-wise.

Lining (make 2 pieces)

Using A, cast on 47 sts and work 6 rows g-st. Break off A and join on B. Using B and beg with a knit row, st st 30 rows, knitting the first 2 and last 2 sts on every purl row.

Begin decreasing

Dec row: K10, (k2tog) twice, k19, (k2tog) twice, k10 (43 sts).

Next row and foll alt row: K2, purl to last 2 sts, k2.

Dec row: K9, (k2tog) twice, k17, (k2tog) twice, k9 (39 sts).

Shape top

Dec row: K8, (k2tog) twice, k15, (k2tog) twice, k8 (35 sts).

Next row and 6 foll alt rows: Purl.

Dec row: K7, (k2tog) twice, k13, (k2tog) twice, k7 (31 sts).

Dec row: K6, (k2tog) twice, k11, (k2tog) twice, k6 (27 sts).

Dec row: K5, (k2tog) twice, k9, (k2tog) twice, k5 (23 sts).

Dec row: K4, (k2tog) twice, k7, (k2tog) twice, k4 (19 sts).

Dec row: K3, (k2tog) twice, k5, (k2tog) twice, k3 (15 sts).

Dec row: K2, (k2tog) twice, k3, (k2tog) twice, k2 (11 sts).

Dec row: K1, (k2tog) twice, k1, (k2tog) twice, k1 (7 sts).

Thread yarn through rem sts, pull tight and secure.

Making up
Tea cozy

Join row ends of tea cozy, leaving g-st edges open. Join row ends of garter st band at lower edge.

Lining

Join row ends as for tea cozy, then with wrong sides together, place lining inside tea cozy. Slip st g-st row ends at both openings and then join cast on sts at lower edge, all the way round.

Teapot stand

Using A, cast on 112 sts.

Dec row: K12, (k2tog) twice, *k24, (k2tog) twice**, rep from * to ** twice, k12 (104 sts).

Next row and 2 foll alt rows: Knit.

Dec row: K11, (k2tog) twice, *k22, (k2tog) twice**, rep from * to ** twice, k11 (96 sts).

Dec row: K10, (k2tog) twice, *k20, (k2tog) twice**, rep from * to ** twice, k10 (88 sts).

Break off A and continue in B.

Dec row: K9, (k2tog) twice, *k18, (k2tog) twice**, rep from * to ** twice, k9 (80 sts).

Next row and 8 foll alt rows: Knit.

Dec row: K8, (k2tog) twice, *k16, (k2tog) twice**, rep from * to ** twice, k8 (72 sts).

Dec row: K7, (k2tog) twice, *k14, (k2tog) twice**, rep from * to ** twice, k7 (64 sts).

Dec row: K6, (k2tog) twice, *k12, (k2tog) twice**, rep from * to ** twice, k6 (56 sts).

Dec row: K5, (k2tog) twice, *k10, (k2tog) twice**, rep from * to ** twice, k5 (48 sts).

Dec row: K4, (k2tog) twice, *k8, (k2tog) twice**, rep from * to ** twice, k4 (40 sts).

Dec row: K3, (k2tog) twice, *k6, (k2tog) twice**, rep from * to ** twice, k3 (32 sts).

Dec row: K2, (k2tog) twice, *k4, (k2tog) twice**, rep from * to ** twice, k2 (24 sts).

Dec row: K1, (k2tog) twice, *k2, (k2tog) twice**, rep from * to ** twice, k1 (16 sts).

Dec row: (K2tog) to end (8 sts). Thread yarn through remaining sts, pull tight and secure.

Making up

Join row ends.

This design has a separate button-on top, so it is easy to gain access to the lid to refresh your brew without taking the whole cozy off the pot. The buttons are an attractive design detail.

All buttoned up

Materials
Stylecraft Nature's Way Chunky, 100% undyed virgin wool (87yd/80m per 50g ball):
2 balls in 3652 Brown
A pair of 5mm (UK6:US8) needles
Cable needle or stitch holder
4 x 25–30mm buttons
Tapestry needle

Tension
Four repeats of the cable pattern (over 24 sts) measure 5in (12.5cm) wide using 5mm needles. Use larger or smaller needles if necessary to obtain the correct tension.

Special abbreviations
Cab4b: Slip two stitches onto cable needle and hold at back of work, k2, then knit stitches from cable needle.
Cab4f: Slip two stitches onto cable needle and hold at front of work, k2, then knit stitches from cable needle.

Sides (make 2)

With 5mm needles, cast on 31 sts and work 4 rows in g-st.

Next row: (K3, inc in next st); rep to last 3 sts, k3 (38 sts).

Next row: Knit across.

Next row: K2, (p4, k2); rep to end. Rep last 2 rows once more.

Cable pattern

Row 1: (K2, cab4f, k2, cab4b); rep to last 2 sts, k2.

Row 2: (K2, p4) to last 2 sts, k2.

Row 3: Knit across.

Row 4: As row 2.

Row 5: As row 3.

Row 6: As row 2.

Rep 6 rows of cable pattern until work measures approx. 4in (10cm) or the height necessary to suit your pot, ending on row 5 if possible.

Next row: (K2tog, p4); rep to last 2 sts, k2tog (31 sts).

Break off yarn, leaving a long end for making up. Leave sts on a spare needle or stitch holder. Make another piece the same but do not break off yarn; cont on same sts.

Join sides

Keeping to cable pattern (k1, cab4f, k1, cab4b), work across sts on needle to last st. Knit together this last st and the first st of the sts of side 2 to join. Work across sts of side 2, keeping to cable pattern (61 sts).

Next 3 rows: Work in g-st.

Cast off, leaving a long end.

Top

With 5mm needles, cast on 26 sts and work 4 rows in g-st.

Next row: K4, cast off 2 sts, k to last 6 sts, cast off 2 sts, k to end.

Next row: K3, p1, cast on 2 sts, p to last 6 sts, cast on 2 sts, p1, k3.

Next row: Knit across.

Next row: K3, p to last 3 sts, k3.

Rep last 2 rows until work measures 3in (7.5cm).

Next row: K11, cast off 4, k to end.

Next row: K3, p to last 3 sts casting on 4 sts over the sts cast off on previous row, k3.

Next row: Knit across.

Next row: K3, p to last 3 sts, k3.

Rep last 2 rows until work measures 2in (5cm) from hole in centre.

Next row: K4, cast off 2 sts, k to last 6 sts, cast off 2 sts, k to end.

Next row: K3, p1, cast on 2 sts, p to last 6 sts, cast on 2 sts, p1, k3.

Work 3 rows in g-st. Cast off.

Making up

Join the garter-stitch sections at the top and bottom of the cozy. Work blanket stitch (see page 360) loosely round hole in lid.

Place the cozy and the lid on the teapot and work out the position for the buttons. Sew on buttons. Weave in all ends.

Tip

The height of this cover is important for a snug fit, so measure your pot before shaping the top.

Geometric

Geometric cozies can be chic or shabby chic, simply elegant or just a good way to use up your yarn stash. From the jolly Big Top to the vintage charm of Granny Squares or a Battenberg Slice, there are plenty of designs to inspire and delight.

Classic stripes are guaranteed to harmonize with almost any decor from rustic and homely to modern and sleek. This simple design could find a place in every tea-lover's home.

Stripy sensation

Materials

Rowan Cashsoft Aran, 10% cashmere, 57% merino wool, 33% acrylic (87m/95yd per 50g ball):
3 balls in Terracotta (A)
1 ball in Ecru (B)
1 ball in Deep Blue (C)
A pair in each of 3.75mm (UK9:US5) and 4.5mm (UK7:US7) needles
Tapestry needle

Tension

19 sts and 25 rows to 4in (10cm) square over st st using 4.5mm needles. Use larger or smaller needles to obtain correct tension.

First half

With 4.5mm needles, A and a one-needle method of casting on, such as the continental (long tail) or thumb method (see page 347), cast on 50 sts and work 6 rows g-st.

Join on B and C and work in st st in stripes, carrying yarn up sides of work.

Row 1: B, knit 1 row.

Rows 2–4: C, beg with a purl row st st 3 rows.

Row 5: A, knit 1 row.

Rows 6–8: B, st st 3 rows.

Row 9: C, knit 1 row.

Rows 10–12: A, st st 3 rows.

Rows 1–12 set the pattern and are rep once more.

Next row: B, knit 1 row.

Next row: C, purl 1 row.

Begin decreasing

Dec row: C *(k10, k2tog) rep from * to last 2 sts, k2 (46 sts).

Next row: C, purl 1 row.

Dec row: A *(k9, k2tog) rep from * to last 2 sts, k2 (42 sts).

Next row: B, purl 1 row.

Place a marker on first and last st.

Shape top

Dec row: B *(k8, k2tog) rep from * to last 2 sts, k2 (38 sts).

Next row: B, purl 1 row.

Dec row: C *(k7, k2tog) rep from * to last 2 sts, k2 (34 sts).

Next row: A, purl 1 row.

Dec row: A *(k6, k2tog) rep from * to last 2 sts, k2 (30 sts).

Next row: A, purl 1 row.

Dec row: B *(k5, k2tog) rep from * to last 2 sts, k2 (26 sts).

Next row: C, purl 1 row.

Dec row: C *(k4, k2tog) rep from * to last 2 sts, k2 (22 sts).

Next row: C, purl 1 row.

Dec row: A *(k3, k2tog) rep from * to last 2 sts, k2 (18 sts).

Next row: B, purl 1 row.

Dec row: B *(k2, k2tog) rep from * to last 2 sts, k2 (14 sts).

Next row: B, purl 1 row.

Dec row: C *(k1, k2tog) rep from * to last 2 sts, k2 (10 sts).

Break yarn and set aside.

Second half

Work as for first half but don't break yarn.

Continue in A.

Join pieces.

With WS facing, purl across sts of second half, and then with the same yarn continue purling across sts of first half, 20 sts.

Dec row: *(K2tog) rep from * to end (10 sts).

Dec row: P1, *(p2tog, p1) rep from * to end (7 sts).

Inc row: K1, *(m1, k1) rep from * to end (13 sts).

Beg with a purl row, work 4 rows st st, ending on a k row.

Cast off k-wise, loosely.

Lining (make 2 pieces)

With 4.5mm needles, A and the one-needle method of casting on, begin at lower edge and cast on 46 sts. Work 6 rows g-st.

Beg with a knit row, st st 30 rows, knitting the first and last st on every purl row.

Begin decreasing

Dec row: *(K9, k2tog) rep from * to last 2 sts, k2 (42 sts).

Next row: K1, purl to last st, k1.

Dec row: *(K8, k2tog) rep from * to last 2 sts, k2 (38 sts).

Next row: K1, purl to last 2 sts, k1.

Place a marker on first and last st of last row.

Shape top

Dec row: *(K7, k2tog) rep from * to last 2 sts, k2, 34 sts.

Next row and foll 6 alt rows: Purl.

Dec row: *(K6, k2tog) rep from * to last 2 sts, k2 (30 sts).

Dec row: *(K5, k2tog) rep from * to last 2 sts, k2 (26 sts).

Dec row: *(K4, k2tog) rep from * to last 2 sts, k2 (22 sts).

Dec row: *(K3, k2tog) rep from * to last 2 sts, k2 (18 sts).

Dec row: *(K2, k2tog) rep from * to last 2 sts, k2 (14 sts).
Dec row: *(K1, k2tog) rep from * to last 2 sts, k2 (10 sts).
Dec row: *(K2tog) rep from * to end (5 sts). Thread yarn through rem sts, pull tight and secure.

Making up and edging
Outer cozy
With right sides together, place halves of tea cozy together, matching edges. Join row ends from top to markers by sewing back and forth one st in from edge. Turn right side out. Work edging for spout and handle. With 3mm needles and A, with RS facing, pick up and knit 58 sts from around each opening between g-st bands.
Cast off k-wise.
Join row ends of g-st bands.

Lining
Join row ends as for tea cozy then with WS together, place lining inside tea cozy. Working from the inside, slip-st lining to tea cozy around both openings for spout and handle. Join cast on sts at lower edge all the way round.

Teapot stand
Teapot stand is worked in g-st.
With 4.5mm needles, A and using the one-needle method of casting on, cast on 104 sts and knit 2 rows.
Dec row: *(K6, k2tog) rep from * to end, 91 sts.
Work 3 rows g-st.
Break off A and join on B.
Dec row: *(K5, k2tog) rep from * to end, 78 sts.
Knit 1 row.
Break off B and join on C.
Work 2 rows g-st.
Dec row: *(K4, k2tog) rep from * to end (65 sts).
Work 3 rows g-st.

Dec row: *(K3, k2tog) rep from *to end (52 sts).
Work 3 rows g-st.
Dec row: *(K2, k2tog) rep from * to end (39 sts).
Work 3 rows g-st.
Dec row: *(K1, k2tog) rep from * to end (26 sts).
Work 3 rows g-st.
Dec row: *(K2tog) rep from * to end (13 sts).
Knit 1 row.
Thread yarn through sts, pull tight and secure.

Making up
Join row ends.

The red and grey of this tea cozy might remind you of traditional school uniforms! The slip stitch tweed pattern is easy to knit and very satisfying as horizontal stripes of colour magically turn into vertical stripes.

School tweed

Materials

Sirdar Country Style DK, 40% nylon, 30%wool, 30% acrylic (348yd/318m per 100g ball):
1 ball in 408 Grey (A)
1 ball in 402 Red (B)
A pair each of 3.25mm (UK10:US3) and 4mm (UK8:US6) needles
Tapestry needle

Tension

11 sts and 15 rows to 4in (10cm) square over st st using 4mm needles. Use larger or smaller needles to obtain correct tension.

Special abbreviations

Sl1p-wise wyib: Slip 1 st purlwise with yarn held at the back of work
Sl1p-wise wyif: Slip 1 st purlwise with yarn held at the front of work

Sides (make 2)

With 3.25mm needles and A, cast on 40 sts and work 9 rows in k2, p2 rib.
Next row: Rib 4, *(m1, rib 2); rep from * to last 2 sts, rib 2 (57 sts). Change to 4mm needles and knit 1 row.
Now foll the 4-row pattern, working 2 rows red and 2 rows grey alternately.

Slip stitch tweed pattern

Row 1: With B, k2, *(sl1p-wise wyib, k3); rep from * to last 3 sts, sl1p-wise wyib, k2.
Row 2: With B, k2, *(sl1p-wise wyif, k3); rep from * to last 3 sts, sl1 p-wise wyif, k2.
Row 3: With A, k4, *(sl1p-wise wyib, k3); rep from * to last st, k1.
Row 4: With A, k4, *(sl1p-wise wyif, k3); rep from * to last st, k1.

Work 12 reps of patt in total. Change to 3.25mm needles and A only.
Next row: Knit, dec 1 st in the centre of row (56 sts).
Work 10 rows in k2, p2 rib.
Next row: *(k2tog, p2tog), rep from * to end (28 sts).

Work 5 rows in k1, p1 rib.
Next row: *(k2tog), rep from * to end (14 sts).
Change to C for the last few rows.
Next row: P2, *(p2tog, p1); rep from * to end (10 sts).
Beg with a purl row, work 5 rows in reverse st st.
Cast off knitwise loosely, using a 4mm needle.

Making up

Join 1¼in (3cm) at the lower edge and 2½in (6cm) at the top for the handle seam. Join 1in (2.5cm) up from lower edge and 4in (10cm) at the top for the spout seam. These are approximate measurements; try the cozy on the teapot and adjust as necessary before fastening off. When joining the halves of the cozy allow the red strip at the top to curl over before sewing down.

This jolly tea cozy has a garter-stitch striped body and brightly coloured flags that are neatly attached as you knit around the top. The jaunty bobble on top completes the circus look.

Big top

Materials

Rowan Pure Wool DK, 100% wool
(136yd/125m per 50g ball):
1 ball in 036 Kiss (A)
1 ball in 013 Enamel (B)
1 ball in 051 Gold (C)
1 ball in 019 Avocado (D)
A pair of 4mm (UK8:US6) needles
Spare needle or stitch holder
Dressmaking pins
Tapestry needle

Tension

20 sts and 38 rows to 4in (10cm) square over g-st using 4mm needles. Note that achieving accurate tension is not crucial for this project as the garter-stitch fabric will stretch to fit.

Pattern notes

Do not cut ends – carry the yarn up the side of the work, twisting the colours together.

Body (make 2 pieces)

With 4mm needles and A, cast on 22 sts.

Rows 1–8: Using A, knit.

Rows 9–16: Using B, knit.

Repeat these 16 rows three times more. Cast off.

Flags (make 4 pieces in C and 4 in D)

Cast on 2 sts.

Row 1: Knit.

Row 2: Inc in each st (4 sts).

Row 3: Knit.

Row 4: Inc in first st, knit to last st, inc in last st (6 sts).

Knit 3 rows.

Inc in first st, knit to last st, inc in last st (8 sts).

Knit 4 rows.

Cut yarn and leave flag on a spare needle or stitch holder.

Top

Turn the body pieces round so that the stripes run vertically. Make sure that the top edge is the one with the loops where the second colour is carried up the work.

With RS facing and B, pick up and knit 4 sts from each vertical stripe (64 sts).

Next row: Purl.

Add flags as follows using B:

Insert needle into first st of flag in C and knit it together with first st of main body. Cont in this way until all sts of first flag are attached to main body. Rep with flag in D and keep adding flags (one in C and one in D) until all flags are attached.

Next row: Knit.

Next row: *(K14, k2tog); rep from * to end of row (60 sts).

Next row: Knit.

Next row: *(K4, k2tog); rep from * to end of row (50 sts).

Next row: Purl.

Next row: Knit.

Next row: Purl.

Next row: Change to C, *(k3, k2tog); rep from * to end of row (40 sts).

Next row: Purl.

Next row: *(K2, k2tog); rep from * to end of row (30 sts).

Next row: Purl.

Next row: Change to B, *(k1, k2tog); rep from * to end of row (20 sts).

Next row: Purl.

Next row: K2tog to end of row (10 sts).

Next row: Purl.

Cut yarn and thread tail through rem 10 sts, pulling up tightly.

Fasten off.

Bobble

With A, cast on 1 st leaving a 6in (15cm) yarn tail.

Row 1: Knit into front, back and front of st (3 sts).

Row 2: Knit.

Row 3: Inc in first st, k1, inc in last st (5 sts).

Row 4: Knit.

Row 5: K2tog, k1, k2tog (3 sts).

Row 6: Knit.

Row 7: Sl1, k2tog, psso (1 st).

Cut yarn leaving a 6in (15cm) tail and draw through rem st to fasten off.

Tie the two yarn tails together to draw bobble into shape and fasten with a few sts.

Making up

Sew up crown of tea cozy. Join sides together at bottom with a short seam. This is easier if you put the tea cozy on your teapot and mark the seams with pins. Cut 15 pieces of yarn approx. 5in (12.5cm) long in colours C and D. Take three pieces of yarn and use them to create contrasting tassels at the bottom of the flags using the photograph as a guide. Sew the bobble to the top of the tea cozy.

This tea cozy is crocheted in shell stitch and has an elegant vintage vibe. Choose your stripe colours to complement a favourite tea set and finish off the project with a co-ordinating button to add contrasting detail.

Shell-pattern stripes

Materials

Rico Design Essentials Merino DK, 100% merino wool (131yd/120m per 50g ball):

1 ball in 005 Red (A)

1 ball in 098 Silver Grey (B)

4mm (UK8:USG/6) crochet hook

2 x 4mm (UK8:US6) double-pointed needles

1 x 1¼in (3.5cm) button

Tapestry needle

Tension

5 V shell sts and 10 rows to 4in (10cm) over V shell pattern using 4mm hook. Use a larger or smaller hook if necessary to obtain the correct tension.

Sides (make 2)

Row 1: With 4mm hook and A, make 36ch.

Row 2: (2tr, 1ch, 2tr) into 6th ch from hook, *miss 2ch, (2tr, 1ch, 2tr) in next ch; rep from * to last 3 sts, miss 2ch, 1tr in last ch, turn (10 V shell clusters).

Row 3: 3ch, *(2tr, 1ch, 2tr) into 1 ch sp; rep from * to end, 1tr in 3rd ch of turning ch, turn (10 V shell clusters).

Row 3 forms the pattern. Follow the following colour sequence:

Row 4: Change to B, rep row 3.

Rows 5–6: Change to A, rep row 3.

Row 7: Change to B, rep row 3.

Rows 8–9: Change to A, rep row 3.

Row 10: Change to B, rep row 3.

Row 11: Change to A, 3ch, 1tr into first shell ch sp, *(2tr, 1ch, 2tr) into next 1 ch sp; rep from * seven times, 1tr in last shell ch sp, 1tr in 3rd ch of turning ch, turn (8 V shell clusters).

Row 12: 3ch, *(2tr, 1ch, 2tr) into 1 ch sp; rep from * to end, 1tr in 3rd ch of turning ch, turn (8 V shell clusters).

Row 13: Change to B, 3ch, 1tr into first shell ch sp, *(2tr, 1ch, 2tr) into next 1 ch sp; rep from * five times, 1tr in last shell ch sp, 1tr in 3rd ch of turning ch, turn (6 V shell clusters).

Row 14: Change to A, 3ch, *(2tr, 1ch, 2tr) into 1 ch sp; rep from * to end, 1tr in 3rd ch of turning ch, turn (6 V shell clusters).

Row 15: 3ch, 1tr into first shell ch sp, *(2tr, 1ch, 2tr) into next 1 ch sp; rep from * three times, 1tr in last shell ch sp, 1tr in 3rd ch of turning ch, turn (4 V shell clusters).

Row 16: Change to B, ch 3, *(2 tr, 1ch, 2 tr) into 1 ch sp; rep from * to end, 1 tr in 3rd ch of turning ch, turn (4 V shell clusters).

Row 17: Change to A, 1tr into first shell ch sp, *(2tr, 1ch, 2tr) into next 1 ch sp; rep from * once, 1tr in last shell ch sp, 1tr in 3rd ch of turning ch, turn (2 V shell clusters). Fasten off and weave in ends.

Making up

With 4mm hook and A, attach yarn at the bottom right-hand edge and dc along the sides and over the top of each tea cozy side.

Join seams using either slip stitch or backstitch, leaving spaces for spout and handle opening.

With 4mm hook and A, attach yarn at the base of the tea cozy and dc in each ch st around the bottom edge of the tea cozy. Fasten off and weave in ends. With B and two 4mm double-pointed knitting needles, make a 12in (30cm) I-cord. Make three loops and secure firmly to the top of the tea cozy using a tapestry needle. Then secure a button in the centre.

This project is a good introduction to the technique of entrelac, which is easier than it looks. It produces a stunning effect and a substantial cozy to keep your tea piping hot.

Elegant entrelac

Materials

Twilley's Freedom Spirit DK, 100% wool (130yd/119m per 50g ball), or any other variegated pure wool DK yarn:
1 ball in 518 Desire (purple mix) (A)
1 ball in 513 Verve (green mix) (B)
A pair of 4mm (UK8:US6) needles
Tapestry needle

Tension

10 sts and 12 rows to 4in (10cm) over st st using 4mm needles. One repeat of the pattern over 32 sts measures approx. 8in (20cm) unstretched. Use larger or smaller needles if necessary to obtain the correct tension.

Entrelac panels (make 2)

With 4mm needles and A, cast on 40 sts loosely.

Work 8 rows in g st.

Next row (dec): K2, (k2tog, k3); rep to last 3 sts, k2tog, k1 (32 sts).

Change to B.

Base triangle

Row 1: *P2, turn.

Row 2: Sl1, k1, turn.

Row 3: Sl1, p2, turn.

Row 4: Sl1, k2, turn.

Row 5: Sl1, p3, turn.

Row 6: Sl1, k3, turn.

Cont in this way, working 1 more st on each purl row until the row 'Sl1, k6, turn' has been worked.

Next row: Sl1, p7 but do not turn*. Using the next 2 sts on the left-hand needle, rep from * to * to form the second base triangle. Rep twice more, ending sl1, p7, turn (four base triangles worked).

First tier

Change to A to work first tier of three rectangles and two edge triangles.

Right edge triangle

Row 1: K2, turn.

Row 2: Sl1, p1, turn.

Row 3: Inc in first st, skpo, turn.

Row 4: Sl1, p2, turn.

Row 5: Inc in first st, k1, skpo, turn.

Row 6: Sl1, p3, turn.

Row 7: Inc in first st, k2, skpo, turn.

Row 8: Sl1, p4, turn.

Row 9: Inc in first st, k3, skpo, turn.

Cont thus until the row 'inc in first st, k5, skpo' has been worked but do not turn (8 sts).

Next row: **Pick up and knit 8 sts along left edge of next triangle, turn.

Next row: Sl1, p7, turn.

Next row: Sl1, k6, skpo, turn.

Rep last 2 rows until all sts of second triangle have been worked, do not turn** (first rectangle).

Rep from ** to ** twice more, to form two further rectangles.

Left edge triangle

Pick up 8 sts from edge of last triangle.

Row 1: P2tog, p6, turn.

Row 2: Sl1, k6, turn.

Row 3: P2tog, p5, turn.

Row 4: Sl1, k5, turn.

Row 5: P2tog, p4, turn.

Row 6: Sl1, k4, turn.

Row 7: P2tog, p3, turn.

Row 8: Sl1, k3, turn.

Row 9: P2tog, p2, turn.

Row 10: Sl1, k2, turn.
Row 11: P2tog, p1, turn.
Row 12: Sl1, k1, turn.
Row 13: P2tog but do not turn.

Second tier

Join in B. Pick up p-wise and purl 7 sts from side of first triangle, turn (8 sts, including st left on needle from previous row).
Row 1: Sl1, k7, turn.
Row 2: Sl1, p6, p2tog, turn.
Rep last 2 rows until all sts of rectangle have been worked (8 sts) but do not turn. ***Pick up p-wise and purl 8 sts from side of next rectangle, turn. Rep rows 1 and 2 to complete next rectangle***. Rep from *** to *** to complete the final two rectangles of the tier.

Third tier

Join in A.
Row 1: K2, turn.
Row 2: Sl1, p1, turn.
Row 3: Inc in first st, skpo, turn.
Row 4: Sl1, p2, turn.
Row 5: Inc in first st, k1, skpo, turn.
Row 6: Sl1, p3, turn.
Row 7: Inc in first st, k2, skpo, turn.
Row 8: Sl1, p4, turn.
Row 9: Inc in first st, k3, skpo, turn.
Row 10: Sl1, p5, turn.
Row 11: Inc in first st, k4, skpo, turn.
Row 12: Sl1, p6, turn.

Row 13: Inc in first st, k5, skpo (8 sts). Do not turn. Pick up and knit 8 sts from edge of next rectangle, turn.
Next row: Sl1, p7, turn.
Next row: Sl1, k6, skpo, turn.
Rep last 2 rows until all sts of rectangle have been worked. Do not turn. Pick up and knit 8 sts from side of next rectangle and complete in the same way. Rep for final rectangle.

Left edge triangle

Pick up 8 sts from side of last rectangle of previous row and complete as for left edge triangle of first tier.

Final tier

Join in B. Pick up p-wise and purl 7 sts from edge of triangle just worked (8 sts, including st left on needle from previous row).
Row 1: Sl1, k7, turn.
Row 2: P2tog, p5, p2tog, turn.
Row 3: Sl1, k6, turn.
Row 4: P2tog, p4, p2tog, turn.
Row 5: Sl1, k5, turn.
Row 6: P2tog, p3, p2tog, turn.
Row 7: Sl1, k4, turn.
Row 8: P2tog, p2, p2tog, turn.
Row 9: Sl1, k3, turn.
Row 10: P2tog, p1, p2tog, turn.
Row 11: Sl1, k2, turn.
Row 12: P2tog, p2tog, turn.
Row 13: Sl1, k1, turn.
Row 14: P2tog, p2tog, turn.

Row 15: Sl1, k1, turn.
Row 16: P2tog (1 st on needle). Pick up p-wise and purl 7 sts from edge of rectangle of previous tier (8 sts, including st left on needle). Rep last 16 rows three times. Fasten off.

Join panels

With 4mm needles and A, with RS facing, pick up and knit 40 sts along top edge of first panel, then pick up and knit 40 sts along top edge of second panel.
Purl 1 row.
Next row: (K8, k2tog) across row (72 sts).
Next row: Purl.
Next row: (K7, k2tog) across row (64 sts).
Cont in this way until there are 32 sts on needle, ending with a purl row.
Next row: (K2tog) across row (16 sts).
Join in B and purl across row.
Next row: Inc in every st (32 sts). Work 16 rows in g st. Cast off.

Making up

Join top and bottom side edges of work and weave in ends.
Place on pot, allowing top of work to roll over.

This quick and easy-to-make design is a great way to use up oddments of double knitting yarn. Use cheerful, bright colours or work in neutral tones for a more sophisticated effect.

Striking stripes

Materials

Patons Fairytale Colour 4 Me DK, 100% wool (98yd/90m per 50g ball):
Approx. 100g in total of 4–5 different shades (item shown uses 04967 Red, 04985 New Lime, 04957 Aqua, 04953 Strawberry and 04960 Lemon)
A pair of 5mm (UK6:US8) needles
Darning needle

Tension

Approx. 16 sts and 30 rows to 4in (10cm) square over st st using 5mm needles and yarn double. Use larger or smaller needles to obtain correct tension.

THE BIG BOOK OF TEA COZIES

Pattern notes

Although this design is easy to work, there will be lots of ends to sew in, so remember that you will need plenty of time for making up.

Side 1

With 5mm needles and yarn double, cast on 28 sts in first shade and work 4 rows in g-st. Change to second shade.

Next row: Inc in first st, k to last st, inc (30 sts).

Working in g-st and changing shade of yarn every 4 rows, cont until work measures approx. 5in (12.5cm).

Break off yarn and set work aside.

Side 2

Work exactly as for side 1, changing yarns in same sequence. Do not break off yarn.

Shape top

Knit across sts on second side, then knit across sts on first side (60 sts).

Work a further 3 rows in g-st.

Next row: (K4, skpo) to end (50 sts). Knit 1 row.

Next row: (K3, skpo) to end (40 sts). Knit 1 row.

Next row: (K2, skpo) to end (30 sts). Knit 1 row.

Next row: (K1, skpo) to end (20 sts). Knit 1 row.

Next row: (Skpo) to end (10 sts).

Next row: Knit once into each strand of yarn, thus working twice into each st (20 sts).

Using the same colour throughout, work 8 rows in g-st.

Cast off loosely.

Making up

Join sides for just under 1in (2.5cm) from the lower edge. Join work from the top down, leaving a gap of approx. 2½in (6cm) for the spout and handle. Allow last eight rows of work to roll over and catch stitch to top of work. Sew in all yarn ends, weaving them neatly through the ridges on the reverse side of work. Using spare yarn, make approx. seven small pompoms (see page 363), leaving a long end when tying them off. Attach pompoms firmly to cozy, clustering them around rolled-over top edge.

This reversible tea cozy has its own knitted-in mat. A choice of stripes or spots makes this a versatile accessory – button it one way and reverse the next day for two different designer looks for the modern teapot.

Stripes and spots

Materials

Rowan Cotton Glacé, 100% cotton (15m/124yd per 50g ball):

2 balls in 746 Navy (A)

1 ball in 810 Blue (B)

1 ball in 802 Gold (C)

1 ball in 741 Red (D)

A pair of 3.25mm (UK10:US3) needles

2 × circular 3.25mm (UK10:US3) needles

4 × ½in (15mm) buttons

Sewing needle and thread

Tension

23 sts and 32 rows to 4in (10cm) square, over st st using 3.25mm needles. Use larger or smaller needles to obtain correct tension.

Pattern notes

This cozy is knitted in one long strip then folded and knitted up into the finished shape on circular needles. This means that there is little sewing up.

Stripes

With 3.5mm needles and A, cast on 34 sts.

Work in st st, changing colour every 2 rows and foll the colour sequence A, B, C, D. Carry yarns loosely up the side. Work 34 rows in this stripe pattern, thus ending with 2 rows in A.

Base

The base is worked in A throughout.

Row 1: Sl1 k-wise *k1, yb sl1 p-wise, rep from * to last st, k1.

Row 2: Sl1 p-wise, purl to end.

Work this 2 row pattern until 38 rows have been worked in total. Now work another 32 rows in the stripe pattern as before, following the colour sequence D, C, B, A.

K2 rows in A. (This will mark the top of the finished cozy.)

Spots

Work 2 rows st st in A followed by 2 rows g-st.

Spot pattern 1

Row 1: Using B, k1 *sl2 p-wise, k4, rep. from * to last 3 sts, sl2 p-wise, k1.

Row 2: P1, *sl2 p-wise, p4, rep from * to last 3 sts, sl2 p-wise, p1.

Rep. these 2 rows twice more then work 2 rows g-st in A.

Spot pattern 2

Row 1: Using C, k4, *sl2 p-wise, K4, rep. from * to end.

Row 2: P4, *sl2 p-wise, p4, rep. from * to end.

Rep these 2 rows twice more then work 2 rows g-st in A.

Work these two spot patterns twice more using the colour sequence D, B, C, D. Use separate strands for each colour pattern.

Finish spot panel with 2 rows st st in A.

Base

Work the 38 rows of the base as before.

2 rows g-st in A.

Now work 6 spot patterns as before, following the colour sequence D, C, B, D, C, B.

2 rows st st in A.

Cast off and weave in ends.

Handle ribbing

With RS facing and a circular needle, pick up and knit 108 sts down one long side, picking up 20 sts for each pattern panel and 14 sts for each base.

Fold the long strip in half, positioning half the picked-up sts at each end of the circular needle.

Holding the two ends of the circular needle together in one hand and a straight 3.25mm needle in the other, work 54 sts in single (k1, p1) rib. You will be working the sts on the circular needles together as you go in a technique similar to that used in a three-needle cast off.

Now work back and forth in k1, p1 rib in the normal way, dec 2 sts in the middle of first and every alternate row by working the centre 4 sts as ssk and k2tog until 42 sts rem.

Cast off in rib.

Spout ribbing

Work as for handle ribbing, but don't cast off.

Button band

Work 6 rows in single (k1, p1) rib on first 10 sts. Cast off these 10 sts in rib.

Buttonhole band

Rejoin yarn to rem 32 sts and cast off
22 sts.

Rib to end, work one more row in k1,
p1 rib on these 10 sts.

Next row: Rib 5 sts, cast off 2 sts, rib
to end.

Next row: Rib 3 sts, cast on 2 sts, rib
to end.

Work 2 more rows in rib and then cast
off in rib.

There will be one short seam
remaining to sew together. Using A,
oversew this together now.

Top ribbing

Using a circular needle and beginning
with the button flap, pick up and knit
80 sts round top, picking up 10 sts for
the button and buttonhole bands, 24
sts for each pattern repeat and 6 sts
for each section of handle rib. This will
join the tea cozy above the handle
while keeping the spout side open.

Work 2 rows k1, p1 rib.

Next row: Rib 3, cast off 2 sts, rib
to end.

Next row: Rib 75 sts, cast on 2 sts, rib
to end.

Work 5 more rows in rib.

Cast off in rib and weave in ends.

Making up

Sew on 4 buttons back to back on
both sides of the button band.

Tea and cakes are a perfect combination, and this simple yet mouthwatering design is inspired by a traditional teatime favourite that should tempt you to get out the knitting needles.

Battenberg slice

Materials

James C Brett Top Value DK, 100% acrylic
(317yd/290m per 100g ball):
1 ball in 8412 Lemon (A)
1 ball in 8421 Pink (B)
A pair of 5.5mm (UK5:US9) needles
Tapestry needle

Tension

16 sts and 22 rows to 4in (10cm) square over st st using 5.5mm needles and double yarn, unstretched. Use larger or smaller needles to obtain correct tension.

Main body (make 2)

With 5mm needles and A double, cast on 24 sts and work two rows in g-st.

Working the squares

Row 1: Using A, k12. Join in B and k to end.

Row 2: P12 in B, pick up A, p to end.

Rep these 2 rows 6 times more.

Next row: Using A, knit.

Next row: Using A, p12. Pick up B and p to end.

Next row: Using B, k12. Pick up A and k to end.

Rep the last 2 rows 4 times more.

Working the decreases

Keeping the square patt as set, dec 1 st at each end of next 5 rows, using shaped decs (14 sts).

Cast off knitwise.

Marzipan trim (make 2)

Using A, cast on 3 sts and work 110 rows in g-st.

Cast off.

Making up

Sew the marzipan strip round the outside edge of the cozy (excluding the bottom), stretching gently if necessary. Join both sides, leaving room for the spout and handle.

This felted design is perfect for odd-shaped pots as it just drops over to accommodate any size. The pattern looks intricate, but is actually a clever cheat that is worked using rainbow-variegated yarn.

Fancy felt

Materials

Rico Creative Filz & Fun, 100% wool (55yd/50m per 50g ball):
2 balls in 6118 Black (A)
Schachenmayr Wash + Filz-it Stripe Color, 100% wool
(55yd/50m per 50g ball):
2 balls in rainbow variegated shade 10 (B)
A pair of 7mm (UK2:US10.5) needles
Darning needle
Cotton lining fabric (optional)

Tension

13 sts and 17 rows to 4in (10cm) square over st st using /mm needles. Use larger or smaller needles to obtain correct tension.

THE BIG BOOK OF TEA COZIES

Sides (make 2)

With 7mm needles and A, cast on 50 sts and work 4 rows in g-st.
Join in B and cont in st st, carrying yarn not in use up side of work.
Work 4 rows in B.
Work 2 rows in A.
Work 2 rows in B.
Now work in diamond pattern below, changing colours as indicated and stranding yarn loosely across back of work.

Diamond pattern

Row 1: K4A, (k2B, k8A) to last 6 sts, k2B, k4A.
Row 2: P3A, (p4B, p6A) to last 7 sts, p4B, p3A.
Row 3: K2A, (k6B, k4A) to last 8 sts, k6B, k2A.
Row 4: P1A, (p8B, p2A) to last 9 sts, p8B, p1A.
Row 5: Using B, knit.
Row 6: Using B, purl.
Row 7: K1A, (k8B, k2A) to last 9 sts, k8B, k1A.
Row 8: P2A, (p6B, p4A) to last 8 sts, p6B, p2A.
Row 9: K3A, (k4B, k6A) to last 7 sts, k4B, k3A.
Row 10: P4A, (p2B, p8A) to last 6 sts, p2A, p4B.
Then continue in stripe pattern. Using A, work 2 rows in st st.
Using B, work 2 rows in st st.

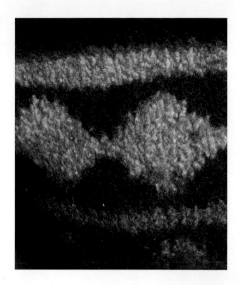

Using A, work 2 rows in st st.
Cont in diamond and stripe pattern until work measures approx. 8½in (21.5cm) from beginning.

Decrease for top

Next row: Skpo, cont in patt to last 2 sts, k2tog (48 sts).
Next row: Purl, keeping to pattern as set.
Rep last 2 rows until there are 40 sts on needle.
Now dec 1 st at each end of every row until there are 24 sts on needle.
Cast off loosely.
Make another piece the same.

Making up

Join sides neatly and sew in all ends.

Felting

Place work in a nylon mesh washing bag or pillowcase. Place in drum of washing machine, adding a bath towel or a pair of jeans to produce the friction necessary for felting. Add a small quantity of washing powder and run through a full 104°F (40°C) cycle. The work should felt sufficiently with just one wash cycle. Remove from drum and pull gently into shape, separating sides if necessary. Allow to dry naturally. Press work using a steam iron.

Lining (optional)

If you wish to line your work, place the completed cozy on a piece of paper and draw round it to make a template. Using the template, cut out cotton lining fabric and join at the top and sides, taking a small seam and snipping edges for ease. Press seam open and place lining inside cozy, making sure raw seam edges are on the inside. Turn back and press lower edge of lining. Catch stitch in place to inside lower edge.

This is the ultimate cozy to give your tea table some extra-bright shabby chic. It's also a great project for using up leftover yarn in any colours, which will help to give your cozy a thrift-style effect.

Pretty pompom

Materials

Rico Design Essentials Merino DK, 100% wool
(131yd/120m per 50g ball):
1 ball in 010 Magenta (A)
1 ball in 071 Lobster (B)
1 ball in 060 Natural (C)
1 ball in 065 Yellow (D)
1 ball in 027 Indigo (E)
1 ball in 042 Green (F)
1 ball in 005 Red (G)
3.5mm (UK9:USE/4) crochet hook
Tapestry needle

Tension

6.5 tr cluster sts and 13 rows to 4in (10cm) over V shell pattern using 3.5mm hook. Use a larger or smaller hook if necessary to obtain the correct tension.

Special abbreviations

MC: Magic circle (see page 359).

Tea cozy

Round 1: With 3.5mm hook and A, make a MC, work 8dc, sl st in first dc to join (8 sts).

Round 2: 3ch, tr in same st, 2tr into each st, join with sl st (16 sts).

Round 3: Change to B, 3ch, 1tr in same st, 1ch, *2tr in next st, 1ch; rep from * 14 times, sl st in 3rd ch (16 clusters).

Round 4: Change to C, 3ch, 2tr in next ch sp, *3tr in next ch sp; rep from * 14 times, sl st in 3rd ch (16 clusters).

Round 5: Change to D, 3ch, 2tr in sp between clusters, *3tr between clusters; rep from * 14 times, sl st in 3rd ch (16 clusters).

Round 6: Change to E, 3ch, 2tr in sp between clusters, 1ch, *3tr between clusters, 1ch; rep from * 14 times, sl st in 3rd ch (16 clusters).

Round 7: Change to F, 3ch, (1tr, 1ch, 2tr) in next ch sp, *(2tr, 1ch, 2tr) in next ch sp; rep from * 14 times, sl st in 3rd ch (32 clusters).

Round 8: Change to G, 3ch, 2tr in next sp, *3tr in next sp; rep from * 30 times, sl st in 3rd ch (32 clusters). Work now divides for the two sides of the tea cozy.

Side 1

Row 1: Change to A, 3ch, 2tr in sp at base of ch, *3tr in next sp; rep from * 12 times, turn (14 clusters).

Row 2: Change to B, 3ch, *3tr in next sp; rep from * 12 times, 1tr in 3rd ch of previous row, turn (13 clusters).

Row 3: Change to C; rep row 1.

Row 4: Change to D; rep row 2.

Row 5: Change to E; rep row 1.

Row 6: Change to F; rep row 2.

Row 7: Change to G; rep row 1.

Row 8: Change to A; rep row 2.

Row 9: Change to B; rep row 1.

Row 10: Change to C; rep row 2.

Fasten off work at the end of this row.

Side 2

Return to the top of the tea cozy.

Row 1: Change to A, miss three clusters of previous round, join yarn in next sp, 3ch, 2tr in sp at base of ch, *3tr in next sp; rep from * 12 times, turn (14 clusters).

Cont to match the pattern for side 1, working rows 2–10.

Row 11: Change to D, 3ch, 2tr in sp at base of ch, *3tr in next sp; rep from * 12 times, then join to first side of tea cozy by working 3tr into first sp of side 1, *3tr in next ch sp; rep from * 12 times, sl st in 3rd ch (28 clusters).

Cont to work in rounds.

Round 1: Change to E, 3ch, 2tr in sp at base of ch, *3tr in next sp; rep from * 26 times, sl st in 3rd ch (28 clusters).

Round 2: Change to B, 1ch, dc in each tr around, sl st in ch (84 sts).

Round 3: 1ch, dc in each dc around, sl st in ch (84 sts).

Round 4: Change to C, 1ch, dc in each dc around, sl st in ch (84 sts).

Round 5: 1ch, dc in each dc around, sl st in ch (84 sts).

Fasten off and weave in all ends.

Pompom

Make a 2in (5cm) pompom using A (see page 363) and sew firmly to the top of the tea cozy.

Whatever the weather, and no matter how grey the skies, this cheerful design will hold the promise of a bright day. Use all the colours of the rainbow as shown, or just use up any oddments from your stash.

Rainbow bright

Materials

Any DK yarn

Approx. 25g in each of the following shades: red, orange, yellow, green, blue, dark blue and violet

1 ball DK yarn in a toning shade for lining

A pair each of 4mm (UK8:US6), 5mm (UK6:US8) and 7mm (UK2.5:US10.5) needles

Tapestry needle

Sewing needle

Tension

Outer cozy: Not critical as pattern is very stretchy.

Lining: 14 sts measure 4in (10cm) in width over st st on 5mm needles, with yarn used double. Use larger or smaller needles to obtain correct tension.

Pattern notes

Yarns are used double throughout.

Sides (make 2)

With 4mm needles and 2 strands of violet, cast on 33 sts and k 1 row. Change to 7mm needles and work in patt, carrying yarns not in use up the side of the work, as folls:

Pattern

Row 1: Using violet, *(k3, wyib, sl1 p-wise); rep from * to last st, k1.
Row 2: K1, *(yf, sl1 p-wise, yb, k3); rep from * to end.
Row 3: Using red, k1, *(wyib, sl1 p-wise, k3); rep from * to end.
Row 4: *(K3, yf, sl1 p-wise, yb); rep from *to last st, k1.
These four rows form the pattern.
Rows 5 and 6: Using orange, rep rows 1 and 2.
Rows 7 and 8: Using yellow, rep rows 3 and 4.
Rows 9 and 10: Using green, rep rows 1 and 2.
Rows 11 and 12: Using blue, rep rows 3 and 4.
Rows 13 and 14: Using dark blue, rep rows 1 and 2.
Cont in patt until 38 rows in total have been worked, ending after a second row in green. Break off all yarn except green.

Next row (dec): *(K2, k2tog); rep from * to last st, k1 (25 sts).
Next row: P.
Next row: *(K2, k2tog); rep from * to last st, k1 (19 sts).
Next row: P.
Next row: *(K2, k2tog); rep from * to last 3 sts, k3 (15 sts).
Next row: P.
Next row: *(K2 tog); rep from * to last st, k1 (8 sts).
Work 6 rows in st st on these 8 sts for spike.
Next row: (K2tog) to end (4 sts).
Break off yarn leaving a long end.
Thread through rem sts and fasten off.

Lining (make 2)

With 5mm needles and 2 strands of DK, cast on 31 sts and work 20 rows in st st. Break off yarn and place sts on a holder.
Complete the second side to match but do not break off yarn.

> ## Tip
> This cozy is ideal for using up oddments of yarn, as each 2-row pattern takes just over a yard (1m) of yarn.

Next row: K30, then k2tog using the last st from this needle and the first st from the spare needle, k across rem sts on spare needle (61 sts).
Purl one row.

Shape top

Next row: *(K8, skpo); rep from * to last st, k1.
Next and alternate rows: P all sts.
Next row: *(K7, skpo); rep from * to last st, k1.
Cont in this way until the row *(k1, skpo); rep from * to last st has been worked.
Cast off very loosely.

Making up
Outer cozy

Join first 6 rows of the lower edge of outer cozy. Join the top spike, then join downwards for approx. 4in (10cm) for the spout side.

Lining

Join the first 2 rows of lower edge. Join lining approx. 4in (10cm) down from the top. Place inside outer cozy and join at handle and spout openings, making sure all ends of yarn carried up the side are hidden by the edge of the lining. Catch lining loosely in place all round lower edge of cozy.

This design brings a modern twist to a traditional tea cozy for an exercise in contemporary chic. It uses the modular knitting technique, which is particularly effective when working with space-dyed yarn.

Tea squares

Materials

Sirdar Bonus Flash DK, 100% acrylic (280m/306yd per 100g ball):
1 ball in 907 Blue and White Mix (A)
1 ball in 969 Blue (B)
A pair each of 4mm (UK8:US6) and 6.5mm (UK3:US10.5) needles
Tapestry needle

Tension

22 sts and 28 rows to 4in (10cm) square over st st using 4mm needles. Use larger or smaller needles to obtain correct tension.

Lining (make 2)

With 6.5mm needles and 3 strands of B held together, cast on 31 sts quite loosely. Work in st st for 12 rows.

Shaping rows

Row 1: K1, *k2tog, k8; rep from * to end (28 sts).

Rows 2–4: St st.

Row 5: K1, *k2tog, k7; rep from * to end (25 sts).

Rows 6–8: St st.

Row 9: K1, *k2tog, k6; rep from * to end (22 sts).

Row 10: Purl.

Row 11: K1, *k2tog, k5; rep from * to end (19 sts).

Row 12: Purl.

Row 13: K1, *k2tog, k4; rep from * to end (16 sts).

Rows 14–16: St st.

Row 17: K1, *k2tog, k3; rep from * to end (13 sts).

Row 18: Purl.

Row 19: K1, *k2tog, k2; rep from * to end (10 sts).

Row 20: *P1, p2tog; rep from * to last st, p1 (7 sts).

Cast off.

Front (make 2)

With 4mm needles and A, work the squares and triangles indicated on the diagram using the mitred square modular technique.

Basic square

Square 1

Row 1: With 4mm needles and A, cast on 19 sts.

Row 2: (WS) K9, p1, k9.

Row 3: K8, slip 2 sts tog, k1, pass slipped sts over tog, (from now on shown as S2kp2) k8 (17 sts).

Row 4: Purl.

Row 5: K7, S2kp2, k7 (15 sts).

Row 6: K7, p1, k7.

Row 7: K6, S2kp2, k6 (13 sts).

Row 8: Purl.

Row 9: K5, S2kp2, k5 (11 sts).

Row 10: K5, p1, k5.

Row 11: K4, S2kp2, k4 (9 sts).

Row 12: Purl.

Row 13: K3, S2kp2, k3 (7 sts).

Row 14: K3, p1, k3.

Row 15: K2, S2kp2, k2 (5 sts).

Row 16: K2, p1, k2.

Row 17: K1, S2kp2, k1 (3 sts).

Row 18: P3tog.

Fasten off or leave stitch on the needle to use as the first st of the next square.

Square 2

With 4mm needles and A, pick up and k9 sts from the L side of square 1, and then cast on 10 sts (19 sts). Work as for square 1, starting with row 2.

Square 3

As square 1.

Square 4

With 4mm needles and A, pick up and k9 sts from the L side of square 3, cast on 1 st, and then pick up and k9 sts from the R edge of square 1 (19 sts). Work as for square 1, starting with row 2.

Square 5

With 4mm needles and A, pick up and k9 sts from the L side of square 4, pick up and k1 st from the top of the centre ridge of square 1, and then pick up and k9 sts from the R edge of square 2 (19 sts). Work as for square 1, starting with row 2.

Square 6

As square 1.

Square 7

With 4mm needles and A, pick up and k9 sts from L side of square 6, cast on 1 st, and then pick up and k9 sts from R edge of square 3 (19 sts). Work as for square 1, starting with row 2.

Square 8

With 4mm needles and A, pick up and k9 sts from the L side of square 7, pick up and k1 st from the top of the centre ridge of square 3, and then pick up and k9 sts from the R edge of square 4 (19 sts). Work as for square 1, starting with row 2.

Square 9

With 4mm needles and A, pick up and k9 sts from the L side of square 8, pick up and k1 st from the top of the centre ridge of square 4, and then pick up and k9 sts from the R edge of square 5 (19 sts). Work as for square 1, starting with row 2.

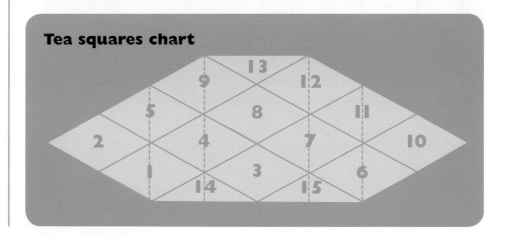

Tea squares chart

Square 10

With 4mm needles and A, cast on 10 sts, and pick up and k9 sts R side of square 6 (19 sts). Work as for square 1, starting with row 2

Square 11

With 4mm needles and A, pick up and k9 sts from the L side of square 10, pick up and k1 st from the top of the centre ridge of square 6, and then pick up and k9 sts from the R edge of square 7 (19 sts). Work as for square 1, starting with row 2.

Square 12

With 4mm needles and A, pick up and k9 sts from the L side of square 11, pick up and k1 st from the top of the centre ridge of square 7, and then pick up and k9 sts from the R edge of square 8 (19 sts). Work as for square 1, starting with row 2.

Basic triangle

Triangle 13

Row 1: Pick up 19 sts as for a square (9 + 1 + 9).
Row 2: K9, p1, k9.
Row 3: K2togtbl, k6, S2kp2, k6, k2tog (15 sts).
Row 4: Purl.
Row 5: K2togtbl, k4, S2kp2, k4, k2tog (11 sts).
Row 6: K5, p1, k5.

Row 7: K2togtbl, k2, S2kp2, k2, k2tog (7 sts).

Row 8: P3tog, p1, p3tog (3 sts).

Row 9: S2kp (1 st).

Fasten off.

Triangle 14

As triangle 13, but worked downwards.

Triangle 15

As triangle 13, but worked downwards.

Making up

Sew in any ends. Sew each front to a lining with the right sides facing outwards. Then sew the two pieces together at the top and the bottom of the sides, leaving holes for the spout and the handle.

Pompom

See page 363 for instructions. Use the end of yarn left over from tying to secure the pompom to the top of the tea cozy.

This pretty tea cozy, with its delicate sugared-almond colours, has bags of vintage charm. You can alter the shades of the granny square motif as necessary to complement your best china.

Granny squares

Materials

Rico Design Essentials Merino DK, 100% merino wool (131yd/120m per 50g ball):

1 ball in 023 Grey Blue (A)

1 ball in 020 Mauve (B)

1 ball in 063 Light Yellow (C)

1 ball in 001 Rose (D)

1 ball in 098 Silver Grey (E)

3mm (UK11:USC/2 or D/3) crochet hook

20in (50cm) × 10mm ribbon

Tapestry needle

Tension

Each granny square motif measures 1¾in × 1¾in (4.5cm × 4.5cm) using 3mm hook. Use a larger or smaller hook if necessary to obtain the correct tension.

Main granny square motif (make 24)

Round 1: With 3mm hook and B, make 4ch, work 11tr in 4th ch from hook, sl st in top of 3rd ch (counts as 12tr). (See diagram, opposite.)

Round 2: 1htr in same st where sl st was made, work 1htr in each of the next 2 sts, 1ch (1htr in next 3 sts, 1ch) rep twice, join with sl st to top of first htr.

Round 3: Change to A and join yarn in 1ch corner sp, 3ch, work 4tr in same sp, 1ch, 5tr in same sp (5tr in the next corner ch sp, 1ch, 5tr in same sp) rep twice, join with sl st to top of 3ch. Fasten off and weave in ends.

Work a further five squares that have yarn B at their centre.

Work six squares each using C, D and E for rounds 1–2 and A for round 3.

In total you will need 24 granny squares.

Making up

With 3mm hook and A, use photographs as a guide and sl st 12 square motifs together for each side. With 3mm hook and A, attach yarn to any stitch on the edge with a sl st, 1ch, work 1dc in each tr and ch around, working 3dc at each corner so that you have worked evenly around the four edges of each side, sl st into ch.

Bottom edge

With WS together using 3mm hook and A, attach yarn to any stitch on the bottom edge with a sl st, 1ch, work 1dc in each dc around, joining both sides of the tea cozy together, sl st into ch. Work a further 2 rows in dc. Fasten off and weave in ends.

Tea cozy top

Round 1: With WS together using 3mm hook and A, attach yarn to any stitch on the top edge with a sl st, 1ch, work 1dc in each dc around, joining both sides of the tea cozy together, sl st into ch (90 sts).

Round 2: 1ch, dc in each st to end, sl st into ch.

Round 3: 3ch, *3tr, tr2tog; rep from * around, sl st into 3rd ch (72 sts).

Round 4: 3ch, *2tr, tr2tog; rep from * around, sl st into 3rd ch (54 sts).

Round 5: 3ch, *1tr, tr2tog; rep from * around, sl st into 3rd ch (36 sts).

Round 6: 3ch, *tr2tog; rep from * around, sl st into 3rd ch (18 sts).

Round 7: 3ch, 1tr into each st, sl st into 3rd ch (18 sts).

Round 8: 3ch, *2tr in next st; rep from * around, sl st into 3rd ch (36 sts).

Round 9: 3ch, *2tr in next st, 1tr; rep from * around, sl st into 3rd ch (54 sts).

Round 10: 3ch, work 4tr in same st at base of ch, 1ch, 5tr in same sp, * miss 3 sts, (5tr, 1ch, 5tr) in next st; rep from * around, sl st in 3rd ch (13 shell clusters). Fasten off and weave in ends. Use the tapestry needle to weave the ribbon through stitches in round 7. Pull the ribbon tight and tie in a bow.

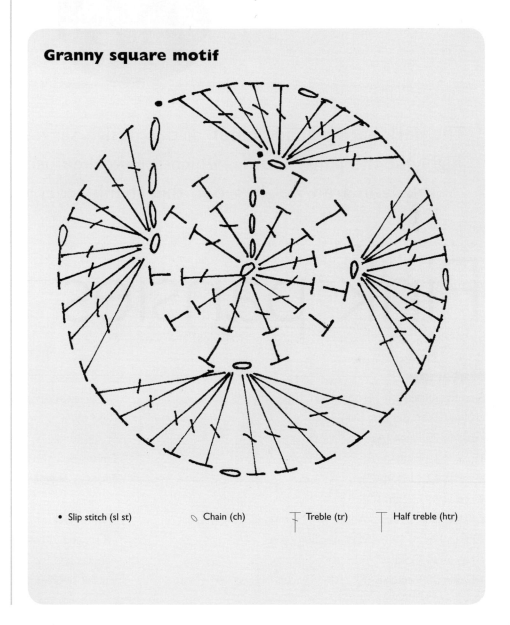

Granny square motif

• Slip stitch (sl st)   ○ Chain (ch)   ⊤ Treble (tr)   ⊤ Half treble (htr)

The dark background colour of this design serves as the perfect canvas to highlight the pansy motifs, which are worked using the intarsia technique. Made in aran-weight wool, this chunky cozy will be well insulated.

Pink pansies

Materials

Rico Essentials Soft Merino Aran, 100% merino wool (109yd/100m per 50g ball):
1 ball in 90 Black (A)
1 ball in 15 Fuchsia (B)
1 ball in 12 Orchid (C)
1 ball in 61 Cream (D)
Debbie Bliss Cashmerino Aran, 55% merino, 33% microfibre, 12% cashmere (98yd/90m per 50g ball):
1 ball in 34 Gold (E)
1 ball in 50 Pistachio (F)

A pair each of 5mm (UK6:US8) and 3mm (UK11:USC/2 or D/3) needles
Spare needle or stitch holder
Embroidery thread in co-ordinating colour
Tapestry needle

Tension

18 sts and 24 rows to 4in (10cm) over st st using 5mm needles and Rico Essentials Soft Merino Aran. Use larger or smaller needles if necessary to obtain the correct tension.

Sides (make 2)

With 5mm needles and B, cast on 43 sts.

Work 5 rows in g st.

Break off yarn and join in A.

Follow 44 rows of chart, shaping as shown on chart.

Cast off.

Pansies (make 3)

Top front petals (2 per flower)

With 3mm needles and C, cast on 5 sts.

Row 1: Knit.

Row 2: P1, M1, p3, M1, p1 (7 sts).

Row 3: K1, M1, k5, M1, k1 (9 sts).

Row 4: Purl.

Row 5: K4 C, k1 B, k4 C.

Row 6: P3 C, p3 B, p3 C.

Row 7: K2 C, k5 B, k2 C.

Row 8: P2tog C, p1 C, p3 B, p1 C, p2tog tbl C. (7 sts).

Row 9: Skpo C, k3 B, k2tog C. (5 sts).

Row 10: P2tog C, p1 B, p2tog tbl C. (3 sts).

Leave sts on spare needle or on stitch holder.

Lower front petal (1 per flower)

With 3mm needles and C, cast on 7 sts.

Row 1: Knit.

Row 2: P1, M1, p5, M1, p1 (9 sts).

Row 3: K1, M1, k7, M1, k1 (11 sts).

Row 4: P3 C, p5 B, p3 C.

Row 5: K2 C, k7 B, k2 C.

Row 6: P2tog C, p1 C, p5 B, p1 C, p2tog tbl C (9 sts).

Row 7: Skpo C, k1 C, k3 B, k1 C, k2tog C (7 sts).

Row 8: P2tog C, p1 C, p1 B, p1 C, p2tog tbl C (5 sts).

Row 9: Skpo C, k1 B, k2tog C (3 sts).

Leave sts on spare needle or on stitch holder.

Top back petals (make 6)

With 3mm needles and B, cast on 5 sts.

Row 1: Knit.

Row 2: P1, M1, p3, M1, p1 (7 sts).

Row 3: K1, M1, k5, M1, k1 (9 sts).

Rows 4 and 6: Purl.

Rows 5 and 7: Knit.

Row 8: P2tog, p5, p2tog tbl (7 sts).

Row 9: Skpo, k3, k2tog (5 sts).

Row 10: P2tog, p1, p2tog tbl. (3 sts).

Leave sts on spare needle or on stitch holder.

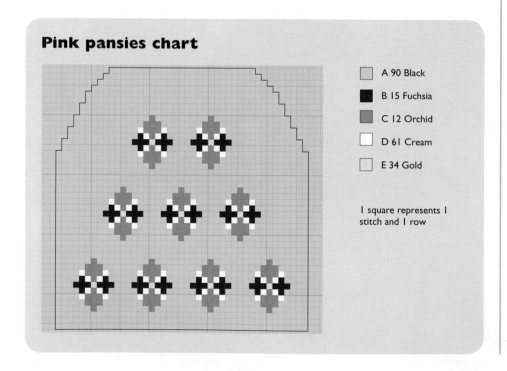

Pink pansies chart

- A 90 Black
- B 15 Fuchsia
- C 12 Orchid
- D 61 Cream
- E 34 Gold

1 square represents 1 stitch and 1 row

Leaves (make 3)

With 3mm needles and F, cast on 3 sts.

Foundation row: K1, p1, k1.

Row 1: K1, M1, k1, M1, k1 (5 sts).

Row 2: K2, p1, k2.

Row 3: K2, M1, k1, M1, k2 (7 sts).

Row 4 and foll even rows: K to centre st, p1, k to end.

Rows 5, 7 and 9: Knit.

Row 11: Skpo, k3, k2tog (5 sts).

Row 13: Skpo, k1, k2tog (3 sts).

Row 15: Sl 1, k2tog, psso, fasten off.

Making up

Using a length of embroidery thread and a tapestry needle, thread through the stitches of the two top front petals and one lower front petal left on a stitch holder, repeat once more, pull yarn together tightly, secure, do not fasten off.

With the two top back petals, thread through stitches left on holder, repeat once more, pull the yarn together, secure, place behind the top front petals overlapping them slightly, sew in place.

Using E, embroider French knots (see page 361) at centre of flowers.

Sew sides and top of main pieces, leaving gaps for the handle and spout. Sew pansies onto top centre, sewing leaves underneath flowers. Weave in all ends.

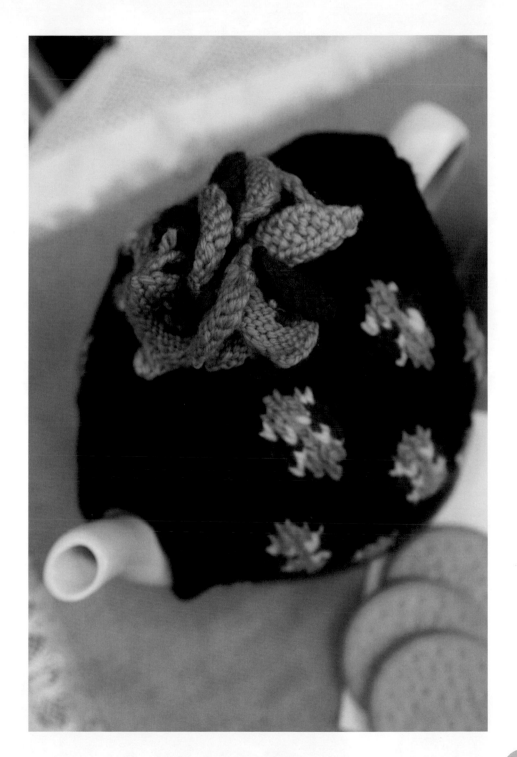

This delightful cozy was inspired by traditional Scandinavian designs, using the shapes of embroidered snowflakes but with wooden beads adding a twist. Using the retro colours suggested will bring a winter folk look to your table.

Winter Fair Isle

Materials
Rowan Kid Classic, 70% lambswool, 26% kid mohair, 4% nylon (153yd/140m per 50g ball):

1 ball in 828 Feather (A)

1 ball in 854 Tea Rose (B)

1 ball in 862 Teal (C)

1 ball in 853 Spruce (D)

A pair of 5mm (UK6:US8) needles

10 small unvarnished wooden beads

Tapestry needle

Tension
18 sts and 23 rows to 4in (10cm) square over st st using 5mm needles. Use larger or smaller needles to obtain correct tension.

Pattern notes

The tea cozy is worked using the Fair Isle method (see page 352) and the intarsia method (see page 353), where separate balls of yarn are used for each block of colour. Read the chart from right to left on right-side rows and from left to right on wrong-side rows.

Main piece (make 2)

With 5mm needles and A, cast on 44 sts. Knit 3 rows. Join in D.

Row 1: K2A, (p1A, p1D) 20 times, k2A.

Row 2: K2A, (k1A, k1D) 20 times, k2A.

These 2 rows set the pattern for chart 1 and g-st edgings.

Continue to follow chart 1, working in st st and g-st edges throughout until 11 rows have been worked.

Starting with a purl row, work 4 rows st st, dec 1 st on last row (43 sts). Cont as follows.

Row 1: K13A, follow row 1 of chart 2, k13A.

Row 2: K2A, p11, follow row 2 of chart 2, p11A, k2A.

These 2 rows set the pattern. Continue to follow chart 2 until 20 rows have been worked.

Shape top

Row 21: K2A, (k2Atog, k2A) 3 times, K5A, follow centre 5 sts of chart 2, k5A, (k2A, k2Atog) 3 times, k2A (37 sts).

Row 22: K2A, p15D; p3A; p15D, k2A.

Row 23: K2A, (k2Atog, k1A) 4 times, k2A, (k1D, k1A) twice, k1D, k2A, (k1A, k2Atog) 4 times, k2A (29 sts).

Working with A only, continue as follows.

Next and foll alt row: K2, p to last 2 sts, k2.

Next row: K2, (k2tog) 6 times, k1, (k2tog) 6 times, k2 (17 sts).

Next row: (K2tog) 4 times, K1, (K2tog) 4 times (9 sts).

Cast off.

Making up

Press pieces according to ball band. Using B and straight stitch, embroider snowflakes around main motif as shown. Sew on wooden beads. Sew side seams, leaving gaps for handle and spout.

Ties

Cut six 30in (76cm) lengths of yarn. Form into a plait, tie in a bow and sew on to top of cozy.

Winter Fair Isle chart 1
(10 sts x 11 rows)

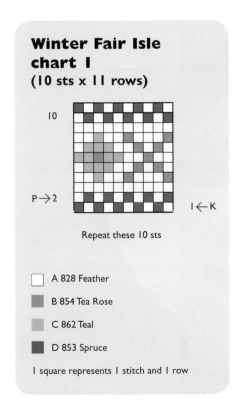

Repeat these 10 sts

☐ A 828 Feather

▨ B 854 Tea Rose

▨ C 862 Teal

▨ D 853 Spruce

I square represents 1 stitch and 1 row

Winter Fair Isle chart 2
(17 sts x 23 rows)

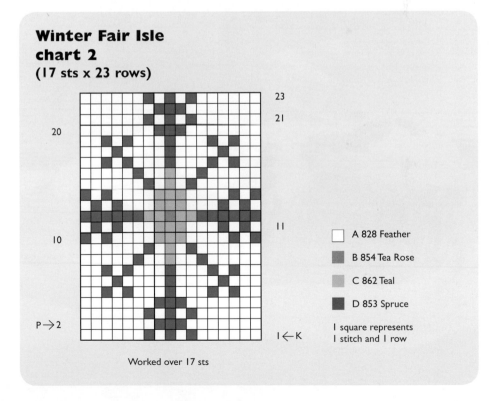

Worked over 17 sts

☐ A 828 Feather

▨ B 854 Tea Rose

▨ C 862 Teal

▨ D 853 Spruce

I square represents 1 stitch and 1 row

Country Life

Bring the great outdoors to your tea table with these fabulous country-themed cozies. Designs range from quaint to sophisticated, from a Loopy Lamb to a Cottage Garden, with lots of lovely cozies that reflect the changing seasons in between.

This cuddly cozy was inspired by Swaledale sheep, the fleece of which were traditionally used in carpet making. The looped pile and matching lining provide excellent insulation for your teapot.

Loopy lamb

Materials

British Breeds Jacob Aran, 100% wool:
(162yd/148m per 100g ball)
3 balls in Cream (A)
1 ball in Grey (B)
A pair of 4.5mm (UK7:US7) needles
Black tapestry wool to embroider the eyes and nose
A small quantity of washable stuffing or wadding
for the nose
A stitch holder, a safety pin large enough to hold 7 sts
and a tapestry needle for sewing up

Tension

18 sts and 24 rows to 4in (10cm) square in st st.
15 sts and 26 rows to 4in (10cm) square in loop stitch.
Use larger or smaller needles if necessary to obtain the correct tension.

Back head

With 4.5mm needles and A, cast on 42 sts.

Row 1: Purl

Row 2: K1 (loop 1 to last st) k1. Rep last 2 rows 14 more times, marking either end of row 9 to assist with sewing up (30 rows).

Row 31: Marking either end of this row with contrasting yarn, p1 (p2tog, 5 times) p20 (p2tog, 5 times) p1 (32 sts).

*Row 32 and every alt row: As row 2.

Row 33: (P6, p2tog) to end (28 sts).

Row 35: (P5, p2tog) to end (24 sts).

Row 37: (P4, p2tog) to end (20 sts).

Row 39: (P3, p2tog) to end (16 sts).

Row 41: (P2, p2tog) to end (12 sts).

Row 42: This will be decreasing and casting off at the same time. P2tog twice. Pass first loop over second, *p2tog, pass prev st over, repeat from * to end.

Front head

As for back until 3 loop rows have been knitted.

Row 7: P5, purl twice into next st (for selvedge). Put these 7 sts onto a safety pin. (They will later be used to knit the RH side of the face.) Cast off 30 sts p-wise (should leave 1 st on RH needle and 5 sts on LH needle. Purl twice into next st, purl to end (7sts on needle).

Row 8: K1, loop 5 sts, k1.

Row 9: Purl.

Row 10: As Row 8

Rows 11–22: As rows 9 and 10 (6 times).

Row 23: Inc 1 st, purl to end of row (8 sts).

Row 24: K1, loop 6, k1.

Row 25: Cast on 2 sts, purl to end of row (10 sts).

Row 26: K1, loop 8, k1.

Row 27: As row 25 (12 sts).

Row 28: K1, loop 10, k1.

Row 29: Cast on 4 sts, purl to end of row (16 sts).

Row 30: K1, loop 14, k1.

Put these 16 sts onto a stitch holder. Replace the 7 sts held on a safety pin onto the needle such that you can commence work with RS facing. Rejoin yarn and knit the LH side of face to match, rows 8–30, reversing the shapings such that the inc are at the end rather than the beginning of the row.

Row 31: P1 (p2tog, 5 times) p5, cast on 10 sts and then cont across the 16 sts for the RH side left on a stitch holder, p5 (p2tog, 5 times) p1. You should now have 32 sts on the needle and the 2 sides of the face should be joined.

Rows 32–43: As given for back.

Face

With 4.5mm needles and B, cast on 36 sts. (**Note:** *This does not correspond to the number of sts left in the front head because of the difference in tension between st st and loop stitch.*)

Rows 1–15: Starting with a purl row, work 15 rows in st st.

Row 16: K2tog, k to last 2 sts, k2tog, marking the 18th stitch with contrasting yarn to guide the positioning of the nose (34 sts).

Rows 17–22: Continue in st st, casting off 2 sts at beg of next 2 rows, 4 sts at beg of next 2 rows, and then 5 sts at beg of foll 2 rows (12 sts).

Row 23: Cast off p-wise.

Nose

With 4.5mm needles and A, cast on 32 sts.

Rows 1–6: Starting with a knit row, work in st st.

Row 7: K2tog to end (16 sts).

Row 8: Purl.

Rows 9–12: Rep rows 7 and 8 twice more (4 sts).

Leaving a long enough tail to sew on the nose, cut the yarn and pull through the remaining 4 sts to secure.

Eyes (make 2)

These are worked from the top down. With A and 4.5mm needles cast on 5 sts.

Row 1: Working in st st, start with a purl row.

Row 2: Inc 1 st at both ends (7 sts).

Row 3: Purl.

Row 4: With RS (k side) of work facing, inc 1 st at beg of row (8 sts).

Rows 5–6: Cont to inc 1 st at same side of work as in row 4 (10 sts on needle).

Row 7: Dec 1 st at beg of row, purl. (9 sts).

Row 8: Knit, dec 1 st at end of row (8 sts).

Row 9: Purl, dec 1 st at both ends (6 sts).

Row 10: Knit to last 2 sts, k2tog (4 sts).

Cast off p-wise, marking the last st with contrasting yarn. This marks the bottom outside corner of the eye where it will be sewn to the face edge. Make another eye, reversing the shaping.

Ears (make 4)

With 4.5mm needles and B, cast on 6 sts.

Starting with a knit row, k2 rows in st st.

Row 3: Inc 1 st at each end, knit (8 sts).

Row 4: Purl.

Rep the last 2 rows twice more (12 sts).

Rows 9–11: Cont straight in st st on 12 sts.

Rows 12–16: Cont in st st, dec 1 st at each end of every row (2 sts).

Row 17: K2tog and pass yarn through rem loop to secure.

Make 3 more the same.

Lining (make 2)

Using A and 4.5mm needles, cast on 50 sts (more than for outside of cozy because of difference in tension).

Rows 1–4: K1, p1 rib.

Rows 5–28: In st st, starting with a knit row.

Row 29: K1 (k2tog, 6 times) k24, (k2tog, 6 times) k1 (38 sts).

Row 30 and each foll alt row: Purl.

Row 31: (K7, k2tog) 4 times, k to end, (34 sts).

Row 33: (K6, k2tog) 4 times, k to end (30 sts).

Row 35: (K3, k2tog) 6 times (24 sts).

Row 37: (K2, k2tog) 6 times (18 sts).

Row 39: K3, k2tog, (k2, k2tog) twice, k3, k2tog (14 sts).

Row 41: Dec and cast off simultaneously: K2tog, k2tog, pass first loop over second, **k2tog, pass previous loop over. Rep from ** to end.

Making up

Block out and very lightly steam all the stocking stitch pieces to facilitate sewing up. Fit the face into the front head and pin to hold in place.

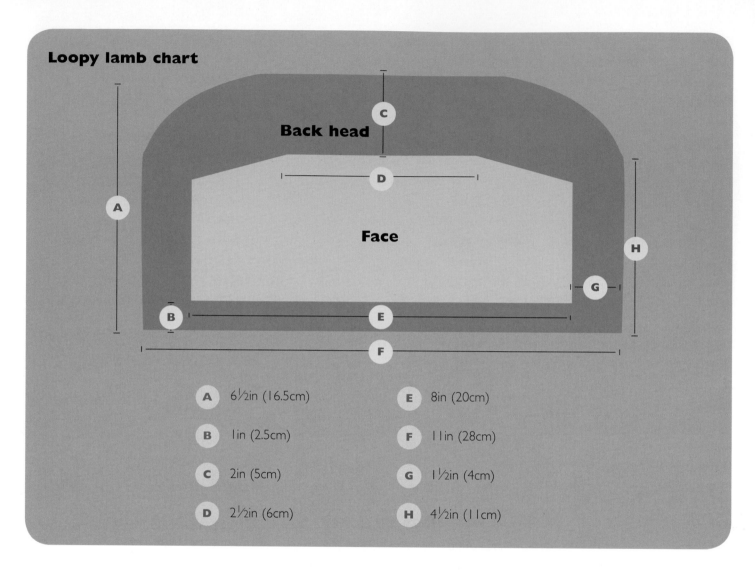

Loopy lamb chart

Back head

Face

A	6½in (16.5cm)	E	8in (20cm)
B	1in (2.5cm)	F	11in (28cm)
C	2in (5cm)	G	1½in (4cm)
D	2½in (6cm)	H	4½in (11cm)

Sew together, fitting it close to the 'roots' of the loops. The best finish is achieved by sewing with the right side facing you.

Join the two straight edges of the nose. Line up the point on the outer, curved edge immediately opposite the seam

you have just made with the marker on the face. That seam should then be at the bottom centre edge of the face. Pin the outer edge to the face in an approximate circle, so that the nose takes a cone shape, and sew to the face leaving sufficient room to insert stuffing. Stuff firmly and sew up the gap.

With the cast-off edge of the eyes at the top, position the eyes at the outer corners of the face and sew on. Using tapestry yarn double, embroider the eyes and nose as shown using a simple straight stitch. Make up the ears by seaming the outer edges, but leaving the bottoms open. Put aside.

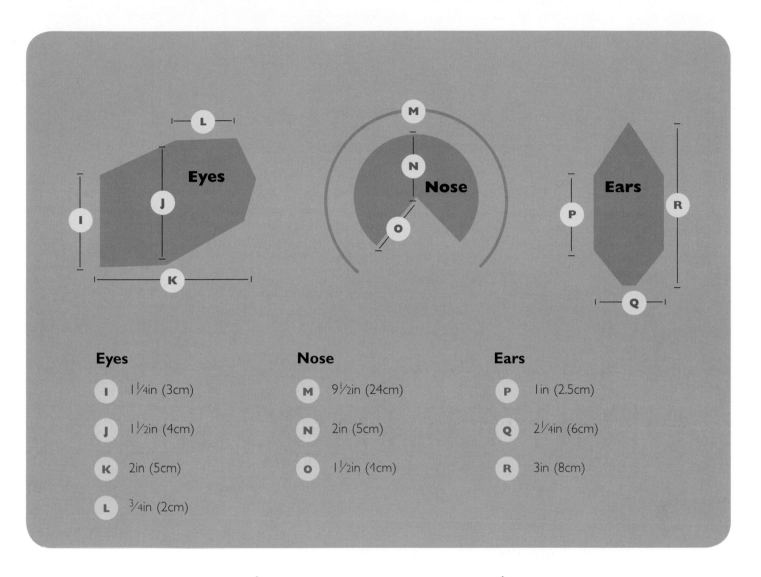

Eyes

I	1¼in (3cm)
J	1½in (4cm)
K	2in (5cm)
L	¾in (2cm)

Nose

M	9½in (24cm)
N	2in (5cm)
O	1½in (4cm)

Ears

P	1in (2.5cm)
Q	2¼in (6cm)
R	3in (8cm)

Using the markers of contrasting yarn as a guide, sew up the two looped outer sides of the cozy leaving an opening between the markers for the handle and spout. Sew the two sides of the lining together in the same way. Take a thread through the top centre of the lining and through the top centre of the outer cozy. The inside of the lining should show the knit side. Pull through to help position the lining and secure. Sew the lining to the outer cozy at the bottom edges and at the spout and handle gaps.

Next fix the ears. Tuck the bottom ⅜in (1cm) of each ear into itself to make a firm base. Fold each ear along its length and catch in this position with a stitch at the base. Position the ears on the seam of the outer cozy and secure.

This charming design evokes light-dappled water, water lilies and the fleeting iridescence of a dragonfly. The cozy was inspired by Monet's famous paintings of water lilies and will bring a touch of summer to any tea-time table.

Summer mood

Materials

Hayfield Bonus DK, 100% acrylic (306yd/280m per 100g ball):
1 ball in each of 0904 Orchard (A) and 0958 Light Pink (B)
Patons Dreamtime 2 ply, 100% wool (372yd/340m per 50g ball):
Small quantity of 0051 White (C) (alternatively, organdie or satin ribbon or felt, cut to shape to mimic dragonfly wings, could be used)
A pair of 3.75mm (UK9:US5) needles
Set of 5 x 3.75mm (UK9:US5) double-pointed needles
2 x 3.25mm (UK10:US3) and 2 x 2.5mm (UK13:US1) double-pointed needles
Fine crochet hook (optional)

4 x ⅛in (4mm) teal beads
6 x ⅛in (4mm) gold beads
Beading needle
Clear sewing thread
Dressmaking pins
Tapestry needle

Tension

22 sts and 25 rows to 4in (10cm) over st st using 3.75mm needles and Hayfield Bonus DK yarn. Use larger or smaller needles if necessary to obtain the correct tension.

Special abbreviations

Kfb: Knit into the front and back of the next stitch.

PB: Place bead by slipping a stitch as it comes off the left needle (purlwise) and onto the right, pushing a bead up the yarn as close to the slipped stitch as possible without slack, then knit the next stitch to secure the bead.

Pattern notes

The basic cozy is knitted in four simple stages, then each water lily is worked, followed by the I-cord with the dragonflies. Leave long cast-on and cast-off tails throughout, as they will be used for sewing up. Unless otherwise directed, use the thumb cast-on method throughout (see page 347).

Basic leaf border

With 3.75mm needles and A, and using thumb method, cast on 8 sts.

Row 1 (RS): K5, yf, k1, yf, k2 (10 sts).
Row 2: P6, kfb, k3 (11 sts).
Row 3: K4, p1, k2, yf, k1, yf, k3 (13 sts).
Row 4: P8, kfb, k4 (14 sts).
Row 5: K4, p2, k3, yf, k1, yf, k4 (16 sts).
Row 6: P10, kfb, k5 (17 sts).
Row 7: K4, p3, k4, yf, k1, yf, k5 (19 sts).
Row 8: P12, kfb, k6 (20 sts).
Row 9: K4, p4, sl1, k1, psso, k7, k2tog, k1 (18 sts).
Row 10: P10, kfb, k7 (19 sts).

Row 11: K4, p5, sl1, k1, psso, k5, k2tog, k1 (17 sts).
Row 12: P8, kfb, k2, p1, k5 (18 sts).
Row 13: K4, p1, k1, p4, sl1, k1, psso, k3, k2tog, k1 (16 sts).
Row 14: P6, kfb, k3, p1, k5 (17 sts).
Row 15: K4, p1, k1, p5, sl1, k1, psso, k1, k2tog, k1 (15 sts).
Row 16: P4, kfb, k4, p1, k5 (16 sts).
Row 17: K4, p1, k1, p6, sl1, k2tog, psso, k1 (14 sts).
Row 18 (WS): P2tog, cast off next 5 sts using p2tog st to cast off first st, p3, k4 (8 sts).
Rep rows 1–18 six times more (7 leaves in total). Cast off.

Sides (make 2)

Pin the leaf border in a circle, RS together and sew up along the garter-st border for around ¾in (2cm) to form a ring. Turn RS out and fold in half with seam just made to the right. Using 3.75mm needles and A, pick up 48 sts evenly on the first half. (It is sometimes easier to do this with a crochet hook, putting them onto the needle one by one facing correctly for a knit row. This is optional; otherwise pick up using the preferred method.)

Row 1 (WS): K4, p to last 4 sts, k4.
Row 2: K4, *p1, k3; rep from * to last 4 sts, k4.
Row 3: K4, *k1, p5, k1, p1; rep from * to last 4 sts, k4.
Row 4: K4, *k2, p1, k3, p1, k1; rep from * to last 4 sts, k4.
Row 5: K4, *p2, k1, p1, k1, p3; rep from * to last 4 sts, k4.
Rep rows 2–5 six times more (7 repeats in all).
With RS facing, put sts onto 3.75mm dpns.

Join sides

Round 1: *P1, k3; rep from * to end of round (96 sts).
Round 2: K3, p1, *k1, p1, k5, p1; rep from * to last 4 sts, k1, p1, k2.
Round 3: K2, p1, k1, *k2, p1, k3, p1, k1; rep from * to last 4 sts, k2, p1, k1.
Round 4: K1, p1, k2, *k3, p1, k1, p1, k2; rep from * to last 4 sts, k3, p1.
Rep rounds 1–4 three more times.

Eyelets

Round 1: Purl.
Round 2: Knit.
Round 3: *K2, yf, k2tog; rep from * to end of round.

Round 4: Knit.

Round 5: Purl.

Picot edging

Rounds 1–2: Knit.

Round 3: *Yf, k2tog; rep from *
to end.

Rounds 4–6: Knit.

Cast off k-wise, leaving a long tail, and
break yarn.

Fold the picot in half to the inside of
the cozy, being careful to ensure that
the picots match to provide an even
crenulation. Pin into place, then catch
the sts down, so that no sts show
on RS.

Water lilies (make 6)

These are made in one long piece of
five small petals then five larger ones.
The large ones form the centre, while
the small petals make the splayed
outer section.

With 3.25mm dpns and B, cast on
7 sts.

Small petals

Row 1: Purl.

Row 2: Knit.

Row 3: Purl.

Row 4: Cast off 5 sts knit-wise, leaving
2 sts on the needles, knit the last st.

Row 5: Purl.

Row 6: Put the right needle
through the first stitch and knit a stitch

(3 stitches on the needle). Cast on 4 sts using cable cast-on method (see page 346) and knit the row (7 sts). Rep rows 1–6 four more times so that there are five small petals in all ending on a row 5.

Large petals

Row 1: Put right needle into first stitch, knit a stitch (3 stitches on the needle). Cast on 5 sts using cable cast-on method and knit the row (8 sts).
Row 2: Purl.
Row 3: Knit.
Row 4: Purl.
Row 5: Cast off 6 sts with 2 rem on the needle, k the last st, turn.
Row 6: P to the end, turn.

Rep last 6 rows four more times so that there are five large petals in all. On the last large petal when reaching row 5, cast off all 8 sts and fasten off, leaving a long tail.

I-Cord and Dragonflies

The I-cord and dragonfly bodies are made in one piece with the wings knitted separately and pushed through the body afterwards. The right and left wings are made in one piece, large and small. Make two large and two small, pairing them as directed.

Small wings (make 2)

Using 2.5mm dpns and C, cast on 17 sts.

Row 1 (WS): P to end.
Row 2: (Sl1, k1, psso) twice, k to the last 4 sts, (k2tog) twice (13 sts).
Row 3: P to end.
Row 4: (Sl1, k1, psso) three times to last 6 sts, (k2tog) three times (7 sts).
Row 5: Cast off p-wise.

Large wings (make 2)

Using 2.5mm dpns and C, cast on 21 sts.

Row 1 (WS): P to end.
Row 2: (Sl1, k1, psso) twice, k to the last 4 sts, (k2tog) twice (17 sts).
Row 3: P to end.
Row 4: (Sl1, k1, psso) four times, k to last 8 sts, (k2tog) four times (9 sts).
Row 5: Cast off p-wise.

I-Cord

Thread four teal beads onto yarn A. With 2.5mm dpns, cast on 4 sts and make I-cord that measures 1¼in (3.5cm).

Change to 3.25mm dpns and work as before until the I-cord measures 2½in (6cm).

Next row (first dragonfly): K1, M1R, k3 (5 sts).
Row 2: K1, PB, k1, PB, k1.
Row 3: K1 to end (as I-cord).
Row 4: Sl1, k1, psso, k1, k2tog (3 sts).
Change to 2.5mm dpns and knit backwards and forwards without turning until work measures

24½in (62cm) excluding the dragonfly just worked.

Change to 3.25mm dpns.

Next row (second dragonfly): K1, M1R, k1, M1L, k1 (5 sts).

Next row: K to end.

Next row: K1, PB, k1, PB, k1.

K (as I-cord) for a further 1in (2.5cm).

Change to 2.5mm dpns.

Next row: Sl1, k1, psso, k3 (4 sts).

K (as I-cord) and work for a further 1¼in (3.5cm).

Cast off, leaving a long tail.

Making up
Wings

Start at top right-hand corner of the large wings. With a yarn tail weave the yarn around the wing edges, gathering only slightly. Fasten off. Repeat with the other large wing and then the small wings. Take the large wings again and with the yarn tail at the bottom left, run it along the back of the wing to the centre. Both wings should have their curves pointing downwards. Place the smaller wing centrally on top, balancing its top edge on the lower edge on the large wing. Pin into place and attach the smaller wing to the large one neatly. To do this, use the bottom left yarn tail on the smaller wing, running it along its edge approximately halfway, and ruche both wings slightly. Fasten off. Repeat with the other wings.

I-cord

Draw the yarn tail up through the centre of the I-cord for approx. 1½in (3.5cm) of tail, work some running stitches around the body in a circle at this point and pull tight. At 1½in (3.5cm) from the bottom of the tail, place the wings by drawing them gently through the body horizontally, using a crochet hook or preferred method. Pull the yarn tail up through the body again for approx. 1in (2.5cm) and repeat the running stitches as above. Repeat this once more, taking the yarn tail to one row above the eyes and work some running stitches in a circle and pull tight. Run the yarn inside the I-cord for a few rows, catch it down, run it back again and fasten off so that the cut yarn does not show. Repeat this at the other end, using the first dragonfly as a template for the second one, to ensure that the tail, body and head divides are evenly executed.

Water lilies

Thread the long yarn tail onto a tapestry needle and work the yarn around each petal to the base of every one from the first large petal to the last small one, gently gathering them to form delicate curves. Fasten off. With the other yarn tail, thread along the base of the petals gathering this to form a flower. The petals may twist in on themselves at this point; if this happens, just untwist them. The five large ones should form the centre with one in the middle and four around it. The five small ones will form a flower shape, cradling the larger centre. Draw the yarn tails neatly through the central hole formed by the gathers, fasten off, then trim. Repeat until all the flowers are complete.

Cozy

Weave in any loose ends and fasten off neatly. With leaf border seam to the right, thread the I-cord through the eyelets so that the tail ends are centrally placed at the front for tying, allowing the dragonflies to 'hover' above the pond. Gather and tie. Place over a teapot, balled towel or similar. Thread a beading needle with invisible thread and pick up a gold bead. Pin the first lily in place and attach with the bead in the centre, running a few stitches underneath the lily pad, fasten off and cut. Repeat with the other lilies, placing them evenly. Remember not to start with the lily pad under the spout, as this is impractical! Start centrally and flank one lily on either side of it.

This pretty felted cozy uses soft colours that really evoke a sense of warmth and homeliness. If dogs aren't your thing, create a stencil of your choice to add your own personal touch.

Country kitchen

Materials

Crystal Palace Yarns Iceland, 100% wool
(99m/109yd per 100g ball):
2 balls 7063 Dutch Blue
Oddment of 5329 Celadon (optional)
2 × 10mm (UK000:US15) circular needles, 16in (41cm) long
5mm (UK6:USH) crochet hook, tapestry needle, felting needles (36 and 40 gauge)
Felting sponge or block
Straight pins (for securing pattern to work area)
Silhouettes of a dog breed, centre cut out to produce a stencil

Fibre, bits of yarn or wool from many sources, some dyed for felting the decorations on cozy after knitting and machine or hand felting the cozy.
Two small button eyes, appropriate size for the dog breed you have chosen, or other figures

Tension

Tension is not critical for this project – the size will be determined by the felting process.

Pattern notes

When felted, the cozy will be approx. 10in (25cm) high and 13in (33cm) wide.

Cozy

Using one of the circular needles, cast on 92 sts, placing a marker on the needle after the 46th st and at beg of the row. Be careful not to twist sts, knit every row. At 3in (7.5cm) a contrasting row can be added. When the knitting is 11in (28cm) long from beg, start dec as follows: Before and after the 2 st markers k2tog on every other row until the overall length from beg is 18in (46cm). There will be 34 sts left on the needles, 17 stitches between the markers.

Turn inside out and place 17 sts on another circular needle. Use 3-needle cast off and cast off all stitches to form the top of the cozy. If you would like the cozy to be larger cast on more stitches and work more rows.

Loop

With 5mm crochet hook, make 16ch. Attach securely to middle of the top of the cosy and weave in the end around the loop three times to make the loop thicker and the base a bigger attachment. Weave in all loose ends.

Felting

Use very hot water (104°F/40°C) and put cozy in a fastened pillowcase to protect the washing machine. Place a small amount (½ tspn) of liquid soap or detergent on the pillowcase and place in the washing machine on high agitation. Check the progress of the felting process every 5–10 minutes and continue to agitate until the piece has felted to your liking. You can hand felt but it may require more patience.

Rinse with cool water when felting is complete to remove the rest of the soap. Roll the finished felted cosy in towels to remove most of the moisture and then lay out to dry. Shaping should be done at this point. If your teapot has decorative sides or is particularly round, the felt will stretch at this point and can be shaped to fit your particular teapot.

Needle felting

Once dry, take a silhouette of the dog breed you prefer and cut out the centre of the silhouette carefully. This will leave the white portion of the paper as a stencil. Put the stencil portion on the felt fabric with the fibre

or wool under the paper. Secure the paper with straight pins to the felting surface or felting block. Do not worry that the fibre or wool extends beyond the stencil edges.

To needle felt to the fabric, hold a felting needle straight up and down. Poke the needle through the yarn and fabric, working along its length until the yarn is felted to the underlying fabric. Begin by needle felting the edges of the

dog and then work in slowly to attach the fibre to the felt. Carefully lift up small sections of stencil and fold the excess fibre or wool into the centre of the pattern, felting as you go around the outside edge. Add fibre anywhere it is needed or to get the look you want.

Add any flowers or other felted decorations freehand with coloured or natural fibre or wool. Sew on button eyes, and the tea cozy is complete.

Dog template
(actual size)

This design is the perfect accessory for a summer tea party with scones, cream and strawberry jam. The wool yarn is used double to keep your cuppa piping hot, and an easy, raised pattern mimics the strawberry pips.

Strawberry fields

Materials

Patons Fairytale Dreamtime DK, 100% wool
(98yd/90m per 50g ball):
1 ball in 04967 Red (A)
Oddment of 04985 New Lime for leaves (B)
A pair of 5mm (UK6:US8) needles
Darning needle

Tension

13 sts and 19 rows to 4in (10cm) square over st st using 5mm needles and yarn double. Use larger or smaller needles to obtain correct tension.

Pattern notes

Yarn is used double throughout.

Side 1

With 5mm needles and A double, cast on 29 sts and work 2 rows in g-st.
Work 3 rows in st st.
Now work in pattern thus:

Row 1: (K5, p1) to last 5 sts, k5.
Row 2: K1, p to last st, k1.
Row 3: Knit.
Row 4: K1, p to last st, k1.
Row 5: K2, (p1, k5) to last 3 sts, p1, k2.
Row 6: K1, p to last st, k1.
Row 7: Knit.
Row 8: K1, p to last st, k1.
These 8 rows form the pattern.

Work a further 16 rows in patt. Work should measure just over 5in (12.5cm). Adjust height at this point if required. Break off yarn and leave sts on a spare needle.

Side 2

With 5mm needles and A double, cast on 29 sts and work as given for first side but begin pattern at row 5. Do not break off yarn.

Join top

Next row: P2tog, p across rem sts, then p across sts on spare needle to last 2 sts, p2tog (56 sts).
Work 2 rows in st st.

Next row (dec): (K5, k2tog) across (48 sts).
Join in B and work thus, changing colours as given and stranding yarn loosely across back of work:
Next row: P3A, (p1B, p5A) to last 3 sts, p1B, p2A.
Next row: (K1A, k2B, k1A, k2togA) 8 times (40 sts).
Next row: P2A, (p2B, p3A) to last 3 sts, p2B, p1A.
Next row: (K3B, k2togA) to end (32 sts).
Next row: (P1A, p3B) to end.
Break off A and cont in B only.
Next row: Using B, (k2, k2tog) to end (24 sts).
Next row: Purl.
Next row: (K1, k2tog) to end (16 sts).
Next row: Purl.
Next row: (K1, k2tog) to last st, k1 (11 sts).
Cast off very loosely.

Making up

Press very lightly. Join the first few rows from lower edge on each side. Join remainder of seam from top down, leaving a gap each side of approx. 3in (7.5cm) for the spout and handle.

Cat lovers will adore this cheerful design with the cute little mouse peering nervously from the top of the lid. Attractive flowers complete the design.

Cat & mouse

Materials

1 x 50g ball of any white DK yarn (A)

1 x 50g ball of any grey-mix DK yarn (B)

Oddment of black and fawn DK yarn for cat and mouse

Oddments of green, yellow, pink, blue and brown DK yarn for leaves and flowers

A pair each of 5mm (UK6:US8), 4mm (UK:US6) and 3.25mm (UK10:US3) needles

3.25mm (UK10:USD/3) crochet hook

Tapestry needle

Small amount of toy stuffing

Tension

Not critical as fabric is very stretchy.

Sides (make 2)

With 5mm needles and one strand of A and one strand of B, mix together and cast on 29 sts and work in pattern:
Row 1: K3, *(p1, k1, p1, k1, p1, k4); rep from * across row, ending last rep k3.
Row 1: P4, *(k1, p1, k1, p6); rep from * across row, ending last rep p4.
Work for 40 rows in total.

Shape top

Row 1: K3, *(k2tog, k2); rep from * to last 2 sts, k2tog (22 sts).
Rows 2 and 4: Purl.
Row 3: K2, *(k2tog, k1); rep from * to last 2 sts, k2tog (15 sts).
Row 5: K1, *(k2tog); rep from * to end (8 sts).
Break yarn and thread through rem sts. Fasten off.

Making up

Sew up 1¾in (2cm) from bottom.
Leave opening for handle and spout.
Sew rem seam to top.

Small leaves (make 3)

With 4mm needles and one strand of green, cast on 8sts.
Next row: K6, turn.
Next row: Sl1, k3, turn.
Next row: Sl1, k to end.
Cast off all sts.

Large leaves (make 7)

With 4mm needles and one strand of green, cast on 12 sts.
Next row: K10, turn.
Next row: Sl1, k7, turn.
Next row: Sl1, k3, turn.
Next row: Sl1, k to end.
Cast off all sts.

Large flower

With 3.25mm hook and one strand of pink, make 5ch and sl st into first ch to form a ring.
Round 1: 4ch, (1tr, 1ch) 7 times into ring, sl st into third of 4ch.
Round 2: Sl st into first ch sp, *(3ch, 3tr, 3ch, sl st into ch sp, sl st into next ch); rep from * to end.
Fasten off.

Small flowers (make 1 blue, 1 yellow)

With 4mm needles, cast on 16 sts.
Next row: (P2tog) to end (8 sts).
Thread yarn through rem sts and fasten off.
Join seam and embroider contrast cross stitch in centre.

Flower stems

With 3.25mm hook and one strand of green, make 15 ch and fasten off. Make another, 10ch long, and fasten off.

Cat

With 4mm needles and one strand of black, cast on 8 sts.
Row 1: Knit.
Row 2: Knit, inc 1 st at each end.
Row 3: Knit.
Rows 4 and 5: As last 2 rows (12 sts).
Work 10 rows in g-st.
Next row: Dec 1 st at each end.
Work 3 rows in g-st.
Next row: Dec 1 st at each end of row (8 sts).
Work 2 rows g-st.
Next row: (K2tog) to end (4 sts).
Next row: Inc in every st (8 sts).
Work 2 rows in g-st.
Next row: Inc 1 st at each end of row (10 sts).
Work 6 rows in g-st.
Dec 1 st at each end of foll 2 rows (6 sts).

Shape ears

Next row: K3, turn.
Knit 1 row.
Next row: K3tog.
Fasten off. Rejoin yarn and complete other ear to match.

Tail

Using black, cast on 16 sts.
Cast off.

Mouse

With 4mm needles and one strand of brown, cast on 6 sts.

Row 1: Inc in every st to end (12 sts).
Beg purl, work 7 rows st st.
Change to 3.25mm needles.

Shape head

Row 9: K2tog, k8, k2tog (10 sts).
Rows 10, 12 and 14: Purl.
Row 11: K2tog, k6, k2tog (8 sts).

Row 13: (k2tog, k1) twice, k2tog (5 sts).
Thread yarn through rem sts.
Fasten off.

Making up

Sew in ends of yarn. Join cover 1¼in (3cm) up from lower edge and approx. 5in (13cm) from top, fitting on pot to check before fastening off. Attach cat to cozy, curving tail as shown.

Assemble 7 large leaves, the large flower and the small blue flower and attach to top. Assemble 3 small leaves, the stems and 4 small flowers and attach as shown.
Sew seam of mouse and stuff. Crochet chain for mouse's tail and make loops for ears. Embroider eyes and nose. Attach to cozy.

In this design, strands of green and white yarn worked together give the effect of a misty spring morning. The leaves and flowers are worked separately and sewn on when the cover is complete.

Spring morning

Materials

Any DK yarn:
1 x 100g ball in green (A)
1 x 50g ball in white (B)
Oddments of yellow and pink
A pair of 5.5mm (UK5:US9) needles
A pair of 4mm (UK8:US6) needles
A 3.25mm (UK10:USD/3) crochet hook
Narrow ribbon for bows
Tapestry needle

Tension

Not critical as garter stitch rib pattern is very stretchy.

Sides (make 2)

Using 5.5mm needles and one strand of green and one strand of white, cast on 29 sts.

Row 1: K to end.

Row 2: *(P1, k3); rep from * to last st, p1.

These two rows form the garter stitch rib pattern. Work in patt for 40 rows.

Shape top

Next row: K3, *(k2tog, k2); rep from * to last 2 sts, k2tog (22 sts).

Next row: *(P1, k2); rep from * to last st, p1.

Next row: K2, *(k2tog, k2); rep from * to last 2 sts, k2tog (15 sts).

Next row: *(P1, k1); rep from * to end, p1.

Next row: K1, *(k2tog); rep from * to end (8 sts).

Break yarn and thread through rem sts. Fasten off.

Leaves (make 16)

With 4mm needles and one strand of A, cast on 2 sts.

Next row: Inc 1, k to end.

Rep last row until there are 8 sts. Work 8 rows in g-st.

Next row: Sl1, k1, psso, k to end.

Next row: K2tog.

Fasten off.

Large crochet flower

Using yellow yarn, make 6ch and join into ring using a sl st.

Round 1: Work (1 dc, 3ch) six times into ring. Join to first dc using a sl st. Change to pink yarn.

Round 2: Ss into first 3-ch sp. Work (1dc, 3ch, 3tr, 3ch, 1dc) into each space. Join to first dc using a sl st. Fasten off.

Chain flower base

With 3.25mm crochet hook and A, make 10ch and ss into first ch to form a loop.

Repeat until there are five loops. Join using a sl st and fasten off.

Small crochet flower

Using pink yarn, make a ring round finger and work (2ch, 2tr, 2ch, 1ss) five times into. Join using a sl st and fasten off. Pull starting thread into a tight ring and fasten off.

Making up

Join both sides of cover for 1¼in (3cm). Leave a 2¼in (5.5cm) gap for handle and spout. Join rem seam on either side.

Layer eight of the leaves and the large crochet flower and attach to top of cover as shown. Join the six small crochet flowers to the flower bases. Arrange the flowers and the rest of the leaves to the cover as shown. Finish off with two small double ribbon bows.

Tip
Changing the flowers will give the cozy a completely different look. Why not have a tea cozy with an appropriate flower for each season?

An idyllic country cottage with flowers and smoke from the chimney gives this cozy a fairy-tale look. You'll look forward to your tea by the fire with a favourite book.

Country cottage

Materials

Artesano 100% Pure Superfine Alpaca DK
(109yd/100m per 50g ball):
1 ball in each of SFN10 Cream (A), C734 Poinsettia (B),
C864 Forget Me Not (C) and C704 Violet (D)
Oddments of CA13 Sweet Pea or any similar yarn (E)
A pair of 3.75mm (UK9:US5) needles
2.5mm (UK12:USC/2) crochet hook
2mm (UK14:USB/1) crochet hook
Darning needle

Tension

21 sts and 28 rows to 4in (10cm) square over patterned st st using 3.75mm needles. Use larger or smaller needles to obtain correct tension.

Pattern notes

The cozy is worked using the Fair Isle method (see page 352) and also the intarsia method (see page 353), where separate balls of yarn are used for each block of colour. Read chart from right to left on right-side rows and from left to right on the wrong-side rows.

Sides (make 2)

With 3.75mm needles and A, cast on 50 sts using the thumb method (see page 347).
Knit 4 rows.

With RS facing for next row, beg with a knit row and working in st st throughout, work from chart until rows 1 to 32 have been completed. With RS facing for next row and at the same time following chart, dec 1 st at each end of next and 3 foll alt rows then on foll 5 rows (32 sts). Cast off 2 sts at beg of next 4 rows (24 sts).
Next row: Cast off 8 sts, place the st left on RH needle and next 6 sts onto a holder. Carry yarn used to cast off the first 8 sts behind work and cast off rem sts.

With RS of work facing, using 3.75mm needles and 2 strands of B, purl across the 7 sts held on holder.
Next row: Purl.
Next row: Knit.
Repeat last 2 rows twice more.
With WS facing, knit 4 rows.
Cast off knitwise on WS.

Smoke twirl

With 2.5mm crochet hook and A,
make a chain length of 26 sts.
Row 1: Work 2 dc into second ch
from hook and every ch to end.
Fasten off.

Making up

Work a large French knot (see page
361) in C as shown on row 13 of chart
for door knob.

Sew up sides of cozy, allowing a gap of
3½in (9cm) for spout and 4in (10cm)
for handle. Sew up sides of chimney pot.
Place smoke twirl inside chimney and
sew in place either side of the inside
of cozy.

Embroidery

With E, embroider French knots
around doorway.

Flowers (make 20)

With 2mm crochet hook and D, make
a slipped ring as follows:
Make a loop by wrapping yarn

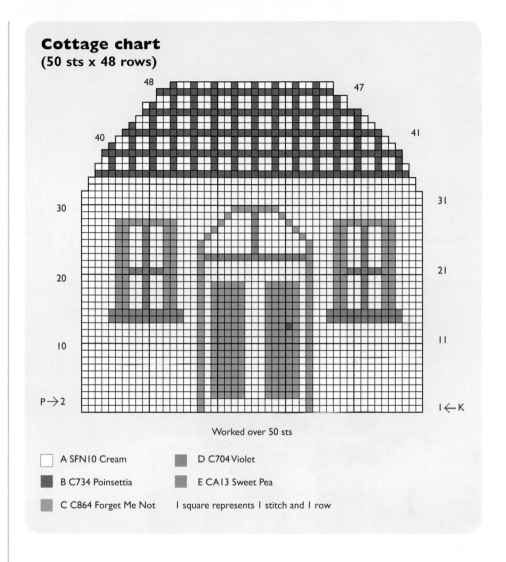

Cottage chart
(50 sts x 48 rows)

Worked over 50 sts

- ☐ A SFN10 Cream
- ■ B C734 Poinsettia
- ■ C C864 Forget Me Not
- ■ D C704 Violet
- ■ E CA13 Sweet Pea

1 square represents 1 stitch and 1 row

around forefinger; take loop off finger
but still hold between thumb and
forefinger; insert hook through loop, yrh
(1 loop on hook), draw through ring,
yrh, and draw through loop (this has
secured the ring).
Now work *2ch, 1tr into ring, 2ch,
sl st into ring (1 petal made); rep

from * until 5 petals have been made.
Fasten off.
Pull the loose end of the slipped ring
firmly to close the centre of the flower.

Making up

Place flowers all around the base of the
tea cozy as in the photo; sew in place.

Relax with a refreshing cup of tea and let this cozy, with its cable and ruffle patterns, remind you of equally relaxing walks in the woods through tall tree trunks under a lush canopy of leaves.

Woodland walk

Materials

Rowan Felted Tweed, 50% merino, 25% rayon, 25% alpaca (191yd/175m per 50g ball):
1 ball in 145 Treacle (A)
Rowan Pure Wool DK, 100% wool (137yd/125m per 50g ball):
1 ball in 050 Pine Needle (B)
A pair each of 3.25mm (UK10:US3) and 4mm (UK8:US6) needles
Cable needle
Darning needle

Tension

22 sts and 30 rows to 4in (10cm) square over st st using 4mm needles and yarn B. Use larger or smaller needles to obtain correct tension.

Special abbreviations

C6B: Slip 2 sts onto the cable needle, leave at the back of the work, k4 sts, p2 sts from cable needle.

C6F: Slip 4 sts onto the cable needle, leave at the front of the work, p2 sts, k4 sts from cable needle.

C4B: Slip 2 sts onto the cable needle, leave at the back of the work, k2 sts, p2 sts from cable needle.

C4F: Slip 2 sts onto the cable needle, leave at the front of the work, p2 sts, k2 sts from cable needle.

Tree trunk (make 2)

With 3.25mm needles and A, cast on 60 sts.

Next row (RS): P6, (k8, p12) twice, k8, p6.

Next row (WS): K6, (p8, k12) twice, p8, k6.

Repeat last 2 rows once more. Change to 4mm needles. Repeat last 2 rows until work measures 2in (5cm) from cast-on edge, ending with a WS row.

Woodland cable pattern

Work next 12 rows as given below or from woodland cable pattern chart.

Row 1: P4, (C6B, C6F, p8) twice, C6B, C6F, p4.

Row 2: (K4, p4) twice, k8, p4, k4, p4, k8, (p4, k4) twice.

Row 3: (P4, k4) twice, p8, k4, p4, k4, p8, (k4, p4) twice.

Row 4: As row 2.

Row 5: P2, (C6B, p4, C6F, p4) twice, C6B, p4, C6F, p2.

Row 6: K2, (p4, k8, p4, k4) twice, p4, k8, p4, k2.

Row 7: P2, (k4, p8, k4, p4) twice, k4, p8, k4, p2.

Row 8: As row 6.

Row 9: P2, k2, C4F, *p4, (C4B, C4F) twice; rep from * once, p4, C4B, k2, p2.

Row 10: (K2, p2) twice, k4, p2, k4, p4, (k4, p2) twice, k4, p4, k4, p2, k4, (p2, k2) twice.

Row 11: (P2, k2) twice, p4, k2, p4, k4, (p4, k2) twice, p4, k4, p4, k2, p4, (k2, p2) twice.

Row 12: As row 10.

Begin shaping

Row 13 (dec): (P2, k2) twice, p1, p2tog, p1, k2, p1, p2tog, p1, k4, p1, p2tog, p1, k2, p4, k2, p1, p2tog, p1, k4, (p1, p2tog, p1, k2) twice, p2, k2, p2 (54 sts).

Row 14: (K2, p2) twice, k3, p2, k3, p4, k3, p2, k4, p2, k3, p4, (k3, p2) twice, k2, p2, k2.

Leafy tree tops

Row 15: Join in B, (p3, cast on 6 sts onto left-hand needle then knit them) 17 times, p3 (156 sts).

Row 16: *K3, p6; rep from * to last 3 sts, k3.

Row 17: *P3, k2tog, k2, k2tog; rep from * to last 3 sts, p3 (122 sts).

Row 18: *K3, p4; rep from * to last 3 sts, p3.

Row 19: *P3, (k2tog) twice; rep from * to last 3 sts, p3 (88 sts).

Row 20: *K3, p2; rep from * to last 3 sts, k3.

Row 21: *P2, sl1, k2tog, psso; rep from * to last 3 sts, p3 (54 sts).

Row 22 (dec): K4, *k2tog, k2; rep from * to last 6 sts, k2tog, k4 (42 sts).

Row 23: (P3, cast on 6 sts onto left-hand needle then knit them) 13 times, p3 (120 sts).

Row 24: *K3, p6; rep from * to last 3 sts, k3.

Row 25: *P3, k2tog, k2, k2tog; rep from * to last 3 sts, p3 (94 sts).

Row 26: *K3, p4; rep from * to last 3 sts, k3.

Row 27: *P3, (k2tog) twice; rep from * to last 3 sts, p3 (68 sts).

Row 28: *K3, p2; rep from * to last 3 sts, k3.

Row 29: *P2, sl1, k2tog, psso; rep from * to last 3 sts, p3 (42 sts).

Row 30 (dec): K3, *k2tog, k1; rep from to last 3 sts, k3 (30 sts).

Row 31: (P3, cast on 6 sts onto left-hand needle then knit them) 9 times, p3 (84 sts).

Row 32: *K3, p6; rep from * to last 3 sts, k3.

Row 33: *P3, k2tog, k2, k2tog; rep from * to last 3 sts, p3 (66 sts).

Row 34: *K3, p4; rep from * to last 3 sts, k3.

Row 35: *P3, (k2tog) twice; rep from * to last 3 sts, p3 (48 sts).

Row 36: *K3, p2; rep from * to last 3 sts, k3.

Row 37: *P2, sl1, k2tog, psso; rep from * to last 3 sts, p3 (30 sts).

Row 38 (dec): (K2tog) 15 times (15 sts).

Row 39: Knit.

Row 40: (K2tog, k1) 5 times (10 sts). Break yarn, thread through remaining stitches, gather up and fasten off. Make another piece the same.

Making up

Join the sides, matching the pattern. Leave an opening for the handle and spout measuring 3in (8cm) from the top and 1¼in (3cm) from the lower edge.

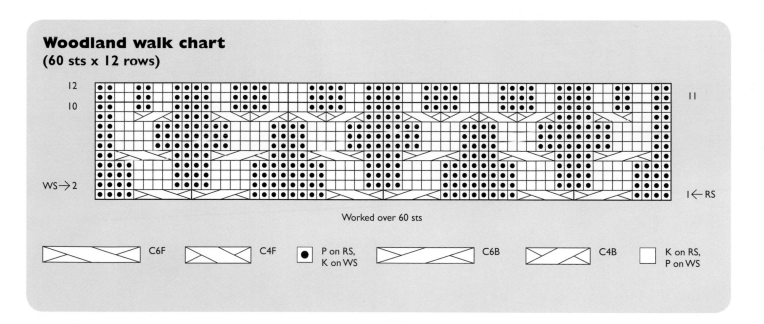

Woodland walk chart
(60 sts x 12 rows)

Worked over 60 sts

C6F | C4F | ● P on RS, K on WS | C6B | C4B | ☐ K on RS, P on WS

This delightful tea cozy uses fresh spring colours to depict an intricate scene of a badger deep in the bluebell wood and a fox among the foxgloves, all garlanded by primroses.

Springwatch

Materials

Jaeger Baby Merino DK, 100% merino
(130yd/120m per 50g ball):
1 ball in each of Pale Green (A) and Primrose (B)
Jaeger Matchmaker DK, 100% merino wool
(130yd/120m per 50g ball):
1 ball in each of Bluebell (C) and Winter White (D)
Small amounts of same yarn in Black (E), Grey (F), Dark
Green (G), Mid Green (H) and Mustard (J).
Debbie Bliss Alpaca Silk DK, 80% alpaca, 20% silk (approx.
114yd/104m per 50g ball):
1 ball in Russet (K)

Small bits of 4-ply yarn in 3 hues of pink for the foxgloves
Jaeger Siena 4 ply cotton – for lining (140m/153yd
per 50g ball): 1 ball in any colour
A pair of 2.75mm (UK12:US2) double-pointed needles.
A pair each of 3.75mm (UK9:US5) (plus 1 spare)
and 2.75mm (UK12:US2) needles.

Tension

22 sts and 30 rows to 4 in (10cm) square using
3.75mm needles. Use larger or smaller needles to
obtain correct tension.

Special abbreviations

KT = knot: using C, cast on 2 sts, cast off 2 sts, all into same st. Also used for badger's eyes in D, and fox's eyes in J.

Before commencing

Wind off separate balls of yarn as follows:
3 each in D and E
2 each in C and A

Method

With 3.75mm needles and A, cast on 56 sts. Work in k1, p1 rib for 3 rows.
Next row (WS): Knit.
Begin with a knit row, work 2 rows st st. Now work rows 1–8 inclusive of chart C, using Fair Isle method and rep the 8 sts 7 times along row, to form primrose border.

Now work 24 rows of chart B, using intarsia method for fox, A for either side of fox, and approx. 30in (76cm) lengths of H for foxglove stems.
At end of 24 rows, leave sts on spare needle, breaking off yarn.

Work second piece in same way, following chart A for 24 rows, again using intarsia method for badger and separate balls of yarn for bluebells either side.
Next row: Using A (but continuing to work foxglove stems in H) knit across all 56 sts, then across 56 sts of first piece.
Next row: Purl across all 112 sts.

Commence shaping

Row 1:: *K5, k2tog, rep from * to end.
Row 2 and foll alt rows: Purl.
Row 3: *K4, k2tog, repeat from * to end.
Continue decreasing in this manner to 32 sts, ending with a purl row.
Next row: K1 *yn fwd k2tog, repeat from * to last st, k1.
Next row: Purl.
Now work 7 rows of chart A, commencing with row 2, rep the 8 sts 4 times across the rows.
Next row (WS): Knit.
Beg with knit row, work 8 rows of st st, then cast off.

Foxgloves

Buds

Make 2 or 3 for top of foxglove stems.
Using size 2.75m needles and pink 4
ply, cast on 2 sts.

Row 1: Knit, inc in both sts.

Rows 2 & 4: Purl.

Row 3: Knit, inc in first and last st.

Row 5: K2tog 3 times.

Row 6: P3tog.

Cut off yarn leaving enough to sew up
side seam and attach to cozy, threading
yarn through rem st to fasten it off.

Gloves

Make 4, 5 or even 6 in appropriate
pink 4 ply yarn.
Using 2.75mm needles, cast on 12 sts.

Row 1: P1, slip next 2 sts p-wise, p9.

Row 2: Sl 1 p-wise, k2, sl 1 p-wise,
turn.

Row 3: P4, turn.

Row 4: Sl 1 p-wise, k3, sl 1 p-wise,
turn.

Row 5: P5, turn.

Row 6: K12.

Row 7: P1, sl 1 p-wise, turn.

Row 8: K2, turn.

Row 9: P2, sl p-wise, turn.

Row 10: K3 turn.

Row 11: P12.

Row 12: K2tog, k to last 2 sts, k2tog.

Row 13: Purl.

Rep last 2 rows until 4 sts rem, ending
with a purl row. Then, k2tog twice, sl
first st over 2nd and fasten off. Again,
leave adequate yarn to sew up seam
and attach to cozy.

Lining (make 2)

With 3.75mm needles and 4 ply
Siena, cast on 49 sts. Work in st st
for 32 rows.

Shape top

Work as for top of cozy, until 21 sts.
Cast off. Sew to inside of cozy, placing
knit side of lining to inside of cozy.

Making up

Press cozy lightly under damp cloth.
Sew on foxglove flowers and buds,
keeping seam to back of work. Sew in
all ends.

Turn three rows of rib at base of cozy
over to form hem, and catch down.
Rep at top of cozy, with eight rows
st st.

Attach lining, then sew up side seams,
leaving gap for handle and spout.

Chart A
(56 sts x 24 rows)

Work in st st. Each square = 1 st and 1 row. Read RS rows from R to L and WS (purl) rows from L to R.

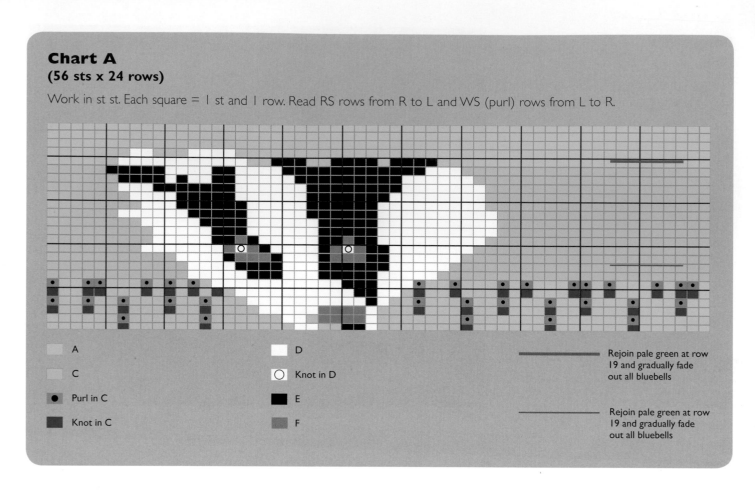

	A			D			Rejoin pale green at row 19 and gradually fade out all bluebells
	C		○	Knot in D			
●	Purl in C		■	E			Rejoin pale green at row 19 and gradually fade out all bluebells
■	Knot in C			F			

Cord

Using A and 2.75mm double-pointed needles, cast on 2 sts.

Next row (RS): K2 – both sts, now on RH needle *slip both sts to opposite end of needle and transfer this needle to LH, without turning work and taking yarn tightly across back of work, knit same 2 sts again – both sts now on RH needle again. Rep from * until cord measures approx. 21in (54cm), k2tog and fasten off.

Thread through eyelet holes, to meet in centre of badger.

Bluebell tassels (make 2)

With 3.75mm needles and C, cast on 16 sts.

Row 1: Knit.
Rows 2, 4, 6 & 8: Purl.
Row 3: K1 *yf, k2tog, rep from * to last st, k1.
Row 5: Knit.

Row 7: Make picot hem by knitting each st along row tog with its corresponding st on cast on edge.
Row 9: K2tog 8 times.
Row 10: P2tog 4 times.

Cut off yarn, leaving enough to sew up side of bell and threading yarn through rem 4 sts, drawing up tightly. Thread a bell onto end of cord, and knot end of cord to secure in place.

Chart B
(56 sts x 24 rows)

Work in st st. Each square = 1 st and 1 row. Read RS rows from R to L and WS (purl) rows from L to R.

	A			Knot in J
	D			K
	E			H Use strands of approx. 76cm (30in) for full length stems

Chart C
(8 sts x 8 rows)

Work in st st. Each square = 1 st and 1 row. Read RS rows from R to L and WS (purl) rows from L to R.

	A
	H
	B
	J

A tea-loving gardener's dream, this unusual design
mixing crochet and embroidered detailing will remind
you of summery warmth all year round.

Cottage garden

Materials

Aran yarn wool/synthetic mix
(approx. 180yd /164m per 100g ball):
1 x 100g ball in cream (A)
Oddments of chunky yarn in purple (B)
Oddments of 4-ply yarn in blue (C) and green (D)
Small oddment of 4-ply metallic yarn
(E – for butterfly body)
Oddments of fancy textured yarn
(for French knot embroidery at base)
3.5mm (UK9:USE/4) and 4.5mm (UK7:US7)
crochet hooks

Tension

18 sts and 24 rows to 4in (10cm) square over st st
using 4.5mm crochet hook. Use larger or smaller crochet
hook to obtain correct tension.

Main body (make 2)

Work 2 pieces alike.

With 4.5mm hook and A, make 39ch. Miss 1ch. Dc in 38ch (add one turning ch at beg of each row).

Work until piece measures 8in (20cm). Fasten off.

Gusset strip

With 4.5mm hook and A, make 16ch. Miss 1ch, dc into 15ch (remembering to add the turning ch at beg).

Work until the strip fits round three sides of the tea cozy. Fasten off.

Flower (make 6)

With 4.5mm hook and B, make 6chs, join into a circle with a sl st. 1ch and 7dc into the ring, sl st to first ch, dc all the way round, ending with a sl st in the first ch and beg each row with 1ch. Work 1 more row. (Another row can be added, if desired.)

Then work 4ch, miss 1dc, dc into next ch, 3ch, dc into next ch, rep until end.

Sl st into base of first st. Fasten off.

Butterfly (small circle) (make 2)

With 3.5mm hook and C, make 6ch, sl st to form a circle. Work 6dc into the ring. (Another row of dc can be added, if desired.) Fasten off with a sl st.

Large wing (large oval) (make 2)

With 3.5mm hook and C, work 8ch, join with a sl st. Work 6dc, 1htr, 1 tr, 8dc into ring. Fasten off.

Body (make 1)

With 3.5mm hook and E double, work 8ch. Work 1 or 2 rows of dc. Fasten off. Any finer thread can be used for the body.

Making up

When the three 3 main parts have been crocheted, start placement of the crochet flowers and wool embroidery.

Positioning of crochet flowers

Find the centre on the two squares. Attach the first flower. When attaching the first flower, attach it on its reversed side so that a bit of a ridge shows in the centre. Back stitch round the centre of the flower so that it is attached firmly to the background square. Place the other two flowers at both sides of the central flower and attach in the same manner. Now embroider the flower stems using D in chain stitch.

Embroider the grass by using straight stitch all along the bottom of the square. Using the fancy yarn, make the

French knots, on the grass stalks. Embroider the two leafy stalks and the stalks with the lilac buds in chain stitch and 3-times chain stitch for the buds.

Join the large wing of the butterfly to the small wing using a small overcast stitch. Repeat this twice. Attach the body to the wings by using small back stitches. Attach the butterfly to the grass, near the lilac buds. Do not make another butterfly on the other square piece. The butterfly is only attached to one side of the work.

Embroider the branch in chain stitch, embroider the buds in chain stitch treble. Then add the sequins.

Gusset strip

Join the gusset strip to the left side of the square using a small back stitch. When this is done, with 4.5mm hook and A, work 4ch, 1dc into both gusset strip and rectangle, leaving a ⅜in (1cm) gap. Repeat the process around the three sides of the square.

Work another row, starting with 4ch, 1dc into next ch, to end. Fasten off. Attach the other square in the same manner to the gusset strip.

Lining

Make the lining by cutting the lining ⅜in (1cm) bigger than the main three pieces. Fold the lining under for ⅜in (1cm) and attach on the wrong side of the tea cozy by using a small overcast stitch.

Tip

It can be tricky to keep crocheted edging even. If you are unhappy with the first attempt, simply unravel and start again.

Inspired by a walk in the autumn countryside, fallen leaves in soft colours are topped with acorns and oak leaves. This cozy brings a taste of the countryside to your tea table, wherever you are.

Falling leaves

Materials

Sublime Cashmere Merino Silk DK, 75% extra fine merino, 20% silk, 5% cashmere (127yd/116m per 50g ball):
1 ball in 03 Vanilla (A)
Sublime Extra Fine Merino Wool DK, 100% extra fine merino (127yd/116m per 50g ball):
1 ball in each of 203 Limone (B) and 019 Waterleaf (C)
Sublime Baby Cashmere Merino Silk DK, 75% extra fine merino, 20% silk, 5% cashmere (127yd/116m per 50g ball):
1 ball in 124 Splash (D)
Small amount of cotton wool for stuffing

A pair each of 3.25mm (UK10:US3), 3.75mm (UK9:US5) and 4mm (UK8:US6) needles
Darning needle

Tension

22 sts and 28 rows to 4in (10cm) square over st st using 4mm needles. Use larger or smaller needles to obtain correct tension.

Pattern notes

The tea cozy is worked using the Fair Isle method (see page 352) and the intarsia method (see page 353), where separate balls of yarn are used for each block of colour. Read chart from right to left on right-side rows and from left to right on wrong-side rows.

Sides (make 2)

With 3.75mm needles and A, cast on 50 sts using the thumb method.
Knit 4 rows.
Change to 4mm needles.
Beg with a knit row and working in st st throughout and following chart, work from row 1 to 32, ending with RS facing for next row.

With RS facing for next row, continuing to work from chart, dec 1 st at each end of next and 3 following alternate rows then on following 5 rows (35 sts).
Cast off 2 sts at beg of next 4 rows (27 sts).
Cast off remaining sts.

Oak leaves (make 3)

With 3.25mm needles and C, cast on 3 sts.

Stem

Rows 1 and 3: Purl.
Rows 2 and 4: Knit.

Leaf

Row 1: Knit.
Row 2: Cast on 3 sts, k4, p1, k1 (6 sts).
Row 3: Cast on 3 sts, knit to end (9 sts).
Row 4: Knit to centre st, p1, knit to end.
Row 5: Knit.
Row 6: Cast off 2 sts, knit to centre st, p1, knit to end (7 sts).
Row 7: Cast off 2 sts, knit to end (5 sts).
Row 8: As row 4.
Row 9: As row 5.
Row 10: Cast on 2 sts, knit to centre st, p1, knit to end (7 sts).
Row 11: Cast on 2 sts, knit to end (9 sts).
Row 12: As row 4.

Row 13: Knit.

Row 14: Cast off 3 sts, p1, knit to end (6 sts).

Row 15: Cast off 3 sts, knit to end (3 sts).

Row 16: As row 10 (5 sts).

Row 17: As row 11 (7 sts).

Row 18: As row 4.

Row 19: Knit.

Rows 20 and 21: Cast off 2 sts, knit to end (3 sts).

Row 22: Knit.

Row 23: K3tog.

Fasten off.

Acorns (make 3)

With 3.25mm needles and C, cast on 5 sts.

Row 1: Knit into front and back of each st (10 sts).

Row 2: Knit.

Row 3: *K1, knit into front and back of next st; rep from * to end (15 sts).

Rows 4, 5 and 6: Knit.

Change to B, beg with a knit row and working now in st st, cont as foll:

Row 7: *K2tog, k1; rep from * to end (10 sts).

Rows 8, 10 and 12: Purl.

Rows 9 and 11: Knit.

Row 13: (K2tog) 5 times (5 sts).

Thread yarn through remaining sts, pull tight and secure.

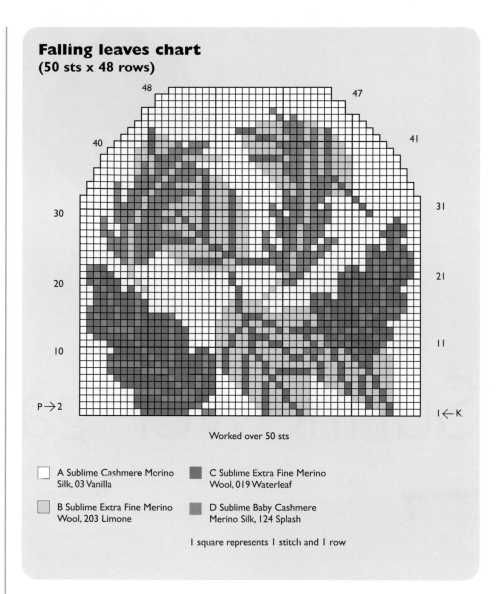

Falling leaves chart
(50 sts x 48 rows)

Worked over 50 sts

A Sublime Cashmere Merino Silk, 03 Vanilla

B Sublime Extra Fine Merino Wool, 203 Limone

C Sublime Extra Fine Merino Wool, 019 Waterleaf

D Sublime Baby Cashmere Merino Silk, 124 Splash

1 square represents 1 stitch and 1 row

Making up

Sew up side seam of acorn to start of st st. Using either a knitting needle or a thick darning needle push cotton wool tightly into the acorn, then complete sewing up.

Sew up sides of cozy allowing a gap of 3½in (9cm) for spout and 4in (10cm) for handle.

Place oak leaves and acorns onto the top centre of cozy as shown and sew in place.

Tiny buttons in the shape of bees inspired this design.
The cheerful sunflowers are worked separately and sewn on,
while the leaves are part of the cable pattern.

Sunflower garden

Materials

Sirdar Country Style DK, 40% nylon, 30% wool, 305 acrylic
(170yd/155m per 50g ball):

Approx. 1 ball in 419 Green (A)

Oddments of yellow (B) and brown (C) 4-ply yarn for
sunflowers

A pair each of 2.75mm (UK12:US2), 3.25mm (UK10:US3)
and 4mm (UK8:US6) needles

Cable needle

Assorted buttons to decorate

Tapestry needle

Sewing needle and green thread

Tension

22 sts and 30 rows to 4in (10cm) over st st using
4mm needles. Use larger or smaller needles to obtain
correct tension.

Special abbreviations

Inc 1: Work into the front, then the back of the next st to inc.

C6R: sSip 3 sts onto a cable needle and hold at back, k3, then p3 from the cable needle.

C6L: Slip 3 sts onto a cable needle and hold at front, p3, then k3 from the cable needle.

Sl1p-wise: Slip 1 stitch with needles held as if to purl.

Wyib: With the yarn in back.

Sides (make 2)

With 3.25mm needles, the long tail method and A, cast on 41 sts and work 9 rows k1, p1 rib.

Next row: (P1, inc1); rep to last st, p1 (61 sts).

Change to 4mm needles and work the background for the sunflowers:

Leaf pattern background

Row 1: K3, p5, (k6, p7) three times; k6, p5, k3.

Row 2: K8, (p6, k7) three times; p6, k8.

Row 3: As row 1.

Row 4: As row 2.

Row 5: K3, p2, (C6R, C6L, p1) four times; p1, k3.

Row 6: K5, (p3, k6, p3, k1) four times; k4.

Row 7: K3, p2, (k3, p6, k3, p1) four times; p1, k3.

Row 8: As row 6.

Row 9: As row 7.

Row 10: As row 6.

Row 11: K3, p2, (k3tog, p6, k3tog, p1) four times, p1, k3 (45 sts).

These 11 rows complete the section. Work the next 7 rows in rev st st with a g-st border thus:

Wrong side rows: Knit.

Right side rows: K3, p to last 3 sts, k3.

Next row: K3, k2tog, k to last 5 sts, k2tog, k3 (43 sts).

Now work 5 rows in slip stitch rib thus:

Slip stitch rib

Row 1: K5, *(p3, k2); rep from * to last 3 sts, k3.

Row 2: K3, p2, *(k1, sl1p-wise wyib, k1, p2); rep from * to last 3 sts, k3.

Change to 3.25mm needles and work another 10 rows slip stitch rib.

Work 8 rows in g-st.

Next row: *(K1, k2tog); rep from * to last st, k1 (29 sts).

Beg with a purl row, work 3 rows in st st.

Next row: *(K2tog, k1); rep from * to last 2 sts, K2tog (19 sts).

Beg with a purl row, work 3 rows in st st.

Knit 2 rows.

Next row: *(K1, k2tog); rep from * to last st, k1 (13 sts).

Knit 1 row.

Next row: *(K1, k2tog); rep from * to last st, k1 (9 sts).

Knit 1 row.

Cast off loosely using a 4mm needle.

Sunflowers (make 8)

With 2.75mm needles and B, cast on 5 sts.

Next step: *Cast off 3sts, K1, turn, K2, cast on 3 sts.

Rep from * until you have knitted a strip of 15 petals.

Cast off, leaving a length of yarn to sew up with. Sew a running stitch along the straight edge of the strip, pull to gather and join the two ends of the strip to complete the petals.

Centre of sunflower

Using C, cast on 2 sts.

Work in g-st, inc1 at the start of each row until there are 8 sts on the needle. Knit 2 rows straight.

Next step: Still working in g-st, k2tog at the start of each row until there are 2 sts on the needle. K2tog and finish off, leaving a length of yarn to sew up with.

Sew a running stitch round the edge of the piece and pull tight to gather. Knot to the end of yarn at the cast-on edge, then attach the centre to the middle of the petals.

Making up

Join 1¼in (3cm) at the lower edge and 2½in (6cm) at the top for the handle seam. Join 1in (2.5cm) at the bottom and 4in (10cm) at the top for the spout seam. These are approximate measurements; after joining it is best to try the cozy on the teapot and adjust seams as necessary before fastening off. Using green yarn sew the sunflowers in place on the tea cozy. Finally, using green sewing thread, attach small buttons of bees and ladybirds if you can get them, or any others that will go well with the cozy.

Tip

It is easier to position the decorative buttons if you place the cozy on the pot first.

This comical shaggy sheep character is perfect for warming the pot. The lovely loopy stitch is extremely effective and makes a very snuggly cozy.

Sheepish look

Materials

King Cole Fashion Aran, 70% acrylic, 30% wool
(218yd/200m per 100g ball):
2 balls in 46 Natural (A)
1 ball in 48 Black (B)
A pair of 5mm (UK8:US6) needles
Tapestry needle
Toy stuffing

Tension

18 sts and 25 rows to 4in (10cm) square over st st using 5mm needles. Use larger or smaller needles to obtain correct tension.

Body (make 2)

Using 5mm needles and A, cast on 44 sts and work 5 rows in single (k1, p1) rib.

Row 6: Knit.

Row 7: K1, *ML, rep from * to last st, k1.

Rows 8 to 29: Rep rows 6 and 7, 11 times, forming loop pattern.

Row 30: K2tog, *k1, rep from * to last st, k2tog (42 sts).

Row 31 and all foll odd rows: As row 7.

Row 32: K2tog, *k1, rep from * to last st, k2tog (40 sts).

Row 34: K2tog, *k1, rep from * to last st, k2tog (38 sts).

Row 36: K2tog. *k1, rep from * to last st, k2tog (36 sts).

Row 38: K2tog, k9 k2tog, k10 k2tog, k9 k2tog (32 sts).

Row 40: K2tog, k8 k2tog, k8 k2tog, k8 k2tog (28 sts).

Row 42: K2tog, k6 k2tog, k8 k2tog, k6 k2tog (24 sts).

Row 44: K2tog, k5 k2tog, k6 k2tog, k5 k2tog (20 sts).

Row 46: K2tog, k4 k2tog, k4 k2tog, k4 k2tog (16 sts).

Row 48: * K2tog, rep from * to end (8 sts).

Cast off.

Head (make 2)

Using B, cast on 6 sts.

Row 1: Inc 1 st into each st across the row (12 sts).

Row 2 and foll even rows: Purl.

Row 3: Inc 1 st into each st across the row (24 sts).

Row 5: K1, m1 k to last st, m1, k1 (26 sts).

Rows 7, 9, 11 & 13: Knit.

Row 15: K1, k2tog, knit to last 3 sts, k2tog, k1 (24 sts).

Row 17: Knit.

Row 19: K1 k2tog, knit to last 3 sts, k2tog, k1 (22 sts).

Row 21: Knit.

Row 23: K1, k2tog, knit to last 3 sts, k2tog, k1 (20 sts).

Row 25: Knit.

Row 27: K1, k2tog, knit to last 3 sts, k2tog, k1 (18 sts).

Rows 29, 31 & 33: Knit.

Row 35: K1, k2tog, knit to last 3 sts, k2tog, k1 (16 sts).

Row 37: K1, k2tog, knit to last 3 sts, k2tog, k1 (14 sts).

Row 39: K1, k2tog, knit to last 3 sts, k2tog, k1 (12 sts).

Row 40: P1, p2tog, p to last 3 sts, p2tog, p1 (10 sts).

Cast off.

Ears (make 2)

Using B, cast on 4 sts.

Row 1 and all foll odd rows: Knit.

Row 2: Inc 1, knit to last st, inc 1, (6 sts).

Row 4: Inc 1, knit to last st, inc 1, (8 sts).

Row 6: Inc 1, knit to last st, inc 1, (10 sts).

Row 8: K4, inc 1, inc 1, k4 (12 sts).

Row 10: K5, inc 1, inc 1, k5 (14 sts).

Row 12: K5, k2tog, k2tog, k5 (12 sts).

Row 14: K4, k2tog, k2tog, k4 (10 sts).

Row 16: K2tog, k6, k2tog (8 sts).

Row 18: K2tog, k4, k2tog (6 sts).

Row 20: K2tog, k2, k2tog (4 sts).

Cast off.

Making up

With loop sides out, put front and back body pieces around teapot and mark openings for spout and handle with safety pins. Join seams, apart from these openings. Sew bound-off edges of the ears onto one of the head pieces. Now sew the front and back head pieces together, so the ear join is concealed in the seam. Leave small opening to stuff with washable toy stuffing, or old scraps of fabric or yarn. Sew opening together. With A yarn, sew eyes onto sheep using satin stitch. Stitch length of yarn through back of head, leaving two long ends. Stitch these ends onto the sheep body to fix in place.

These colourful crocheted butterflies are sure to brighten up any teatime, no matter what the weather, as the sky-blue cozy they rest on keeps your tea nice and warm.

Butterflies

Materials
Rowan Pure Wool DK, 100% wool
(137yd/125m per 50g ball):
1 ball in 006 Pier (A)
Any DK yarn in 3 colours (B, C and D) for each butterfly
Oddment of DK yarn in black (E) for the butterfly body
3mm (UK11:USC/2 or D/3) and 4mm (UK8:USG/6)
crochet hooks
Darning needle

Tension
9 sts and 10½ rounds to 4in (10cm) over treble st using 4mm hook. Use larger or smaller hook to obtain correct tension.

Special abbreviations
To increase:
Tr2inc: 2tr into next stitch.
Htr2inc: 2htr into next stitch.
Dc2inc: 2dc into next stitch.

Cozy

With 4mm hook and A, wind yarn round finger twice to form a ring.

Round 1: Into ring work 1dc, 2ch (to count as first tr), 17tr, sl st to second of 2ch. Pull tightly on short end to close ring (18 sts).

Round 2 (inc): 3ch (to count as first tr), 1tr, tr2inc, *1tr, (tr2inc) twice; rep from * 4 more times, 1tr, sl st to third of 3ch (30 sts).

Round 3 (inc): 3ch (to count as first tr), (tr2inc, 2tr) 9 times, tr2inc, 1tr, sl st to third of 3ch (40 sts).

Round 4 (inc): 3ch (to count as first tr), (tr2inc, 3tr) 9 times, tr2inc, 2tr, sl st to third of 3ch (50 sts).

Round 5 (inc): 3ch (to count as first tr), (tr2inc, 4tr) 9 times, tr2inc, 3tr, sl st to third of 3ch (60 sts).

Round 6 (inc): 3ch (to count as first tr), (tr2inc, 5tr) 9 times, tr2inc, 4tr, sl st to third of 3ch (70 sts).

Round 7: 3ch (to count as first tr), 1tr in each st.

Divide for side openings

The following is worked in rows:

Row 8: 3ch (to count as first tr), 34tr, turn (35 sts).

Rows 9–11: 3ch (to count as first tr), 1tr in next 33 sts, 1tr in third of 3ch, turn.

Row 12 (inc): 3ch (to count as first tr), 5tr, (tr2inc, 10tr) twice, tr2inc, 5tr, 1tr in third of 3ch, turn (38 sts).

Rows 13–15: 3ch (to count as first tr), 1tr in next 36tr, 1tr in third of 3ch, turn. Fasten off and, with RS facing, rejoin yarn to the other side. Work from rows 8–15 to match the first side.

Join sides

The following is worked in rounds:

Round 16: 3ch (to count as first tr), *1tr in next 36tr, 1tr in third of 3ch*, 1tr in first tr of other side to join; rep from * to *, sl st to third of 3ch at beg of round 16 to join other side.

Rounds 17–18: 3ch (to count as first tr), 1tr in next 75tr, sl st to third of 3ch. Fasten off and weave in ends.

Large butterflies (make 6)

Upper wing

With 3mm hook and B, make 4ch and join with sl st to first ch to form a ring.

Round 1: 3ch (to count as first tr), 11tr into ring, sl st to third of 3ch (12 sts).

Round 2: Join in C, 1ch (does not count as a stitch), (dc2inc) 3 times, htr2inc, tr2inc, (1tr, 1dtr) in next st, (1dtr, 1tr) in next st, tr2inc, htr2inc, (dc2inc) 3 times, sl st to first dc (24 sts).

Round 3: Join in D, 1ch (does not count as a stitch), (1dc, dc2inc) 4 times, 1htr, tr2inc, 1tr, (1tr, 1dtr) in next st, (1dtr, 1tr) in next st, 1tr, tr2inc, 1htr, (dc2inc, 1dc) 4 times, sl st to first dc

(36 sts). Fasten off and make another to match the first.

Lower wing

With 3mm hook and C, make 4ch and join with sl st to first ch to form a ring.

Round 1: 1ch (does not count as a stitch), into ring work 3dc, 2htr, 2tr, 2htr, 3dc, sl st to first dc (12 sts).

Round 2: 1ch (does not count as a stitch), (dc2inc) 3 times, (htr2inc) twice, (tr2inc) twice, (htr2inc) twice, (dc2inc) 3 times, sl st to first dc (24 sts).

Round 3: Join in D, 1ch (does not count as a stitch), (dc2inc, 1dc) 12 times, sl st to first dc (36 sts).
Fasten off and make another small wing to match the first.

Large body

With 3mm hook and E, make 12 ch.

Round 1: 1dc into second ch from hook, 1dc in each of next 9ch, 2dc in end ch, 1dc down other side of ch to end (22 sts).

Round 2: Work 1dc in each st to end. To join the seam, sl st together the back loops only of the 11 sts on both sides of the work. Fasten off.

Small butterflies (make 4)

Upper wing

Begin with 3mm hook and B.

Round 1: Work as for round 1 of lower wing of large butterfly.

Round 2: Join in C and work as for round 2 of lower wing of large butterfly.

Round 3: Join in D and work as for round 3 of lower wing of large butterfly. Fasten off and make another to match the first.

Lower wing

With 3mm hook and C.

Round 1: Work as for round 1 of lower wing of large butterfly.

Round 2: Join in D and work as for round 2 of lower wing of large butterfly. Fasten off and make another to match the first.

Small body

With 3mm hook and E, make 8ch. Work 1dc into second ch from hook, 1dc in each of next 5ch, 2dc in end ch, 1dc down other side of ch to end (14 sts).

To join the seam, sl st together the back loops only of the 7 sts on both sides of the work. Fasten off.

Making up

To make up the butterflies, weave in the ends of the wings and the body. Place the large wing so that it overlaps the top of the small wing at a slight angle and stitch in place. Repeat for the other pair so that they mirror the first pair. Attach the wings so the overlap meets the body a third of the way down and the seam of the body sits on the underside. Sew the butterflies onto the cozy, positioning them while the cozy is on a teapot.

Butterflies

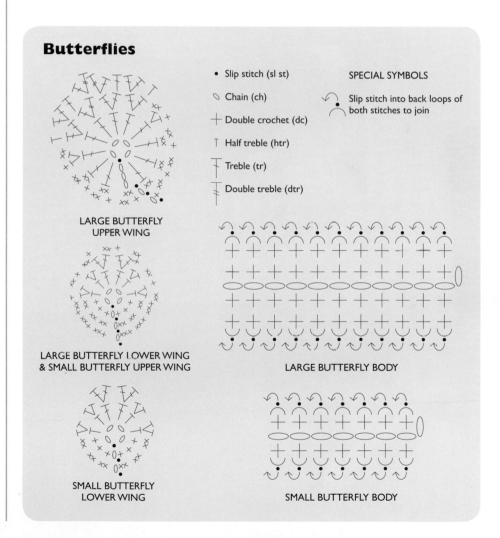

- • Slip stitch (sl st)
- ◦ Chain (ch)
- + Double crochet (dc)
- ⊤ Half treble (htr)
- ⊤ Treble (tr)
- ⊤ Double treble (dtr)

SPECIAL SYMBOLS

Slip stitch into back loops of both stitches to join

LARGE BUTTERFLY UPPER WING

LARGE BUTTERFLY LOWER WING & SMALL BUTTERFLY UPPER WING

SMALL BUTTERFLY LOWER WING

LARGE BUTTERFLY BODY

SMALL BUTTERFLY BODY

Crocheted in rounds, these fruity treats, nestling in their wickerwork
basket, are easy to create and make a wonderful decorative display,
as well as keeping your tea lovely and warm.

Fruit basket

Materials

Debbie Bliss Prima, 80% bamboo, 20% merino
(109yd/100m per 50g ball):
1 ball in 19 Soft Yellow (A)
Debbie Bliss Andes, 65% alpaca, 35% silk (109yd/100m
per 50g skein):
1 skein in each of 05 Fawn (B) and 06 Gold (C)
Oddments of DK yarn in red, pale green, dark green, orange,
yellow and white for the fruit
3mm (UK11:USC/2 or D/3) and 4mm (UK8:USG/6)
crochet hooks
Darning needle

Tension

9 sts and 8½ rounds to 4in (10cm) over treble st using 4mm
hook. Use larger or smaller hook to obtain correct tension.

Special abbreviations

Tr2inc: 2tr into next stitch (to increase).
Dc2inc: 2dc into next stitch (to increase).

Basket

With 4mm hook and A, wind yarn round finger a couple of times to form a ring.

Round 1: 1dc, 2ch into ring (to count as first tr), 17tr, sl st to second of 2ch. Pull tightly on short end to close ring (18 sts).

Round 2 (inc): 3ch (to count as first tr), 1tr, tr2inc, (1tr, (tr2inc) twice) 5 times, 1tr, sl st to third of 3ch (30 sts).

Round 3 (inc): 3ch (to count as first tr), (tr2inc, 2tr) 9 times, tr2inc, 1tr, sl st to third of 3ch (40 sts).

Round 4 (inc): 3ch (to count as first tr), (tr2inc, 3tr) 9 times, tr2inc, 2tr, sl st to third of 3ch (50 sts).

Round 5 (inc): 3ch (to count as first tr), (tr2inc, 4tr) 9 times, tr2inc, 3tr, sl st to third of 3ch (60 sts).

Round 6 (inc): 3ch (to count as first tr), (tr2inc, 5tr) 9 times, tr2inc, 4tr, sl st to third of 3ch (70 sts).

Round 7: 3ch (to count as first tr), 1tr in each st.

Divide for side openings

The following is worked in rows:

Row 8: 3ch (to count as first tr), 16tr, tr2inc, 17tr, turn (36 sts). Join in B.

Row 9: 3ch (to count as first tr), 1tr in next 35 sts, 1tr in third of 3ch, turn.

Row 10: 3ch (to count as first tr), 1tr in next 2tr, *(inserting hook into the space between the next 2 sts 2 rows below, work 1tr drawing up a long loop) 3 times, 1tr in next 3tr; rep from * 5 times, (inserting hook into the space between the next 2 sts 2 rows below, work 1tr drawing up a long loop) 3 times, turn.

Row 11: 3ch (to count as first tr), 1tr in next 35 sts, 1tr in third of 3ch, turn.

Row 12: 3ch (to count as first tr), (inserting hook into the space between the next 2 sts 2 rows below, work 1tr drawing up a long loop) twice, *1tr in next 3tr, (inserting hook into the space between the next 2 sts 2 rows below, work 1tr drawing up a long loop); rep from * 5 times, 1tr in next 3tr, turn.

Rows 13–14: Repeat rows 9 and 10. Fasten off and, with RS facing, rejoin yarn to the rem sts. Work from rows 8–15 to match the first side.

Join sides (work in rounds)

Round 15: 3ch (to count as first tr), *1tr in next 35tr, 1tr in third of 3ch*, 1tr in first tr of other side to join; rep from * to *, sl st to third of 3ch at beg of round 16 to join other side (72 sts). With RS facing, join in C.

Round 16: 3ch (to count as first tr), (inserting hook into the space between the next 2 sts 2 rows below, work 1tr drawing up a long loop) twice, *1tr in next 3tr, (inserting hook into the space between the next 2 sts 2 rows below, work 1tr drawing up a long loop); rep from * 11 times, 1tr in next 3tr, sl st to third of 3ch. Fasten off.

Apples (make 2 in red and 2 in green)

With 3mm hook and red or green, wind yarn round finger to form a ring.

Round 1: Into the ring work 1dc (does not count as a stitch), 10dc (10 sts).

Round 2: (Dc2inc) 10 times, pull on short end to close the ring (20 sts).

Round 3: (Dc2inc, 1dc) 10 times (30 sts).

Round 4: Dc2inc, 2dc, join in white, dc2inc, 2dc, with main colour (dc2inc, 2dc) 8 times (40 sts).

Round 5: 1dc in each st.

Round 6: (Dc2inc, 3dc) 10 times (50 sts).

Stalk and leaf

Join in green, 4ch, sl st to second ch from hook, sl st down next 2ch, sl st into the dc of the apple. Do not fasten off.

Next round: 6ch, 1dc into second ch from hook, 1htr in next ch, 1tr in next ch, 1htr in next ch, 1dc in last ch, 1dc into apple. Fasten off.

Pears (make 2)

With 3mm hook and yellow or green, wind yarn round finger to form a ring.

Rounds 1–3: Work as for apple.

Round 4: 5ch, 1dc into second ch from hook, 1dc into next 3ch, 1dc in each of next 30dc, 1dc into each st of other side of ch (38 sts).

Round 5: Dc2inc, 8dc, join in white, 5dc, use main colour, work 23dc, dc2inc (40 sts).

Round 6: Dc2inc, 9dc, (dc2inc, 1dc) 10 times, 9dc, dc2inc, sl st to next st (50 sts).

Leaf and stalk

Work as for apple.

Oranges (make 2)

Work as for apple, with orange yarn, from rounds 1 to 6 substituting the white yarn for yellow. Join in dark green and work 2ch. Sl st to second ch from hook, sl st into orange. Fasten off.

Cherries (make 2)

With 3mm hook and red, wind yarn round finger to form a ring.

Round 1: Into the ring work 1dc (does not count as a stitch), 8dc, in white work 2dc (10 sts).

Round 2: With red (dc2inc) 10 times (20 sts), pull on short end to close the ring, sl st to next st and fasten off.

Leaves (make 2)

With 3mm hook and dark green yarn, work 6ch.

Next row: 1dc into second ch from hook, *1htr into next ch, 1tr in next ch, 1htr in next ch*, 3dc in end ch, work from * to * down other side of chains, 1dc in next ch, sl st to first dc. Fasten off.

Stalk

1dc into top of first cherry, 3ch, 1dc into end of first leaf, 1dc into end of second leaf, 3ch, 1dc into top of second cherry. Fasten off.

Making up

Sew the fruit to the top of the cozy.

Fruit basket

CHERRY　　CHERRY LEAF

- Slip stitch (sl st)
- Chain (ch)
- Double crochet (dc)
- Half treble (htr)
- Treble (tr)

SPECIAL SYMBOLS

Wind yard round finger to form a ring

APPLE, STALK AND LEAF

PEAR, STALK AND LEAF

Quirky

Our selection of whimsical patterns includes a magical mermaid, a retro pineapple,
a friendly nurse and a comforting cat, plus lots more delightfully dotty designs to choose from.
Each one is guaranteed to brighten up your tea table, no matter what the weather!

Bring the opulence of eighteenth-century fashion into your home with this delightful crocheted cozy. Assembly will require some attention to detail, but your hard work will pay off and you will be able to enjoy it for years to come.

Rococo

Materials

1 x 50g ball of any 4-ply yarn in 3 shades of fresh greens (A, B and C), 1 x 50g ball of 4-ply yarn in cream (D), oddment of 4-ply yarn in white (E)
Embroidery threads or oddments of yarn in metallic silver, blue and red
3.5mm (UK9:USE/4), 2.5mm (UK12:USC/2) and 2mm (UK14:USB/1) crochet hooks
Tapestry needle
Toy stuffing

Tension

3 finished scallops and 8½ rows of scallops to 4in (10cm) square using 3.5mm hook. Use larger or smaller hook to obtain correct tension.

Rococo

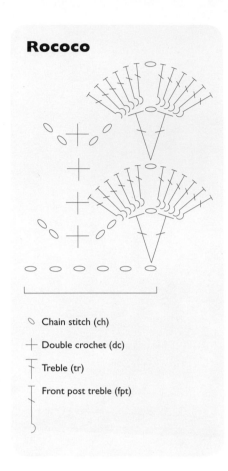

○ Chain stitch (ch)

+ Double crochet (dc)

⊤ Treble (tr)

⌇ Front post treble (fpt)

Special abbreviations

Htr2tog: Work 2 half trebles together. (Yrh, insert hook into ring, yrh, draw back through ring) twice (5 loops on hook), yrh, draw through all 5 loops.

6fptr: Front post treble 6 times. (Yrh, insert hook around the post of the next treble by taking it behind the stitch then back around to the front of the work, yrh, draw through (3 loops left on hook), yrh, draw through 2 loops (2 loops left on hook), yrh, draw through remaining 2 loops on hook (1 loop on hook). Repeat from * 5 more times.)

Dc2dec: Work 2 dc together (to decrease).

Dc2inc: Work 2 dc into next st (to increase).

Skirt

With 3.5mm hook and A, work 45ch.

Row 1: Miss 5ch, *(1tr, 1ch, 1tr) into next ch, 2ch, miss 2ch, 1dc into next ch, 2ch, miss 2ch; rep from * 6 times, (1tr, 1ch, 1tr) into next ch, 2ch, miss 2ch, 1dc into next ch, turn.

Row 2: 1ch (does not count as a stitch), 1dc into last dc of previous row. *6fptr down the post of the first tr, 1ch, 6fptr up the post of the second tr; 1dc in next dc; rep from * finishing with 1 dc in the third of the 5ch of row 1, turn.

Row 3: 1ch (does not count as a stitch), 1dc into first dc, 2ch, *(1tr, 1ch, 1tr) into next 1ch sp, 2ch, 1dc into next dc, 2ch; rep from * 6 times, (1tr, 1ch, 1tr) into next 1ch sp, 2ch, 1dc into last dc, turn.

Row 4: 1ch (does not count as a stitch), 1dc into last dc of previous row. *6fptr down the post of the first tr, 1ch, 6fptr up the post of the second tr; 1dc in next dc; rep from * finishing with 1dc in the last dc, turn.

Rep last 2 rows twice more.

Next row: Join in B and work rows 3 and 4 four times.

Next row: Join in C and work rows 3 and 4 four times.

Next row: Join in D and work rows 3 and 4 twice.

Make another piece to match the first.

Head and body

With 2mm hook and E, starting at the top of the head, work 4ch and join with a sl st to first ch to form a ring.

Round 1: 1ch (does not count as a stitch). Into ring work 5dc (5 sts).

Round 2: (Dc2inc) 5 times (10 sts).

Rounds 3–7: 1dc into each st.

Shape shoulders

Round 8 (inc): (Dc2inc, 1dc) 5 times (15 sts).

Rounds 9–10: 1dc into each st.

Join in yarn A.

Rounds 11–17: 1dc into each st.

Shape base

Round 18: Working into back loops only, 1dc into each st.

Round 19: Working into both loops, (dc2dec, 1dc) 5 times (10 sts).

Fasten off leaving long lengths of yarn. Stuff the head first and run a gathering st along round 7, before the shaping. Draw up to accentuate the neck.

Stuff the body. Run a row of gathering sts around the opening at the base, draw up tightly to close and fasten off.

Arms (make 2)

With 2mm hook and E, work 16ch.

Row 1: 1dc into second ch from hook, 1dc in each ch to end (15 sts), turn.

Rows 2–3: 1ch (does not count as a stitch), 1dc in each dc, turn.

Fold lengthways, 1ch (does not count as a stitch), sl st the back loops of each st on both sides to join. Fasten off leaving a length of yarn with which to stitch to the shoulders of the body. The arm will curve slightly as the sl sts are tighter than the dc sts. The join will therefore be the inner arm.

Collar

With 2.5mm hook and C, work 21ch. Join with a sl st to first ch to form a ring.

1ch, sl st into each ch to end. Fasten off. Sew the collar neatly around the neck edge of the bodice leaving the shoulders free. The collar sits slightly off the shoulder.

Powdered wig

Main piece

*With 2.5mm hook and D, wind yarn around finger a couple of times to form a ring.

Round 1: Into ring work 1dc (does not count as a stitch), 6dc (6 sts).

Round 2: (Dc2inc) 6 times (12 sts). Pull on the short end of the yarn to close the ring.

Round 3: 1dc into each dc.

Round 4: (Dc2inc) 12 times (24 sts)*.

Rounds 5–6: 1dc into each dc.

Round 7: (Dc2dec, 1dc) 8 times (16 sts).

Fasten off leaving a long length of yarn. Run a gathering st around the edge, stuff lightly and fit to the head. Stitch the wig on so the back sits at the nape of the neck.

Middle piece

Work as for main piece from * to *.

Round 5: 1dc in each st.

Round 6: (Dc2dec) 12 times (12 sts). Fasten off, leaving a long length of yarn to run a gathering stitch around the edge. Stuff the piece lightly and gather only a little, leaving a small opening. Stitch in place, slightly to the back of the main piece. Work a couple of stitches through the top to flatten it a bit.

Top piece

With 2.5mm hook and D, wind yarn around finger a couple of times to form a ring.

Round 1: 1dc into the ring (does not count as a stitch). Work a further 6dc into the ring (6 sts).

Round 2: (Dc2inc) 6 times (12 sts). Pull tight on the short end of the yarn to close the ring.

Rounds 3–4: 1dc into each st. Fasten off and gather slightly, as for the middle piece, and sew to the centre top of the wig.

Curly locks

With 2.5mm hook and D, join the yarn with a dc into a st in the last round of the main piece of the wig at the side of the head.

Work 11ch, 2dc into second ch from hook, *sl st into next ch, 2dc into next ch. Rep from * to end. Sl st into the wig where the yarn was joined. Weave in the ends and twist the curl into shape. Repeat on the other side of the head.

Bow

With 2.5mm hook and B, work 6ch. Work 1dc into second ch from hook, dc into each ch to end.

Fasten off leaving a long length of yarn. Weave it through to the centre of the piece and wind it around the middle a few times to form the knot and shape the bow. Work a few stitches in to secure. Sew to the wig between the main and middle pieces, winding the yarn around the hair at the join before stitching in place.

Wind more of the same colour around the join between the top and middle pieces to indicate another ribbon. Sew in place.

Flower

With 2.5mm hook and C, work 4ch and join with sl st to first ch to form a ring.

Petals

(2ch, htr2tog, 2ch, sl st into ring) 4 times (4 petals).

Fasten off leaving a length of yarn to thread onto a needle and work a stitch between each petal to accentuate the shape. Sew the flower to the hands and, with an oddment of metallic silver yarn, work a French knot (see page 361) into the centre of the flower to finish it off.

Making up

Embroider the eyes and mouth with oddments of blue and red yarn or embroidery thread. Sew the side seams of the skirt joining the top 4 and bottom 2 rows of scallop, leaving an opening on each side for the handle and spout of the teapot. Weave in any loose ends. Run a gathering stitch around the top of the skirt and draw up to fit the body. Sew in place ensuring the openings sit on each side.

This cheeky elephant design makes an ideal teacozy – the spout forms a perfect trunk! The designer added a touch of bling with a beaded, gold-trimmed headdress and bell-shaped tassels.

Circus act

Materials

Sirdar Balmoral DK, 72% wool, 25% alpaca, 3% silk (135yd/123m per 50g ball):
2 balls in 0474 Grey (A)
Twilley's Goldfingering, 80% viscose, 20% polyester (109yd/100m per 25g ball):
1 ball in WG2 Gold (B)
Small quantities of red (C) and cream (D) for headdress and tusks; oddment of black (E) for eyes
Gold embroidery thread

A pair each of 4mm (UK8:US6), 3.75mm (UK9:US5) and 3mm (UK11:US2/3) needles
A set of 3.25mm (UK10:US3) double-pointed needles
1.1mm (UK11:US6) crochet hook (or similar)
Darning, beading and sewing needles

Tension

17 sts and 37 rows to 4in (10cm) square over moss stitch using 4mm needles. Use larger or smaller needles to obtain correct tension.

Pattern notes

The sides are worked from bottom to top and joined. The ears are worked as left- and right-facing pieces resembling a square with the corner missing, and sewn into shape before attaching to the cozy. An I-cord gathers the top.

Sides (make 2)

With 4mm needles and A, cast on 40 sts using the thumb method. Work in moss stitch pattern:

Moss stitch pattern

Row 1: P1, k1 to end.
Row 2: K1, p1 to end.
These two rows form patt. Rep until work measures 7¼in (18.5cm).

Eyelet section

Row 1: Knit to end.
Row 2: Purl to end.
Row 3 (eyelets): : K4, *(yo, k2tog, k2); rep from * to last 4 sts, yo, k4.
Row 4: Purl to end
Row 5: Knit to end.
Cont in moss st patt for a further 1⅓in (3cm), ending with a RS row. At this point the side should measure 9in (23cm). Cast off, leaving a long tail. Make another piece the same.

Left-facing ear

*With 4mm needles and A, cast on 25 sts and work in m-st patt for 2⅓in (6cm), ending on a WS row.
Now begin to dec on RS of work only, keeping decs in patt by knitting or purling sts tog as appropriate.*
Next row 1 (dec): M-st 23, work 2 sts tog (24 sts).
Next and every alt row: Work in m-st without dec.
Next row (dec): M-st 22, dec over last 2 sts (23 sts).
Cont in this way until 14 sts rem, ending on a RS row.
Cast off, leaving a long end.

Right-facing ear

Work as for left-facing ear from * to *.
Next row: Work 2 sts tog, m-st 23 (24 sts).
Next row: Work in m-st without dec. Cont thus, dec 1 st at beg of each RS row until 14 sts rem, ending on a RS row. Cast off, leaving a long end.

Tusks (make 2)

With 3.75mm needles and D, cast on 4 sts and work 4 rows st st.
Row 5: Knit, inc 1 st each end (6 sts).
Row 6 and every alt row: Purl.
Row 7: Knit.
Row 9: As row 5 (8 sts).
Row 11: Knit.
Row 13: As row 5 (10 sts).
Row 15: Knit.
Row 17: As row 5 (12 sts).
Row 19: As row 5 (14 sts).
Cast off k-wise, leaving a long tail. The tusk should measure approx. 3in (7.5cm) and will curl when sewn up.

Main headdress

With 3.75mm needles and C, cast on 7 sts.
Row 1 and every alt row: Knit.
Row 2: K1, m1, k6 (8 sts).
Row 4: K1, m1, k7 (9 sts).
Row 6: K1, m1, k8 (10 sts).
Row 8: K1, m1, k9 (11 sts).
Row 10: K1, m1, k10 (12 sts).
Row 12: K1, m1, k11 (13 sts).
Row 14: K1, m1, k12 (14 sts).
Row 16 (dec): K1, k2tog, k to end of row (13 sts).
Cont to dec thus on every alt row until 7 sts rem.
Cast off.

Central panel

With 3mm needles and B, cast on 3 sts. Beg k1, p1, k1, work in moss-st until the panel measures approx. 7in (7.5cm). Cast off.

Scalloped border

With 3mm needles and B, cast on 2 sts, leaving a long tail. Work the first scallop thus:
Row 1 and every alt row: Knit.

Row 2: K1, m1, k1 (3 sts).
Cont to inc on every alt row until
there are 6 sts.
Rows 9, 11 and 13: Knit.
Row 10: K1, k2tog, k3 (5 sts).
Row 12: K1, k2tog, k2 (4 sts).
Row 14: K1, k2tog, k1 (3 sts).
Row 15: K1, k2tog (2 sts).
Row 16: K2.
Beg the patt again from row 2 and
work to row 16. Rep until there are 16
scallops in total. Cast off.

Assembling the headdress

Sew beads and sequins to the narrow
central panel using invisible thread,
placing approx. ½in (1cm) apart. Leave
the top sequin until later, as it will help
to hide the join between the panel and
the braid. Position gold braid round the
red cap, cast-off edge uppermost. The
central point should be flanked by two
braid points to which securing loops
will be attached. There should be a
braid point on either side of the
pointed section of the red cap. Pin
braid in place, then sew using gold
thread. Pin and stitch central panel in
place and position final sequin on join.
Thread six gold beads and a drop on
invisible thread and attach to centre
front of headdress. Using 3mm needles
and B, cast on 2 sts, leaving a long tail.
Work the first scallop thus:

Securing loops (make 2)

With the assembled headdress RS
facing, work a loop into the RH of the
3 scallops at the top edge thus:
Insert a 1.1mm crochet hook into the
central point of the scallop. Make 10ch,
1ss into central point to form a loop.
Work 16dc around loop to form a
teardrop shape. Fasten off.
Make second loop in the LH scallop at
the top edge.

I-cord

Using two 3.25mm double-pointed
needles, cast on 3 sts and work in
I-cord for approx. 24in (60cm).
Cast off.

Bells (make 2)

Using 4mm needles and C, cast on 15
sts leaving a long tail.
Rows 1–4: Purl.
Beg knit, work in st st until work
measures approx. 1¼in (3cm) ending
on a WS row. Do not cast off. Cut yarn
leaving a tail of approx. 8in (20cm).
Thread tail on needle. Draw yarn in a
circle; ease each st onto it but do not
gather yet. Secure a strand of B to cast-
on edge and bind around the first st.
Using backstitch, bind B around each
cast-on st to end to make a decorative
pattern. Bind around the last st (17 gold
sts in total). Using the cast-on tail, join
the back seam to form the bell shape.

Eyes (make 2)

With 3mm needles and E, cast on
12 sts. Knit 1 row but do not cast off;
break yarn leaving a long end and
thread onto a darning needle. Pass
yarn through each st in turn and join
in a ring, joining cast-on edges tog to
form a circle. Leave yarn end for
attaching eyes.

Making up
Sides

Join the sides of the cozy from the
lower edge, leaving gaps for handle and
spout, then join upper seams, leaving a
gap in central back seam to form an
extra eyelet. Thread the I-cord through
eyelets, beginning and ending at handle
seam, and catching the securing loops
from the headdress in the appropriate
position. Tie a knot in each end of the
I-cord, then ease the ring of cast-off sts
at the top of a bell over each knot.
Draw up the sts and sew in place,
covering the knot. Place the cozy on
the teapot ready to pin the ears, tusks,
and eyes in place.

Ears

Using A, gather along the decreased
incline (the short diagonal) using
running stitches. Fasten off securely.
Make two folds on either side of the
centre of the gathered edge, creating
an upside-down 'V'-shape, and stitch to

secure. This provides the characteristic floppy shape. Run yarn back to end and use to attach ear to the head. Position the ears approx. 3in (8cm) down from gathers and 4¼in (11cm) from spout gap edge. Sew in place using small stitches.

Tusks

Thread the cast-on tail onto a darning needle and draw the narrow ends in a circle. Close seam using mattress stitch (see page 355). Place tusks approx. 2⅓in (6cm) apart and 1⅓in (3.5cm) from the edge of the cozy, slanting outwards slightly. Sew in place.

Eyes

Attach eyes to front of the cozy, approx. 5in (12.5cm) apart. Using the tail end, overstitch or blanket stitch around the outer edge. Fasten off.

Tip

When washing the cozy, it is best to remove the headdress and launder separately, reshaping while drying flat.

This cheerful design might just be the ultimate in kitsch: it is inspired by the plastic buckets that were popular for keeping ice cool during the 1960s, though fortunately this has the opposite effect!

Pineapple

Materials

Patons Fairytale Colour 4 Me DK, 100% wool
(98yd/90m per 50g ball):
2 balls in 4960 Yellow (A)
Twilleys Freedom Spirit, 100% wool
(131yd/120m per 50g ball):
Oddment of 514 Nature for crown (B)
A pair of 5.5mm (UK5:US9) needles for main pieces
A pair of 3.25mm (UK10:US3) needles for leaves
Darning needle

Tension

Approx. 18 sts and 18 rows to 4in (10cm) square over pattern using 5mm needles and yarn A double. Use larger or smaller needles to obtain correct tension.

Pattern notes

Yarn A is used double throughout.

Side 1

With 5.5mm needles and A double, cast on 32 sts and knit 1 row.

Now work in pattern thus:

Row 1 (WS): Purl, wrapping yarn twice for each st.

Row 2: *Sl4 sts and drop extra wraps, replace these 4 long sts on left needle, (k4tog, p4tog) twice into long sts; rep from * to end.

Row 3: P2, p28 wrapping yarn twice for each st, p2.

Row 4: K2, *sl4 sts and drop extra wraps, replace 4 long sts on left needle, (k4tog, p4tog) twice into long sts; rep from * to last 2 sts, k2.

These 4 rows form patt.

Rep until work measures approx. 4½in (11.5cm) ending with row 2 of patt.

Adjust length if necessary by working extra rows in groups of 4.

Break off yarn and leave sts on a holder.

Side 2

Complete second side to the same point as side 1, but do not break off yarn.

Join for top

Next row: P2, purl across sts of side 2 wrapping yarn twice for each st, purl across sts of side 1 wrapping yarn twice for each st, p2.

Next row: K2, *sl4 sts and drop extra wraps, replace 4 long sts on left needle and (k4tog, p4tog) twice into long sts; rep from * to last 2 sts, k2.

Next row: Purl, wrapping yarn twice for each st.

Next row (dec): *Sl4 sts and drop extra wraps, replace 4 long sts on left needle and (k4tog, p4tog) once into long sts; rep from * to end (32 sts).

Next row: Purl.

Next row: K2tog to end (16 sts).

Next row: Purl.

Next row (eyelets): K2tog, *(yf, k2tog); rep from * to end (15 sts).

Work 3 rows in st st.

Cast off very loosely.

Crown

Lower set of leaves

With 3.25mm needles and B, cast on 6 sts.

Next row: Knit.

Next row: **Sl1, k to last st, inc in last st (7 sts).

Next row: Knit.

Next row: Sl1, k to last st, inc in last st (8 sts).

Continue in this way until there are 11 sts on the needle.

Next row: Cast off 5 sts, k to end (6 sts).**

Rep from ** to ** six times more (7 leaves made).

Cast off rem 6 sts.

Middle set of leaves

With 3.25mm needles and B, cast on 8 sts.

Next row: Knit.

Next row: **Sl1, k to last st, inc (9 sts).

Next row: Inc in first st, k to end (10 sts).

Next row: Sl1, k to last st, inc (11 sts).

Cont in this way until there are 16 sts on needle.

Knit 1 row.

Next row: Cast off 8 sts, k to end (8 sts).**

Rep from ** to ** five times more (6 leaves made)

Cast off rem 8 sts.

Top set of leaves

With 3.25mm needles and B, cast on 10 sts.

Next row: Knit.

Next row: **Sl1, k to last st, inc (11 sts).

Next row: Inc in first st, k to end (12 sts).

Next row: Sl1, k to last st, inc (13 sts).

Cont in this way until there are 18 sts on needle.

Knit 1 row.
Next row: Cast off 8 sts, k to end (10 sts).**
Rep from ** to ** five times more (6 leaves made).
Cast off rem 10 sts.

Making up

Fold back the rows of st st at the top and catch in place to form a picot edge. Join from the top edge down to form holes for the spout and handle. Join the first few rows at the lower edge for about 1in (2.5cm).

Crown

Join each of the leaf sections into a circle. Layer one circle on top of the next with the shorter leaves outermost. Catch stitch layers together at lower edge, easing if necessary. Insert crown in top of work and sew firmly in place behind picot edge.

Plump grapes nestle on a latticework vine to keep your teapot snug and warm. Crochet your grapes in the colour that evokes your favourite wine and who knows – perhaps you'll end up wanting something extra to drink!

Grapevine on trellis

Materials

Any DK yarn in various shades of green for main part
(each green square takes around 7½yd/7m)

DK yarn in off-white (A)

4-ply yarn in shades of purples and greens for the grapes

4-ply yarn in green (B) for the vine leaves

3.5mm (UK9:USE/4) and 2.5mm (UK12:USC/2) crochet hooks

Darning needle

Toy stuffing

Tension

1 x square motif measures 3 x 3in (7.5 x 7.5cm) using 3.5mm hook. Use larger or smaller hook to obtain correct tension.

Special abbreviations

Dc2inc: Work 2dc into next stitch (to increase).

Dc2dec: Work 2dc together (to decrease).

Main part

Patch (make 13)

With 3.5mm hook and green, wind yarn round finger a couple of times to form a ring.

Round 1: Into ring work 1dc, 2ch (to count as first tr), 19tr. Join with sl st into second of 2ch. Pull tight on the short end of yarn to close ring (20 sts).

Round 2: 1ch (to count as first dc), 1htr in next st, (1tr, 1ch, 1tr) in next st, 1htr in next st, 1dc in next st, *1dc in next st, 1htr in next st, (1tr, 1ch, 1tr) in next st, 1htr in next st, 1dc in next st; rep from * twice more. Join with sl st to first ch.

Round 3: 3ch (to count as first tr), 1tr into each of next 2 sts, (2tr, 1ch, 2tr) into corner 1ch sp, *1tr into each of next 6 sts, (2tr, 1ch, 2tr) into corner 1ch sp. Rep from * twice more, 1tr into each of next 3 sts, sl st into third of 3ch.

Round 4: Join in A and work 1dc in each st and 2dc into each 1ch sp at corner. Sl st to next st, fasten off.

Corner patch (make 2)

With 3.5mm hook and green, wind yarn around finger a couple of times to form a ring.

Round 1: Into the ring work 1dc and 2ch (to count as first tr), 10tr. Pull tight on the short end to close ring (11 sts).

Round 2: 3ch (to count as first tr), 1tr in same st as 3ch, 1htr in next st, dc2inc, 1htr in next st, (1tr, 1ch, 1tr) in next st, 1htr in next st, dc2inc, 1htr in next st, 2tr in third of 3ch in next st, turn.

Round 3: 3ch (to count as first tr), 1tr in same sp, 1tr in next 6 sts, (2tr, 1ch, 2tr) in next 1ch sp, 1tr in next 6 sts, 2tr in third of 3ch, turn.

Round 4: Join in A, 1ch (does not count as a stitch), 1dc into first st, work 12dc evenly across the diagonal edge of the corner patch, 1dc into the same st as the previous dc.

Work 1dc into each st along the straight edges of the patch, working 2dc into the 1ch sp at the corner, and 1dc into the first dc worked in this round. Fasten off.

Grapes (make 8 sets of 8 grapes)

With 2.5mm hook and green or purple 4-ply yarn, wind yarn around finger a couple of times to form a ring.

Round 1: Into ring work 1dc (does not count as a stitch), 5dc (5 sts).

Round 2: (Dc2inc) 5 times. Pull short end of yarn to close ring (10 sts).

Rounds 3–6: 1dc in each st.

Round 7: (Dc2dec, 3dc) twice (8 sts). Break yarn and thread yarn through rem sts, stuff grape, gather up and fasten off. Weave in ends.

Leaves (make 8)

**With 2.5mm hook and B, make 5ch. Join with a sl st to first ch to form a ring.

Round 1: 3ch (counts as first tr), 3tr into ring, 9ch, (4tr, 9ch) twice, sl st to third of 3ch.

Round 2: *1dc into next 2tr, miss next tr, (9tr, 2ch, 9tr) into next 9ch loop, miss first dc.* Rep from * to * twice more, sl st to first dc, turn.

Round 3 (WS): 1ch (does not count as a stitch), *(1dc) 9 times, 2dc into 2ch sp, (1dc) 9 times, miss 2dc*. Rep from * to * twice more**, turn.

Join in the grapes

Work 1dc into the first dc of round 3. 3ch, 1dc into top of first grape (at the gathered end), 1dc into second grape,

3ch, 1dc into each of next three grapes, 3ch, 1dc into each of next 2 grapes, 3ch, 1dc into last grape. Sl st up each ch, missing out the dc sts. Sl st into the dc at the top of the leaf. Fasten off leaving a length of yarn to sew the leaf to the trellis.

Making up

Press the work lightly on the wrong side with a warm iron over a damp cloth. Lay the patches out in the desired order. See layout chart below right.

Using 3.5mm hook and A, join patches with WS together, by inserting the hook under all 4 loops of both stitches and working 1dc. Repeat across all the stitches, joining the patches horizontally and then vertically, leaving the outer edges open for the handle and spout. Fasten off.

Join side edges

With 3.5mm hook and A, join the lower side edges by working 1dc into each of the last 4 sts of both front and back patches, as before. Repeat for the other side.

Edging

Work 2 rows of 1dc in each st across the lower edge.

Leaf and stalk

Work from ** to ** for the leaf, sl st to next st, fasten off and weave in the ends.

For the stalk, using the same yarn and hook, make 12ch, join with sl st to form a ring, 1ch.

Into the ring work 22dc, sl st to first dc, fasten off leaving a long length of yarn. Sew the stalk to the centre of the RS of the leaf. Stitch to the centre top of the cozy. Attach bunches of grapes with just a few stitches so as to let them hang freely.

Vine leaf

- Slip stitch (sl st)
- Chain (ch)
- Double crochet (dc)
- Treble (tr)

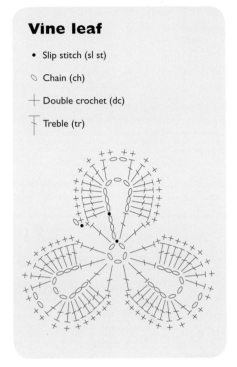

Layout of patches

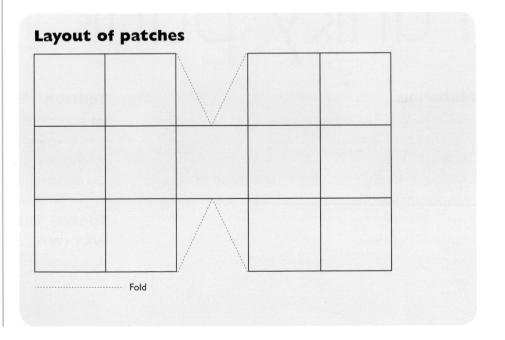

Fold

Who says tea cozies have to be boring? There's nothing traditional about this amazing felted creation, so get out your needles and take a walk on the wild side.

Funky punk

Materials
Elle Merino Solids, 100% merino wool
(76yd/70m per 50g ball):
2 balls in 17 Black
Cascade 220 Heathers DK, 100% Peruvian Highland wool
(220yd/201m per 100g ball):
1 ball in 2426 Red
1 ball in 7825 Orange
A pair of 6mm (UK4:US10) bamboo needles
Tapestry needle

Tension
Elle Merino: approx. 15 sts to 9cm square over st st and 15 rows to 7cm after felting. Use larger or smaller needles to obtain correct tension.
Cascade tension not crucial.

Special abbreviations
W&T (Wrap and turn): Yf, sl next st k-wise, turn. Place sl st back onto R needle. On foll rows, knit wrap and sl st tog.

Pattern notes

The cozy sides are sewn together before felting. Spikes are made from a triangle shape formed using short row shaping, and are attached before felting.

Cozy (make 2)

With 6mm needles, cast on 40 sts and work 5 rows g-st.
Beg with a knit row, work 25 rows st st.

Shape top

Row 1: *K6 k2tog, rep from * to end (35 sts).
Next and every alt row: Purl.
Row 3: Knit.
Row 5: *k5 k2tog, rep from * to end (30 sts).
Row 7: Knit.
Row 9: *k4 k2tog, rep from * to end (25 sts).
Row 11: Knit.
Row 13: *k3, k2tog, rep from * to end (20 sts).
Row 15: *k2, k2tog, rep from * to end (15 sts).
Row 17: *k1, k2tog, rep from * to end (10 sts).
Row 19: *k2tog, rep from * to end (5 sts).
Row 20: Purl
Break off yarn and thread through rem sts. Draw up and fasten off.

Making up

Join back and front down both sides, leaving holes for the spout and handle.

Spikes (make 5 red and 5 orange)

Cast on 13 sts.
Row 1: K11, W&T.
Row 2 and every alt row: Purl to end.
Row 3: K9, W&T.
Row 5: K7, W&T.
Row 7: K5, W&T.
Row 9: K4, W&T.
Row 11: K3, W&T.
Row 12: K2, W&T.
Row 13: K1, W&T.
Row 15: Knit across all sts, picking up the loops below the slipped sts and knitting them with the slipped sts.
Cast off all 13 sts.
Roll each triangle round to form a cone (the stitches will run round the cone and it will be a bit wiggly, but this does not matter. Attach cones to cozy along top seam and under handle by stitching round the base of each cone.

Felting

Place the cozy in a washing machine with a small amount of washing powder and a heavy item such as a pair of jeans or a bath towel – this will provide the friction necessary for the felting to take place. Run through a full cycle at 104°F (40°C) to felt. Stretch into shape straight after washing and pull the spikes straight. Place on the teapot and dry in a warm place to keep the shape.

Tip
The washing process can be repeated if you feel that the cozy has not felted sufficiently.

If you enjoy the company of cats, sharing your
well-earned break with this delightful fluffy friend
means tea times will always be lively.

Feline friend

Materials

Any feather-style yarn:

1 x 50g ball in each of black (A), white (B) and mixed
(black/grey/white) (C)

A pair of 5mm (UK6:US8) needles

19½in (50cm) cotton fabric

19½in (50cm) polyester wadding

Clip-on or screw-in eyes (from craft shops)

Pink and brown embroidery silks, for nose and mouth

White mohair wool for whiskers

Strong darning needle

Tension

Tension not critical for this project.

Special abbreviations

M1: Pick up loop before next stitch and knit through
back of loop.

Pattern notes

Any colour scheme of the feather-style yarn works well with this pattern.

Body

With 5mm needles and A, cast on 60 sts and k10 rows.
Using C, knit 2 rows.
Using A, knit 6 rows.
Rep last 8 rows until work measures 17in (43cm).
Using B knit 4 rows and cast off.

Head

Using C, cast on 20 sts and knit 4 rows.
Row 5 (inc): Using A, (k4, m1) 4 times, k to end (24 sts).
Row 6: Knit.
Row 7 (inc): (K3, m1) 7 times, k to end (31 sts).
Knit 3 rows.
Row 11 (inc): Using C, (k3, m1) 9 times, k4 to end (40 sts).
Row 12: Knit.
B knit 4 rows.
Row 17: A k15, B k10, A k15.
Row 18: A k15, B p10, A k15.
Row 19 (inc): C k15, B (k2, m1) 4 times, k to end of B sts, C k15 (44 sts).

Row 20: C k15, B purl to end of B sts, C k15.
Row 21 (inc): A k15, B (k3, m1) 4 times, k to end of B sts, A k15 (48 sts).
Row 22: A k15, B purl to end of B sts, A k15.
Row 23 (inc): A k13, B (k5, m1) 4 times, k2, A k13 (52 sts).
Row 24: A k11, B purl (30 sts), A k11.
Row 25 (dec): With same colours (k6, k2tog) 6 times, k to end (46 sts).
Row 26: A knit, B purl, A knit.
Row 27 (dec): Using C and B (k4, k2tog) 7 times, k to end (39 sts).
Row 28: C knit, B purl, C knit.

Row 29 (dec): Using A and B (k4, k2tog) 6 times, k to end (33 sts).
Row 30: A knit, B purl, A knit.
Row 31: A k11, B k11, A k11 (33 sts).
Row 32: A k13, B p7, A k13.
Row 33 (dec): Using A and B (k2, k2tog) 8 times, k to end (25 sts).
Row 34: A knit, B purl, A knit.
Row 35 (dec): Using C and B (k3, k2tog) 5 times (20 sts).
Row 36: C knit to end.
Row 37 (dec): A (k2, k2tog) 5 times (15 sts).
Row 38: A knit.
Row 39 (dec): A (k1, k2tog) 5 times (10 sts).
Cast off loosely.

Tail

Using A, cast on 20 sts and knit until work measures 6in (12cm).
A dec 1 st at each end of every alt row until work measures 7in (16cm).
B cont to knit and dec as before until 1 st left, cast off.

Ears (knit 2)

Using A, cast on 12 sts and knit until work is a small square and cast off.

Making up

Fold squares for ears in half and stitch sides. Stitch up sides of head and stuff with scraps of wadding. Place eyes, attach ears, stitch nose and mouth, and stitch in whiskers. Fold body in half and fold in top corners and overstitch one side leaving other side open for attaching head later.

Cut out lining and padding – lining 4in (10cm) extra to allow 2in (5cm) bottom hem. Pin and tack the padding and lining together, folding lining hem over the padding. Joint top sides and bottom hems with permanent stitching (can be machined). Place inside cat's body and pull to shape before tacking into place. Stitch lining and padding to the body side openings, overstitch side seams.

Stitch up tail and stuff with scraps of wadding. Attach tail at the left side and either stitch to the body or use Velcro strips. Firmly attach head to the right opening, stitching through lining and wadding. Make a loop (optional) to attach for hanging.

The variety of stitch techniques and yarns evoke a sense of movement and life in this fun cozy. The mermaid is knitted in pieces, so take time when assembling her to achieve the best results.

Mermaid

Materials

Rowan Pure Wool DK (137yd/125m per 50g ball):
1 ball in 013 Enamel (A)
Debbie Bliss Cashmerino DK (120yd/110m per 50g ball):
1 ball in 028 Duck Egg (B)
Rowan Felted Tweed (191yd/175m per 50g ball):
1 ball in 159 Carbon (C)
Rowan Siena 4 ply (153yd/140m per 50g ball):
Oddment in 652 Cream (D)
Rowan Shimmer (191yd/175m per 25g ball):
1 ball in 093 Titanium (E)
Oddments of blue and red yarn for eyes and lips

Debbie Bliss Andes (109yd/100m per 50g skein):
Oddment in 06 Gold (F)
A pair each of 2.25mm (UK13:US1), 3.25mm (UK10:US3) and 4mm (UK8:US6) needles
Darning needle
Toy stuffing

Tension

22 sts and 30 rows to 4in (10cm) square over st st using 4mm needles. Use larger or smaller needles to obtain correct tension.

Special abbreviations

M1: Pick up the horizontal loop in between the stitch just worked and the next stitch and knit into the back of it.
Kfb: Knit into the front and back of the next stitch (to increase).

Pattern notes

When yarn A or B is not being used, carry it up the side of the work with the stitch at the beginning and end of each row.

Sea and rock

With 3.25mm needles and A, cast on 51 sts.
Row 1 (WS): Knit.
Row 2 (RS): Purl.
Work 3 more rows in rev st st, as above.
Change to 4mm needles and join in B. Continue in pattern as follows:
Row 6 (RS): With B, k2tog, (k3, m1, k1, m1, k3, sl1, k2tog, psso) 4 times, k3, m1, k1, m1, k3, k2tog.
Row 7: Purl.
Rows 8–15: Repeat rows 6 and 7 four more times.
Row 16: With A, work as for row 6.
Row 17: Knit.
Row 18: Purl.
Row 19: Knit.
Rows 20–33: Repeat rows 6 to 19.

Shape top

Row 34 (dec): Join in C, k2tog, (k3, m1, k1, m1, k2, sl2tog, k2tog, p2sso) 4 times, k3, m1, k1, m1, k3, k2tog (47 sts).
Row 35: Purl.
Row 36: K2tog, (k3, m1, k1, m1, k2, sl1, k2tog, psso) 4 times, k3, m1, k1, m1, k3, k2tog.
Row 37: Purl.
Rows 38–39: Repeat rows 36 and 37.
Row 40 (dec): K2tog, k3, (m1, k1, m1, k2, sl1, k3tog, psso, k2) 4 times, m1, k1, m1, k3, k2tog (43 sts).
Row 41: Purl.

Row 42: K2tog, k3, (m1, k1, m1, k2, sl1, k2tog, psso, k2) 4 times, m1, k1, m1, k3, k2tog.
Row 43: Purl.
Rows 44–45: Repeat rows 42 and 43.
Row 46 (dec): K2tog, k4, (m1, k2, sl1, k2tog, psso, k3) 4 times, m1, k3, k2tog (38 sts).
Row 47: Purl.
Row 48: K2tog, k2, (m1, k1, m1, k2, sl1, k2tog, psso, k1), 4 times, m1, k1, m1, k3, k2tog.
Row 49: Purl.
Rows 50–51: Repeat rows 48 and 49.

Next row: Cast off 2 sts, k to end
(9 sts).
Next row: K2tog, k to last 2 sts, k2tog
(7 sts).
Next row: Cast off 2 sts, k to last 2
sts, k2tog (4 sts).
Cast off 4 sts *.
With RS facing, rejoin yarn to the
remaining sts.
Next row: K to end (9 sts).
Next row: K twice in first st, k8
(10 sts).
Work from * to * matching the other
side of tail end.
Gather the cast-on edge and stitch to
the end of the mermaid's tail. Weave
in the ends.

Arms (make 2)

With 2.25mm needles and D, cast on
5 sts.
Work 20 rows in st st.
Break yarn and thread end of yarn
through the 5 sts, gather up and secure.
Stitch arm seam. Attach to shoulders
with the seams facing in towards the
body. Weave in the loose ends.

Bikini top

With 2.25mm needles and E, cast on
5 sts.
Rows 1–2: Knit.
Row 3 (dec): K2tog, k1, K2tog (3 sts).
Break yarn and thread through rem sts,
draw up and fasten off.
Make another and stitch each triangle
shape, upside down, next to each other
on the body.

Hair

With 3.25mm needles and F, cast on
12 sts.
Row 1 (inc): K5, kfb in next 7 sts
(19 sts).
Row 2 (dec): Cast off 14 sts, k5
(5 sts).
Row 3: K5.
Row 4 (inc): Cast on 7 sts, kfb in next
7 sts, k5 (19 sts).
Row 5 (inc): K5, kfb in next 14 sts
(33 sts).
Row 7 (dec): Cast off 28 sts, k5
(5 sts).
Row 8: As row 3.
Row 9 (inc): As row 4.
Cast off.
Run a gathering stitch along the short
edge, draw up to gather and attach to
the head with the gathered end at the
front. Stitch around the head so the
hair fits into the neck and the curls
sit neatly down the back and over
the shoulders.

Making up

Stitch the side seams, matching the
pattern and leaving an opening on
both sides 1½in (4cm) from the
bottom edge and 3in (8cm) from
the top for the handle and spout.
Embroider eyes and lips on the
mermaid. Sit the mermaid on the
rock and sew her in place.

This cozy was inspired by the porcelain dolls and elegant fashions of times gone by. Let this lady bring the tradition and grace of afternoon tea to your own table.

Striped dress

Materials

Rowan Pure Wool DK, 100% wool (137yd/125m per 50g ball):
2 balls in 004 Black (A) and 1 × 50g ball in 012 Snow (B)
Rowan Siena 4 ply, 100% cotton (153yd/140m per 50g ball):
Oddments in 652 Cream (C), 674 Black (D), 651 White (E)
Oddments of any 4-ply yarn in pink
Oddments of blue, red and metallic silver yarn or embroidery thread
A pair each of 2.25mm (UK13:US1), 3.25mm (UK10:US3) and 4mm (UK8:US6) needles

Double-ended needle
Darning needle
Small amount of toy stuffing

Tension

22 sts and 30 rows to 4in (10cm) square over st st using 4mm needles. Use larger or smaller needles to obtain correct tension.

Special abbreviations

Kfb: Knit into the front and back of the next stitch (to increase).

Skirt (make 2)

With 3.25mm needles and A, cast on 86 sts.

Work 3 rows in g-st.

Change to 4mm needles and join in B. Work in patt as follows:

Row 1 (RS): K1A, *k6B, k6A; rep from * to last st, k1B.

Row 2 (WS): K1B, *k6A, k6B; rep from * to last st, k1A.

Rep these 2 rows until the work measures 6¾in (17cm), ending with RS facing for next row.

Shape top

Next row (RS) (dec): K1A, *k2togB, k2B, k2togB, k2togA, k2A, k2togA; rep from * to last st, k1B (58 sts).

Next row (WS): K1B, *k4A, k4B; rep from * to last st, k1A.

Next row (dec): K1A, *(k2togB) twice, (k2togA) twice; rep from * to last st, k1B (30 sts).

Next row: K1B, *k2A, k2B; rep from * to last st, k1A.

Next row (dec): K1A, *k2togB, k2togA; rep from * to last st, k1B (16 sts).

Next row: *K1B, k1A; rep from * to end.

Break yarns and thread through remaining sts.

Leave the sts on the yarns.

Head and body

With 2.25mm needles and C, cast on 10 sts and work 8 rows in st st.

Shape shoulders

Next row (inc): Join in D and kfb first, third, fourth, seventh, eighth and tenth sts (16 sts).

Next row: Work in st st for 15 rows. Cast off leaving a long length of yarn in both colours.

Join the back seam of the body up to the shoulder shaping with the black yarn, then sew up the cast-off edge with the seam just stitched sitting at the centre back of the work. Stuff the body, then work a running st around the neck and draw up to gather. Stitch to secure and fasten off. With the cream length of yarn, sew the back seam of the head. Stuff, then run a gathering st around the top of the head, draw up and secure with a few stitches.

Arms (make 2)

With 2.25mm needles and C, cast on 5 sts.

Work 10 rows in st st.

Leave the sts on a spare double-ended needle.

Sleeves (make 2)

With 2.25mm needles and D, cast on 10 sts.

Row 1 (WS): Purl.

Row 2: (K2tog) 5 times (5 sts).

Row 3: Purl.

Row 4: With D and WS of sleeve over RS of arm, knit together each st of the sleeve and those of the arm on the spare needle to join.

Row 5: P1, (kfb) 3 times, p1 (8 sts).

Next row: Work 8 rows in st st. Fasten off and thread end of yarn through these 8 sts, gather up and secure. Stitch the sleeve, cuff and arm seams – no need to stuff. Attach to shoulders with seams facing in towards the body. Weave in loose ends.

Bow

With 2.25mm needles and E, cast on 4 sts.

Rows 1–3: Knit.

Row 4: (K2tog) twice (2 sts).

Row 5: (Kfb) twice (4 sts).

Rows 6–7: Knit.

Cast off leaving a long length of yarn. Weave the yarn through to the decreased centre and wind it around the middle to form the knot. Secure with a couple of stitches and sew to the front of the body at the neck.

Hat

With 2.25mm needles and D, cast on 10 sts and work in g-st for 8 rows.

Row 9 (inc): Kfb in each st (20 sts).

Row 10: Knit.

Row 11: (Kfb, k1) 10 times (30 sts).

Rows 12–13: Knit.

Cast off loosely. Pull the brim into shape and stitch the hat in place, tilting it slightly towards the back of the head.

Flowers

With 2.25mm needles and E, *cast on 4 sts.

Next row: (Cast off 3, cast on 3) 5 times.

Fasten off leaving a length of yarn. Thread the end into the first stitch to join and form the flower shape. Run gathering stitches around the centre and draw up to close the hole*.

Sew onto the hat.

With 2.25mm needles and an oddment of pink 4ply yarn, rep from * to * and stitch to the hands.

Into the centre of each flower, embroider a French knot (see page 361) using an oddment of metallic yarn or embroidery thread. Embroider the features with blue and red yarns or threads.

Making up

Stitch the side seams leaving an opening on both sides 1½in (4cm) from the bottom edge and 2½in (6.5cm) from the top for the handle and spout.

Gather the top of the skirt to fit around the body and attach, ensuring that the openings are arranged at each side of the figure.

Softly coloured sea creatures float across this cotton cozy, while tactile twirls of coral sit on the top. It's the ideal cozy for a tea party by the sea or to remind you of the summer as you snuggle by a winter fire.

Sea life

Materials

Rowan Handknit Cotton, 100% cotton
(93yd/85m per 50g ball):
1 ball in each of 251 Ecru (A), 352 Sea Foam (B)
and 350 Florence (C)
A pair each of 3.75mm (UK9:US5) and 4mm
(UK8:US6) needles
3mm (UK11:USC/2 or D/3) crochet hook
Darning needle

Tension

20 sts and 28 rows to 4in (10cm) square over st st using 4mm needles. Use larger or smaller needles to obtain correct tension.

Pattern notes

The tea cozy is worked using the intarsia method (see page 353), where separate balls of yarn are used for each block of colour. Read chart from right to left on right-side rows and from left to right on wrong-side rows.

Sides (make 2)

With 3.75mm needles and A, cast on 50 sts.

Knit 3 rows.

Change to 4mm needles and with RS facing follow chart from row 1 until row 32 has been completed.

With RS facing for next row and at the same time following chart, decrease 1 st at each end of next and 3 foll alt rows then on foll 5 rows (32 sts).

Cast off 2 sts at the beg of next 4 rows.

Cast off remaining 24 sts.

Twirls (make 5)

With C and 3mm crochet hook, make 19 ch.

Row 1: Work 1 dc into 2nd ch from hook and each of the remaining ch, turn.

Row 2: 1 ch, 4dc into each dc to last 3dc of row, sl st into each of the remaining dc.

Fasten off.

Twist each twirl to tighten the curl.

Making up

Press sides as given on ball band.

Sew up sides of the cozy leaving a gap of 3½in (9cm) for the spout and 4in (10cm) for the handle, also leaving centre top 1¼in (3cm) open.

Gather together all the twirls with the narrower end at the base. Using a length of yarn, thread through all the twirls, wrapping the yarn around to form a bundle, pull tight and secure.

Place this bundle into the 1¼in (3cm) space left open at the top of the cozy.

Close up the gap and sew up, securing the twirls at the same time.

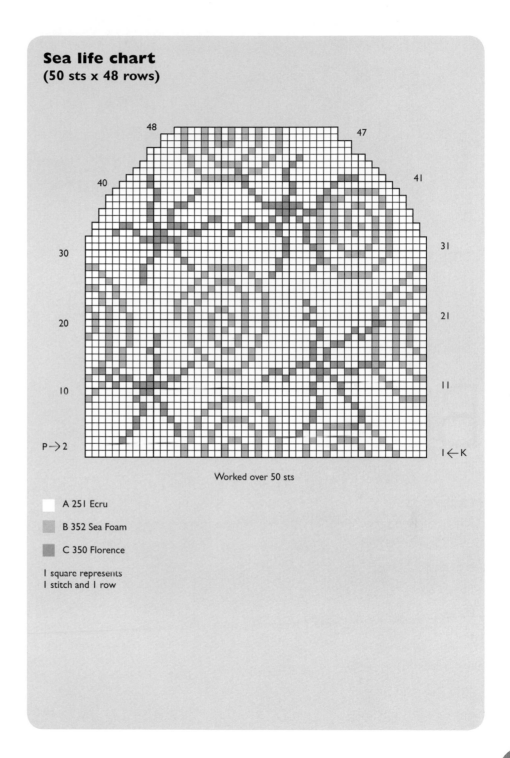

Sea life chart
(50 sts x 48 rows)

Worked over 50 sts

☐ A 251 Ecru

▨ B 352 Sea Foam

▨ C 350 Florence

1 square represents
1 stitch and 1 row

This attractive tea cozy is in the style of a beach hut in bright, fresh colours which sits on the sand under the sun, with seagulls flying around. After a bracing walk on the beach, it's the perfect time for a nice cup of tea!

Beach hut

Materials

Rowan Handknit Cotton, 100% cotton
(93yd/85m per 50g ball):
2 balls in 251 Ecru (A)
1 ball in each of 349 Ochre (B), 219 Gooseberry (C) and
352 Sea Foam (D)
Small amount of black for embroidery
A pair of 5mm (UK6:US8) needles
Darning needle

Tension

17 sts and 23 rows to 4in (10cm) square over st st using 5mm needles and yarn double. Use larger or smaller needles to obtain correct tension.

Pattern notes

Yarn is used double throughout. The tea cozy is worked using the Fair Isle method (see page 352) and also the intarsia method (see page 353), where separate balls of yarn are used for each block of colour. Read chart from right to left on right-side rows and from left to right on wrong-side rows.

Sides (make 2)

With 5mm needles and B double, cast on 39 sts.
Knit 3 rows.
Break off B, join in A.
Row 1: K14A, work next 11 sts as set in chart row 1, k14A.
Row 2: K1A, p13A, work next 11 sts as set in chart row 2, p13A, k1A.
These 2 rows set the pattern. Continue to follow chart to row 20, ending with RS facing for next row.

Shape top

Row 21: Using A, k1, (k2tog, k2) 3 times, k1, work next 11 sts as set in chart, using A, k1, (k2, k2tog) 3 times, k1 (33 sts).
Rows 22–24: Work rows from chart as set.
Row 25: Using A, k1, (k2tog, k1) 3 times, k1, work next 11 sts as set in chart, using A, k1, (k1, k2tog) 3 times, k1 (27 sts).

Rows 26–28: Work rows from chart as set.

Cont using A only.

Row 29: K1, (k2tog) 5 times, k5, (k2tog) 5 times, k1 (17 sts).

Rows 30–32: Work 3 rows in st st.

Row 33: K1, (k2tog) 3 times, sl1, k2tog, psso, (k2tog) 3 times, k1 (9 sts).

Row 34: K1, p to last st, k1.

Cast off.

Making up

Press pieces according to ball band instructions.

Embroider birds in black around top of beach hut using one long straight stitch then a small stitch to secure it, pulling it down to form wing shapes.

Sew side seams for 1⅕in (4cm) from cast-on edge, leaving openings of approx. 4in (10cm) for handle and spout, join rem seam.

Pompom

Cut two circles of card measuring 1¾in (4.5cm) outside, ¾in (2cm) inside. Make a pompom approx. 2in (5cm) in size (see page 363). Sew securely to top centre.

Beach hut chart
(11 sts x 28 rows)

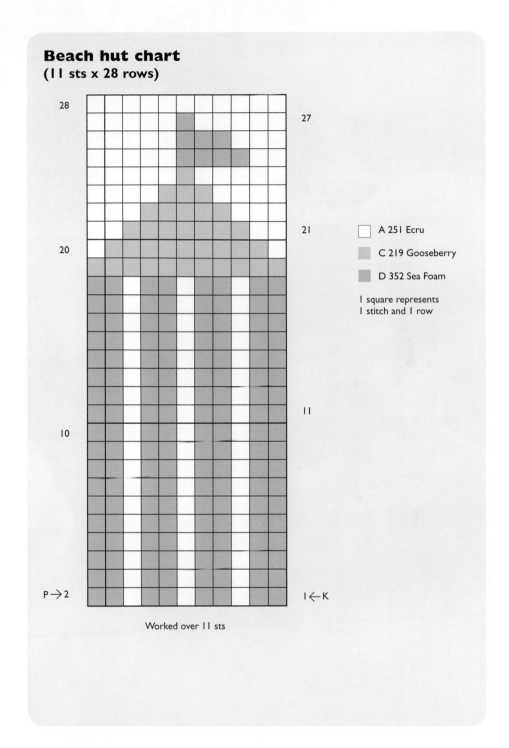

A 251 Ecru

C 219 Gooseberry

D 352 Sea Foam

1 square represents
1 stitch and 1 row

Worked over 11 sts

This charming owl made in a crocheted cluster pattern will bring
a smile to everyone's face at the breakfast table. Sewn-on buttons
enhance the roundness of his eyes, and the chirpy beak adds character.

Wise owl

Materials

Rico Design Fashion Nature DK, 80% acrylic, 10% wool,
5% alpaca, 5% viscose (254yd/233m per 50g ball):
1 ball in 008 Camel (A)
1 ball in 001 Beige (B)
Rico Design Essentials Merino DK, 100% merino wool
(131yd/120m per 50g ball):
Small amount in 023 Grey Blue (C)
Rico Design Essentials Soft Merino Aran, 100% merino wool
(109yd/100m per 50g ball):
Small amount in 070 Mandarin (D)
4mm (UK8:USG/6) crochet hook

3.5mm (UK9:USE/4) crochet hook
2 × ½in (1.25cm) buttons
Tapestry needle
Sewing needle
Sewing thread in co-ordinating colour

Tension

9 V granite clusters sts and 18 rows to 4in (10cm) square
over V granite pattern using 4mm hook and Rico Design
Fashion Nature DK. Use a larger or smaller hook if necessary
to obtain the correct tension.

Special abbreviations

MC: Magic circle (see page 359).

Tea cozy sides (make 2)

Row 1: With 4mm hook and A, make 36ch.

Row 2: (1dc, 1ch, 1dc) in 3rd ch from hook, *miss 1ch, (1dc, 1ch, 1dc) in next ch; rep from * to last ch st, 1dc in last ch, turn (17 V shell clusters).

Row 3: 1ch, *1dc, 1ch, 1dc into 1 sp of next cluster; rep from * to end, 1dc in turning ch, turn (17 V clusters). Row 3 forms the pattern. Follow the following colour sequence:

Rows 4–6: Work 3 rows in patt.

Rows 7–9: Change to B, work 3 rows in patt.

Rows 10–14: Change to A, work 5 rows in patt.

Rows 15–17: Change to B, work 3 rows in patt.

Rows 18–22: Change to A, work 5 rows in patt.

Row 23: Change to B, 1ch, 1dc into first ch sp, *(1dc, 1ch, 1dc) into 1 ch sp of next cluster; rep from * 14 times, 1dc in last ch sp, 1dc in turning ch, turn (15 V clusters).

Row 24: 1ch, miss 1dc *(1dc, 1ch, 1dc) into 1 ch sp of next cluster; rep from * in rest of ch sps, miss 1dc, 1dc in turning ch, turn (15 V clusters).

Row 25: 1ch, *(1dc, 1ch, 1dc) into 1 ch sp of next cluster; rep from * to end, 1dc in turning ch, turn (15 V clusters).

Row 26: Change to A, 1ch, 1dc into first ch sp, *(1dc, 1ch, 1dc) into 1 ch sp of next cluster; rep from * to last ch sp, 1dc in last ch sp, 1dc in turning ch, turn (13 V clusters).

Row 27: 1ch, miss 1dc *(1dc, 1ch, 1dc) into 1 ch sp of next cluster; rep from * in rest of ch sps, miss 1dc, 1dc in turning ch, turn (13 V clusters).

Row 28: 1ch, 1dc into first ch sp, *(1dc, 1ch, 1dc) into 1 ch sp of next cluster; rep from * to last ch sp, 1dc in last ch sp, 1dc in turning ch, turn (11 V clusters).

Row 29: 1ch, miss 1dc *(1dc, 1ch, 1dc) into 1 ch sp of next cluster; rep from * in rest of ch sps, miss 1dc, 1dc in turning ch, turn (11 V clusters).

Row 30: 1ch, 1dc into first ch sp, *(1dc, 1ch, 1dc) into 1 ch sp of next cluster; rep from * to last ch sp, 1dc in last ch sp, 1dc in turning ch, turn (9 V clusters).

Row 31: 1ch, miss 1dc *(1dc, 1ch, 1dc) into 1 ch sp of next cluster; rep from * in rest of ch sps, miss 1dc, 1dc in turning ch, turn (9 V clusters).
Fasten off and weave in ends.

Eyes (make 2)

Round 1: With 3.5mm hook and C, make an MC, work 8dc, sl st in first dc to join (8 sts).

Round 2: 3ch, 1tr in same st, 2tr into each st, join with sl st (16 sts).

Round 3: Change to B, 3ch, 1tr in same st, 1tr in next st, * 2tr in next st, 1tr in next st; rep from * six times, sl st in 3rd ch, join with sl st (24 sts). Fasten off and weave in ends.

Beak

Row 1: With 4mm hook and D, make 2ch.

Row 2: 2dc in 2nd ch from hook, turn (2 sts).

Row 3: 1ch, 2dc in each st, turn (4 sts).

Row 4: 1ch, 2dc in first st, 1dc in next 2 sts, 2dc in last st, turn (6 sts).

Row 5: 1ch, dc to end, turn (6 sts).

Row 6: 1ch, dc to end (6 sts).
Fasten off and weave in ends.

Making up

Join seams using either slip stitch or whip stitch (see page 356), leaving spaces for the spout and handle openings.
Place eyes on one side of the tea cozy and, using co-ordinating thread, sew to the tea cozy using whip stitch.
Using co-ordinating thread, sew a button to the centre of each eye.
Using co-ordinating yarn, sew the beak to the same side of the tea cozy using whip stitch.

This cozy is adorned with a friendly nurse and is bound to cheer up the recipient. Why not swap the colours for other yarns to make different characters, or use different accessories?

Get well soon

Materials

Sirdar Hayfield Bonus DK, 100% acrylic
(306yd/280m per 100g ball):
1 ball in 961 White (A)
1 ball in 969 Bluebell (B)
1 ball in 963 Flesh Tone (C)
Sirdar Funky Fur, 100% polyester (98yd/90m per 50g ball):
1 ball in 548 Chocolate (D)
Oddments of red and black yarn to embroider face
A pair each of 3.75mm (UK9:US5) and 4mm (UK8:US6) needles

Spare needle or stitch holder
Toy stuffing
'Watch' button
Red crayon or blusher
Tapestry needle

Tension

22 sts and 28 rows to 4in (10cm) square over st st using 3.75mm needles and Sirdar Hayfield Bonus DK. Use larger or smaller needles if necessary to obtain the correct tension.

Body (make 2)

With 3.75mm needles and B, cast on
42 sts.

Work in g st for 4 rows.

Row 5: Knit.

Row 6: K2, p38, k2.

Rep rows 5–6 three more times.

Change to A and work in g st for
4 rows.

Rep rows 5–6 for 16 rows.

Work in g st for 4 rows.

Change to B and rep rows 5–6 until
piece measures 5in (12.5cm) from cast-
on edge (or to fit your teapot).

Dec as follows:

Next row: *K5, k2tog; rep from * to
end (36 sts).

Next row: Purl.

Next row: *K4, k2tog; rep from * to
end (30 sts).

Next row: Purl.

Next row: *K3, k2tog; rep from * to
end (24 sts).

Next row: Purl.

Now hold the yarn double to give
strength to the neck.

Next row: *K2, k2tog; rep from * to
end (18 sts).

Break yarn and leave sts on spare
needle or stitch holder.

Work a second piece to match but
do not break yarn.

Head

Using B and holding yarn double, purl
across both sets of sts (36 sts).

Change to C, holding yarn double,
work in st st for 2 rows.

Next row: Now holding yarn single,
*k2, inc; rep from * to end (48 sts).

Work in st st for 23 rows.

Next row: K2tog to end (24 sts).

Next row: P2tog to end (12 sts).

Break yarn, leaving a long tail,
thread tail through these sts and
fasten off securely.

Hair

With 4mm needles and D, cast on
12 sts.
Row 1: K2tog; k to last 3 sts, turn.
Row 2: K to last st, inc in last st.
Row 3: K to last 2 sts, turn.
Row 4: Knit.
Row 5: K across all sts.
Row 6: Knit.
Rep these 6 rows ten times.
Cast off.

Collar

With 3.75mm needles and A, cast on
40 sts.
Work in g st for 3 rows.
Next row: *K2, k2tog; rep from * to
end (30 sts).
Cast off.

Bow

With 3./5mm needles and A, cast on
4 sts.
Work in g st for 8in (20cm).
Cast off.

Hat

With 3.75mm needles and A, cast on
54 sts.
Work in st st for 4 rows.
Cont in st st, cast off 8 sts at beg of
next 2 rows (38 sts).
Dec 1 st at each end of next and every
foll row until 24 sts rem.
Work in st st for 28 rows.
Work in g st for 2 rows.
Cast off.

Bib

With 3.75mm needles and A, cast on
12 sts.
Work in g st for 2 rows.
Work in st st for 11 rows.
Work in g st for 2 rows.
Cast off.

Making up

Sew up the sides of the cozy body,
leaving room for the handle and spout
of the teapot.
Sew up the side of the head.
Stuff and run a gathering thread around
the neck, but do not pull too tight.
Embroider the eyes and mouth, using
the photograph as a guide.
Pinch in nose and catch with a stitch.
Blush cheeks using red crayon
or blusher.
Sew cast-on and cast-off edges of hair
together. The wavy set of row ends is
the face edge. Gather opposite sets of
row ends tightly and fasten. Place onto
head and sew in place (attach each
point of wave to face with a stitch).
Place the collar around the neck and
sew the ends together.
Sew the bib in place at front of body
(as picture). Attach 'watch' button to
one corner.
Join short straight sets of row ends of
hat. Place on head with the seam at the
back. Stitch into place, onto hair. Fold
the hat back and join the cast-off edge
and the cast-on edge. Shape as
in picture.
Make the garter-stitch strip into a bow
and sew onto back of dress, as in
photograph.
Weave in all ends.

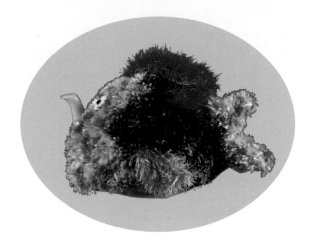

This funky fish cozy uses furry yarn to create a
fluffy texture and bright colours to ensure that this
design is bursting with cheeky character.

Fluffy fish

Materials

Fun fur-look yarn (approx. DK):
2 x 50g balls in each of pink mix (A), blue (B)
1 x 50g ball in magenta (C)
Smooth DK:
Oddments in white and black
A pair of 4mm (UK8:US6) needles
3mm (UK11:USC/2 or D/3) crochet hook

Tension

22 sts and 30 rows to 4in (10cm) square over st st using
4mm needles. Use larger or smaller needles to obtain
correct tension.

Main body (make 2)

With 4mm needles, cast on 36 sts in A, 24 sts in B (60 sts total).

Work in intarsia technique (see page 353) as chart; weave in yarn when changing colours to prevent gaps. Work second side in reverse.

Dec for top:

Next row: *K2tog, k3 rep from * to end.

Next row: Work 1 row.

Next row: *K2tog, k2 rep from * to end.

Next row: Work 1 row.

Next row: *K2tog, k1 rep from * to end.

Next row: Work 1 row.

Next row: *K2tog rep from * to end.

Next row: Work 1 row.
Cast off.

Small fin (make 2)

Using C, cast on 12 sts and work 1 row in g-st.

Next row: K2tog, work to last st, inc 1.

Next row: Inc 1 st, k9 sts, k2tog. Work these 2 rows 5 times (10 rows). Cast off and leave length of yarn to attach fin to main body.

Large fin (make 1)

Using C, cast on 20 sts and work 1 row in g-st.

Next row: K2tog, work to last st, inc 1.

Next row: Inc 1 st, work 17 sts, k2tog. Work these 2 rows 5 times (10 rows). Work 1 row.

Next row: K2tog, work to last st, inc 1.

Next row: Inc 1 st, work 17 sts, k2tog. Work these 2 rows 5 times (10 rows). Work 1 row then cast off.

Fold over and sew together open short ends. Leave long edge open to attach to top of main body closing the opening.

Tail (make 2)

Using A, cast on 20 sts and work 4 rows in g-st.

Next row: K9 k3tog, knit to end. Working on first 9 sts:

Next row: Knit.

Next row: K7 k2tog.

Next row: K6 k2tog.

Next row: K5 k2tog.

Next row: K4 k2tog.

Next row: K3 k2tog.

Next row: K2 k2tog (3 sts).

Fluffy fish chart
60 sts x 36 rows

Work in st st. Each square = 1 st and 1 row.

Read RS rows from R to L and WS (purl) rows from L to R.

Second side to be worked in reverse.

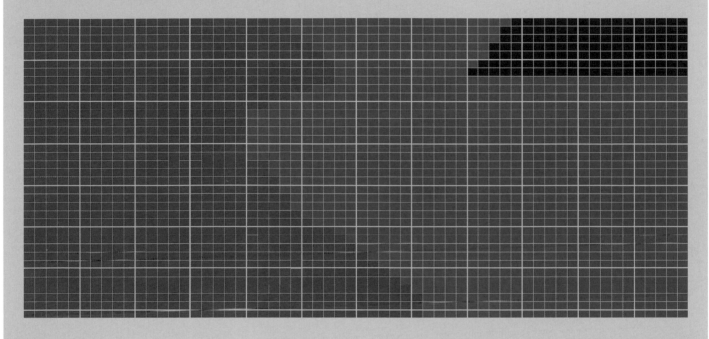

■ A

■ B

■ C

Next row: K3tog.

Re-join yarn at centre and complete the other side with first dec row on first row: K2tog k7.

Next row: Knit 1 row etc.

Eyes (make 2)

With 3mm hook, work a white circle in dc until 1in (2.5cm) across. Work a large French knot in black in centre of eye. You can make the eye from white felt and embroider a black centre.

Making up

Sew up main body leaving holes for the handle and spout. Attach eyes and fins. Make sure that the pattern is symmetrical on both sides to look like a fish.

This quirky striped octopus design is worked in a pretty feather and fan pattern. Not only will it keep your tea hot, it is guaranteed to bring a smile to your face at any time of day.

Octopus

Materials

Sirdar Snuggly DK, 55% nylon, 45% acrylic
(191yd/175m per 50g ball):
1 ball 0392 Party Mix Pink (A)
Sirdar Snuggly Pearls DK, 53% nylon, 43% acrylic, 4% polyester
(186yd/170m per 50g ball):
1 ball in 0302 Pearly Pink (B)
A pair of 3.25mm (UK10:US3) needles
A set of 3.25mm (UK10:US3) double-pointed needles
1 x large black buttons
Oddment of red yarn
Stuffing

Tension

Not critical for this project. One rep of patt measures just over 6¼in (16cm) in width.

Legs (make 4 in each colour)

Using double-pointed needles, cast on 1 st.

Row 1: Knit into each st twice (2 sts).

Row 2: Push the 2 sts to the end of the needle. RS still facing k1, m1, k1.

Row 3: Push the 2 sts to the end of the needle. RS still facing k2, m1, k1.

Row 4: Push the 2 sts to the end of the needle. With RS still facing k3, m1, k1.

Row/round 5: K2 onto first dpn, k2 onto second dpn, k into final st twice using the third dpn. Place a marker after the sts on the third needle.

Round 6: Knit.

Round 7: K1, m1, k1 on needle 1, knit rest of round.

Round 8: K3, k1, m1, k1 on needle 2, knit rem sts.

Round 9: K6, k1, m1, k1 on needle 3.

Round 10: K2, m1, k1 on needle 1, knit rem sts.

Round 11: K4, k2, m1, k1 on needle 2, knit rem sts.

Round 12: K8, k2, m1, k1 on needle 3. Cont in this way, inc 1 st on each round, until there are 36 sts in total. Work in rounds without dec until leg measures 5in (13cm).

Finishing legs

Slip 6 sts from the middle needle onto each of the other needles. Stuff leg lightly. Hold the two needles parallel and, taking 1 st from each needle, k2tog across row. Place rem sts on a holder.

Body (make 2)

With 3.25mm needles and A, cast on 74 sts and work in feather and fan pattern throughout the body.

Feather and fan pattern

(Alternate between A and B every 4 rows)

Row 1 (RS): Using A, knit.

Row 2: Purl.

Row 3: K1, *(k2tog) 3 times, (yo, k1) 6 times, (k2tog) 3 times; rep from * to last st, k1.

Row 4: Purl.

These 4 rows form patt.

Grafting on the legs

Row 5: Using B, k1, then foll the k2tog method used to seal the legs, *(graft a light pink leg to work over foll 18 sts; graft a dark pink leg to work over the next 18 sts) rep from * to last st, k1.

Row 6: Purl.

Row 7: K1, *(k2tog) 3 times, (yo, k1) 6 times, (k2tog) 3 times; rep from * to last st, k1.

Row 8: Purl.

Beg with row 1, rep the feather and fan patt, changing cols as appropriate and ending with a 4th row, until work measures just over 5in (13cm).

Shape top

Row 1 (RS): Knit.

Row 2: Purl.

Row 3: K1, *(k2tog) 3 times, k1, (yo, k1) 5 times, (k2tog) 3 times; rep from * to end.

Row 4: Purl.

Row 5: Knit.

Row 6: Purl.

Row 7: K1, *(k2 tog) 3 times, (yo, k1) 4 times. (k2tog) 3 times; rep from * to last st, k1.

Row 8: Purl.

Row 9: Knit.

Row 10: Purl.

Row 11: K1, *(k2tog) 3 times, (yo, k1) twice, (k2tog) 3 times; rep from * to last st, k1.

Row 12: Purl.

Row 13: Knit.

Row 14: Purl.

Row 15: K1, *(k2tog) twice, (yo, k1) twice, (k2tog) twice; rep from * to last st, k1.

Row 16: Purl.

Row 17: Cont with colour from the previous row, k2tog to end.

Cast off.

Making up

Press the two sides, avoiding the legs. Join, leaving gaps for spout and handle. Attach the buttons to one side at the point where decs began. Using red yarn, chain stitch the mouth.

This mouthwatering trio of designs look good enough
to eat. The fondant fancy makes the perfect complement
to good old-fashioned tea and cakes.

Fondant fancy

Materials

Tawny Family Favourites DK, 100% acrylic
(328yd/300m per 100g ball):
1 ball in 0001 White 1 (A)
James C Brett Top Value DK, 100% acrylic
(317yd/290m per 100g ball):
1 ball in 8412 Lemon, 8421 Pink or 8410 Brown (B)
Oddments of dark brown or white yarn for the stitched
icing drizzle
A pair of 5.5mm (UK5:US9) needles

Tension

16 sts and 22 rows to 4in (10cm) square over st st using
5.5mm needle and double yarn, unstretched. Use larger or
smaller needles to obtain correct tension.

Next row: Purl.
Next row: K2, *(k2tog, k1); rep from * to last 4 sts, k2tog, k2 (21 sts).
Next row: Purl.
Next row: (k2tog) five times, k1, (k2tog) five times (11 sts).
Cut yarn leaving a long tail and draw through sts, pulling tight.

Nobble

Using B double, cast on 20 sts.
Beg knit, st st 2 rows.
Next row: K2tog across row (10 sts).
Cut yarn leaving a long tail.
Draw yarn through sts and pull tight, then sew up seam.

Making up

Sew down top seam to match the other side. Join lower edge to allow room for handle and spout. Attach the nobble to top of cake. Using dark brown or white yarn, embroider the icing drizzle in chain stitch.

Tip
The cozy is shown in all three colour variations but you can choose your own. The 'nobble' can be made in red to look like a cherry if you prefer!

First side

Yarns are used double throughout.
Using 5mm needles and A double, cast on 34 sts using the thumb method.
Work 20 rows in k1, p1 rib.
Break off yarn.
Change to B used double.
Next row: Knit 5, *(k2tog, k5); rep from * to last 8 sts, k2tog, k6 (30 sts).
Next row: Purl.
Beg knit, st st 6 rows.**
Break off yarn and leave sts on a holder.

Second side

Work as for first half to **.
Next row: With RS facing, knit across all sts from both halves (60 sts).
Next row: Purl.
Next row: K2, *(k2tog, k4); rep from * to last 4 sts, k2tog, k2 (50 sts).
Next row: Purl.
Next row: K2, *(k2tog, k3); rep from * to last 3 sts, k2tog, k1 (40 sts).
Next row: Purl.
Next row: K1, *(k2tog, k2); rep from * to last 3 sts, k2tog, k1 (30 sts).

Techniques

Here you'll find out everything you need to get started, including materials and equipment.
Also covered are all of the techniques used for knitting, crocheting, sewing up your work
and for adding those finishing touches that make your tea cozy look truly special.

Getting started

Tension

Tension is important as just a slight difference can have a noticeable effect on the size of the finished cozy. If you are a new knitter, it is a good idea to start a habit that will save a lot of time in the end: work a swatch using the chosen yarn and needles. These can be labelled and filed for future reference. The tension required is given at the beginning of each pattern.

Working a swatch

To work a tension swatch, cast on at least 24 stitches using your chosen yarn and needles. Work for about 30 rows until you have produced a piece that is roughly square, then cast off. Press lightly, following the instructions on the ball band. Lay the swatch flat and measure carefully across the central section to check that your stitch count matches that of the pattern.

Materials and equipment

Yarn

Cozies may be made in a huge variety of yarns. Wool or wool-mix yarns have the best insulating properties, but cotton or silk are also good. If you are using acrylic yarn, you may prefer to choose one of the thicker designs, or one that has a lining. Cozies are also an ideal way to use up oddments of yarn.

Substituting yarn

It is relatively simple to substitute different yarns for any of the projects in this book. One way to do this is to work out how many wraps per inch (wpi) the yarn produces (see table). It is important to check your tension, so begin by working a tension swatch. Then wind the yarn closely, in a single layer, round a rule or similar object, and count how many 'wraps' it produces to an inch (2.5cm). For a successful result, choose a yarn that produces twice, or slightly more than twice, the number of wraps per inch as there are stitches per inch in the tension swatch.

Needles and hooks

Most of the designs in this book are worked back and forth on standard knitting needles. Bamboo needles are useful if you are using a rough-textured yarn as they are very smooth and will help to prevent snags. You may also need double-pointed needles. Where crochet hooks are used, these are standard metal hooks that are widely available.

Tension required	Number of wraps per inch produced by yarn
8 sts per in (4-ply/fingering)	16–18 wpi
6.5 sts per in (DK/sport)	13–14 wpi
5.5 sts per in (chunky/worsted)	11–12 wpi

Knitting techniques

Simple cast-on

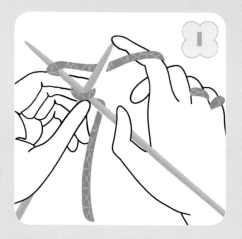

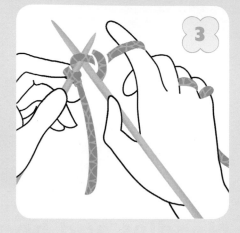

1 Form a slip knot on the left-hand needle. Insert the right-hand needle into the loop and wrap the yarn round it as shown.

2 Pull the yarn through the first loop to create a new one.

3 Slide it onto the left-hand needle. There are now two stitches on the left-hand needle. Continue until you have the required number of stitches.

Cable cast-on

For a firmer edge, cast on the first two stitches as shown above. When casting on the third and subsequent stitches, insert the needle between the cast-on stitches on the left needle, wrap the yarn round and pull through to create a loop. Slide the loop onto the left needle. Repeat to end.

Thumb method cast-on

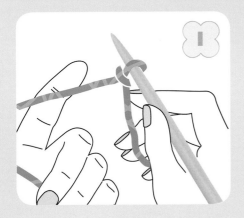

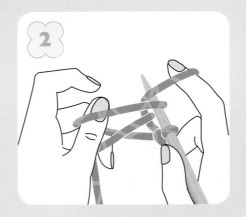

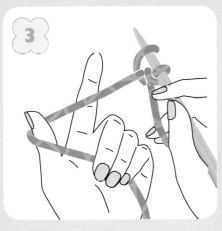

1 Make a slip knot some way from the end of the yarn and place on the needle. Pull the knot tight.

2 Hold the needle in your right hand and wrap the loose tail end round the left thumb, from front to back. Push the needle point through the thumb loop from front to back. Wind the ball end of the yarn round the needle from left to right.

3 Pull the loop through the thumb loop, then remove your thumb. Gently pull the new loop tight using the tail yarn. Repeat until the desired number of stitches are on the needle.

Casting off

1 Knit two stitches onto the right-hand needle, then slip the first stitch over the second and let it drop off the needle (one stitch remains).

2 Knit another stitch so you have two stitches on the right-hand needle again. Repeat this process until only one stitch remains on the left-hand needle. Break the yarn and thread through the remaining stitch.

Knit stitch

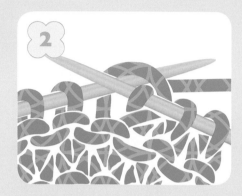

1 Hold the needle with the cast-on stitches in your left hand. Place the tip of the empty right needle into the first stitch and wrap the yarn round as for casting on.

2 Slip the newly made stitch onto the right needle.

3 Pull the yarn through to create a new loop.

Continue in the same way for each stitch on the left-hand needle.

To start a new row, turn the work to swap the needles and repeat steps.

Purl stitch

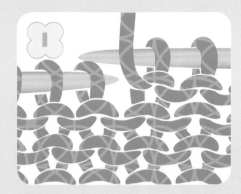

1 Hold the yarn at the front of the work as shown.

2 Place the right-hand needle into the first stitch from front to back. Wrap the yarn around right-hand needle anti-clockwise as shown.

3 Bring the needle back through the stitch and pull through.

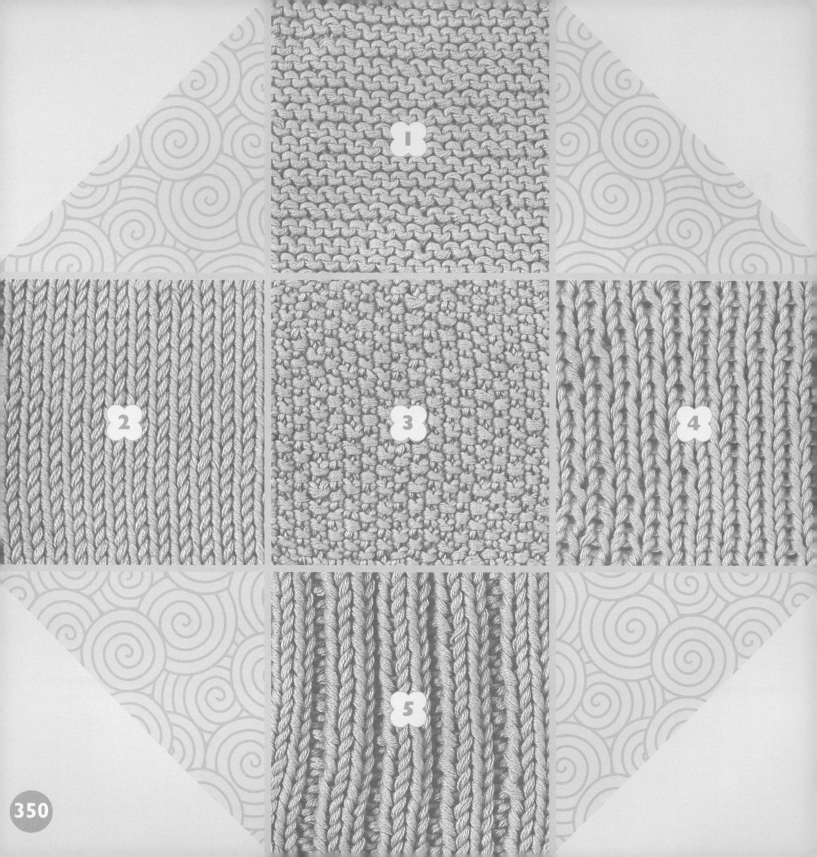

1 Garter stitch

Knit every row.

2 Stocking stitch

Knit on right-side rows and purl on wrong-side rows.

3 Moss stitch

With an even number of stitches:

Row 1: (K1, P1) to end.

Row 2: (P1, K1) to end.

Repeat rows 1 and 2 to form pattern.

With an odd number of stitches:

Row 1: *K1, P1, rep from * to last st, K1.

Repeat to form pattern.

4 Single rib

With an even number of stitches:

Row 1: *K1, p1* rep to end.

Repeat for each row.

With an odd number of stitches:

Row 1: *K1, p1, rep from * to last st, k1.

Row 2: *P1, k1, rep from * to last st, p1.

5 Double rib

Row 1: *K2, p2, rep from * to end.

Repeat for each row.

Colour knitting

Fair Isle

Fair Isle knitting uses the stranding technique, which involves picking up and dropping yarns as they are needed but, unlike intarsia, they are then carried across the row. Loops are formed along the back of the work, which should not exceed about 5 stitches in length. Make sure the loops are of even tension, otherwise your fabric may pucker.

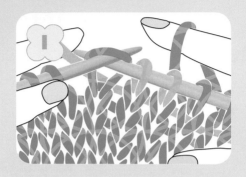

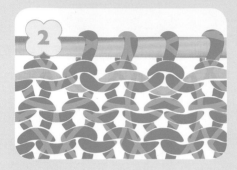

1 Start knitting with the first colour (A), which is dropped when you need to incorporate the second colour (B). To pick up A again, bring under B and knit the next stitch with A.

2 To pick up B again, drop A, bring B over A and knit the next stitch with B.

Reading charts

Most charts are shown in squares, with each square representing one stitch. Charts are usually marked in sections of ten stitches, which makes counting easier. When working in stocking stitch on straight needles, read the chart from right to left on knit (RS) rows and from left to right on purl (WS) rows. Check carefully after every purl row to make sure pattern stitches are in the right position.

Intarsia

Blocks of colour are created by using the intarsia technique of twisting the yarns at the back of the work with each colour change (see diagram above). It is better to wind a small amount of yarn onto bobbins rather than using whole balls to prevent tangling. They are smaller and can hang at the back of the work out of the way. Once finished, the ends are woven in at the back and pressed carefully under a damp cloth to help neaten any distorted stitches.

Felting

Sew in yarn ends carefully. Place items to be felted in a net bag or pillowcase in the drum of a washing machine. Add a bath towel or a pair of jeans to provide the friction necessary for felting. Add a small quantity of washing powder and run through one full cycle at 104°F (40°C). Remove the felted item(s) and check that they have felted sufficiently. Pull gently into required shape and leave to dry naturally.

Felting will reduce the size of a knitted item by up to one third. If work does not felt sufficiently on one cycle, repeat the process. If items seem too small after felting, ease gently to make them bigger. Remember that perfect results can be guaranteed only when using natural, untreated wool yarn. 'Superwash' treated wool will not felt, and wool blends may not felt. If in doubt, test a sample square of your chosen yarn.

Cable stitch

With the help of a cable needle, these decorative stitches are quite straightforward. Stitches are slipped onto the needle and then knitted later to create the twists.

Front cable worked over 4 sts (cab4f)

1 Slip the next 2 sts onto a cable needle and hold in front of work.

2 Knit the next 2 stitches from the left needle as normal, then knit the 2 sts from the cable needle.

Back cable worked over 4 sts (cab4b)

Slip the next 2 sts onto a cable needle and hold at back of work.

Knit the next 2 sts from the left needle as normal, then knit the 2 sts from the cable needle.

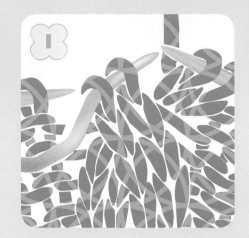

Loop stitch

K1 without slipping st off L needle. Bring yarn to front (yf) between needles. Wrap yarn around left thumb to form a loop. Bring yarn to back (yb), between the needles, and knit the same stitch again, this time slipping to R needle (2 sts now on R needle). Lift first st over second st and drop it off the needle.

Finishing off

Sewing up seams

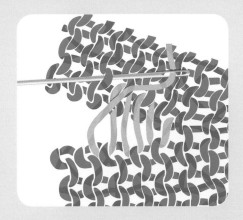

Stocking-stitch joins

When joining stocking-stitch pieces, use mattress stitch for an invisible seam and a neat finish. After pressing, place the pieces side by side with right sides facing. Starting at the bottom, secure the yarn and bring the needle up between the first and second stitch on one piece. Find the corresponding point on the other piece and insert the needle there. Keep the sewing-up yarn loose as you work up the seam, then pull tight.

Garter-stitch joins

It is easier to join garter stitch as it has a firm edge and lies flat. Place the edges of the work together, right sides up, and see where the stitches line up. Pick up the bottom loops of the stitches on one side of the work and the top loops of the stitches on the other side. After a few stitches, pull gently on the yarn. The stitches should lock together and lie completely flat. The inside of the join should look the same as the outside.

Slip stitch

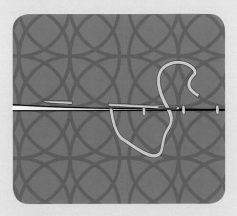

This stitch is used to join two folded edges or to fasten a lining inside a knitted project. Fasten the thread and working from right to left bring the needle up through one folded edge and then back through the other piece of fabric to make a tiny stitch. Continue along the row, running the thread between the fold so that it doesn't show.

Whip stitch

1 Start with the right sides of your pieces facing and the edges to be seamed together. Use matching yarn for an invisible seam. Insert the sewing needle from the right side through the first edge stitch on the right-hand piece and through the first stitch on the left-hand piece from the wrong side.

2 Pull the yarn through. Carry the yarn over the top of the work and insert needle into next stitch on each piece in the same way.

3 Repeat this process, taking up one stitch from each edge with each stitch.

Backstitch

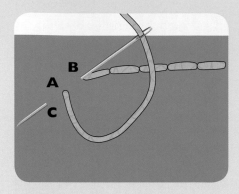

Make a knot to secure yarn at back of work. Bring the needle up to point A, insert at point B, and bring back up at point C. Repeat, keeping the stitches an even length.

Crochet techniques

Chain stitch (ch)

1 With hook in right hand and yarn resting over middle finger of left hand, pull yarn taut. Take hook under then over yarn.

2 Pull the hook and yarn through the loop whilst holding slip knot steady. Repeat action to form a foundation row of chain stitch.

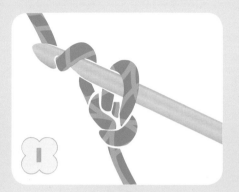

Slip stitch (sl st)

1 Slip the crochet hook under the top two strands of the V of the first stitch of the row.

2 Wrap the yarn around the hook and draw it back through both the V and the loop on the hook.

Double crochet (dc)

1 Start by placing hook into a stitch. Wrap new yarn round the hook and draw loop back through work towards you. There should now be two loops on the hook.

2 Wrap the yarn around hook once more, then draw through both loops. There should now be one loop left on the hook. One double crochet stitch is now complete. Repeat as required.

Half treble (htr)

1 Wrap yarn around hook and then place into a stitch. Wrap yarn around hook and then draw the loop through. Three loops should now be on the hook.

2 Wrap yarn around hook again and draw through the three loops. There should be one loop remaining on the hook.

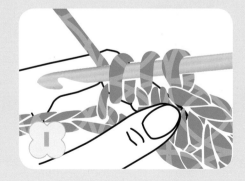

Treble crochet (tr)

Follow instructions for half treble until there are three loops on the hook.

1 Catch the yarn with hook amd draw through two of the loops.

2 Catch yarn again and draw it through the remaining two loops.

Double treble (dtr)

Follow instructions for half treble until there are three loops on the hook.

1 Wrap yarn around hook twice and then place into a stitch.

2 Wrap yarn around hook and then draw the loop through (four loops should now be on the hook).

3 Catch the yarn and draw through two of the loops.

4 Catch yarn again and draw it through two loops.

5 Catch the yarn once more and draw through the remaining two loops.

Magic circle

Use a magic circle to make a very tight centre.

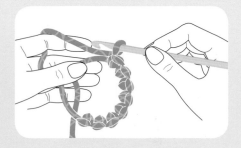

1 Make a half-formed slip knot.

2 Make all the first-round stitches into the circle.

3 Pull the end tight after completing one round.

Finishing touches

Blanket stitch

Work from left to right. The twisted edge should lie on the outer edge of the fabric to form a raised line. Bring needle up at point A, down at B and up at C with thread looped under the needle. Pull through. Take care to tighten the stitches equally. Repeat to the right. Fasten the last loop by taking a small stitch along the lower line.

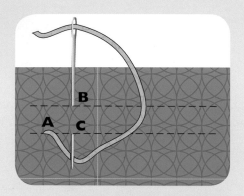

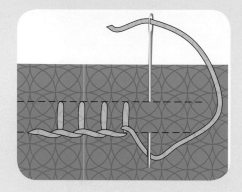

Cross stitch

1 Start from the top left of the stitch, then bring the needle through from the bottom, holding the tail at the back of the thread.

2 Bring the thread down to the lower right corner.

3 Take it back up through the upper right and down through the lower left, forming an X. Each time you should pull the thread all the way through so that it is flush with the fabric surface.

4 Start your next stitch so it uses two of the same holes as the first one.

French knots

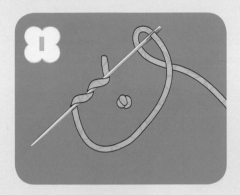

Work in any direction.

1 Bring needle to RS of fabric. Holding thread taut with finger and thumb of left hand, wind thread once or twice around needle tip.

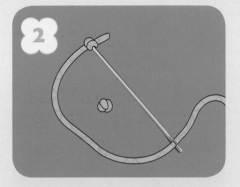

2 Still holding thread, insert needle tip close to the point where you brought the needle out to the RS of work and pull needle to back so that the twist lies neatly on the fabric surface. Repeat as required.

Satin stitch

Make a knot to secure yarn at back of work. Bring needle to front of work. Insert needle from front to back, forming a stitch the length required. Repeat until there are enough stitches for the motif you are doing.

Making an I-cord

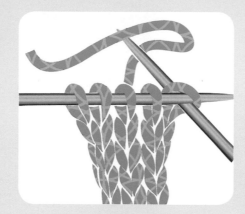

Using double-pointed needles, cast on the required number of sts – typically 5 sts. Do not turn work. Slide sts to the opposite end of the needle, then take the yarn firmly across the back of work. Knit sts again. Repeat to desired length. Cast off, or follow instructions in pattern. An I-cord is often grafted to stitches left on a needle after working another part of the pattern.

Making a pompom

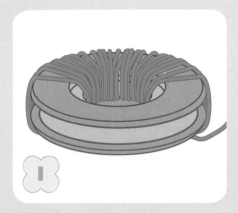

1 Cut out two cardboard circles a little smaller in diameter than the pompom you want. Make a hole in the middle of both about a third of the diameter. Place both circles together and thread lengths of yarn through the central hole, wrapping evenly round the outer edge until the card is completely covered. Use one or more colours for different effects. Continue working in this way until the centre hole is only a pinprick.

2 With sharp-ended scissors, cut all around the edge of the circle, slicing through all the strands of yarn.

3 Now ease a length of yarn between the card discs and tie very firmly around the centre, leaving a tail for sewing. You have now secured all the strands of yarn around the middle. Ease the card discs away from the pompom and fluff out all the strands. Trim any loose or straggly ends.

Making a tassel

1 Cut a piece of stiff card so the height is the required length of your tassel. Wrap the yarn round it several times, depending on how full you require the tassel to be. Secure this bundle with a separate length of yarn threaded through at one end and tied to leave long ends. Cut through the bundle at the opposite end.

2 Keeping the strands folded in half, remove the card. About a quarter of the way down from the fold, wind a separate length of yarn a few times round the whole bundle, including the long ends of the tie, to form the head of the tassel. Tie the two ends of this length of yarn together tightly. Trim all the ends of yarn at the base of the tassel to give a tidy finish.

Abbreviations

alt	alternate
approx.	approximately
beg	beginning
blo	back loop only
cab4b	cable over four stitches holding two stitches at back of work
cab4f	cable over four stitches holding two stitches at front of work
ch	chain stitch
ch sp	chain space
cm	centimetre(s)
cont	continue
dc	double crochet
dec	decrease
dpn(s)	double-pointed needle(s)
foll	following
g	gram(s)
g-st	garter stitch
htr	half treble
in	inch(es)
inc	knit into front and back of stitch
k	knit
k2tog	knit two stitches together
k2tog tbl	knit two stitches together through the back loop
k3tog	knit three stitches together
k-wise	knit-wise

m	metre(s)
M1	make stitch by picking up strand of yarn that runs between stitch just worked and next stitch on LH needle
M1L	insert left-hand needle, from front to back, under strand of yarn that runs between stitch just worked and next stitch on the left-hand needle. Knit this stitch through the back loop
M1R	insert left-hand needle, from back to front, under strand of yarn that runs between stitch just worked and next stitch on the left-hand needle. Knit this stitch through the front loop
MB	make bobble
MC	magic circle
mm	millimetre(s)
p	purl
p2tog	purl two stitches together
p3tog	purl three stitches together
patt	pattern
PB	place bead
pm	place marker
psso	pass the slipped stitch over
p-wise	purl-wise
rem	remain(ing)
rep	repeat
rev	reverse

RS	right side
skpo	slip one stitch, knit one stitch, pass the slipped stitch over
sl	slip
sl2, k1, p2sso	slip two stitches, knit one stitch, then pass both slipped stitches over the knit stitch
sm	slip marker
sl st	slip stitch
sp	space
ssk	slip two stitches knitwise; knit these two stitches together through the back of the loops
st st	stocking stitch
st(s)	stitch(es)
tbl	through back of loop
tog	together
tr	treble
tr2tog	treble two stitches together
W&T	wrap and turn
WS	wrong side
wyf	with yarn in front
yb	yarn back
yd	yards
yf	yarn forward
*	work instructions following *, then repeat as directed
( )	repeat instructions inside brackets as directed

Conversions

Knitting needle sizes

UK	Metric	US
14	2mm	0
13	2.25mm	1
12	2.75mm	2
11	3mm	–
10	3.25mm	3
–	3.5mm	4
9	3.75mm	5
8	4mm	6
7	4.5mm	7
6	5mm	8
5	5.5mm	9
4	6mm	10
3	6.5mm	10.5
2	7mm	10.5
1	7.5mm	11
0	8mm	11
00	9mm	13
000	10mm	15

Crochet hook sizes

UK	Metric	US
14	2mm	B/1
12	2.5mm	C/2
11	3mm	–
10	3.25mm	D/3
9	3.5mm	E/4
8	4mm	G/6
7	4.5mm	7
4	1mm	10

UK/US yarn weights

UK	US
2-ply	Lace
3-ply	Fingering
4-ply	Sport
Double knitting	Light worsted
Aran	Fisherman/worsted
Chunky	Bulky
Super chunky	Extra bulky

UK/US crochet terms

UK	US
Double crochet	Single crochet
Half treble	Half double crochet
Treble	Double crochet
Double treble	Triple crochet

Acknowledgements

The publishers would like to thank the following people for their contributions to this book:

DESIGNS

Susan Ainslie
Big top *page152*

Frankie Brown
Double diamonds *page 88*
School tweed *page 148*
Stripes and spots *page168*
Sunflower garden *page 258*

Sian Brown
Beach hut *page 318*
Country cottage *page 236*
Fair Isle hearts *page 30*
Falling leaves *page 254*
Folk flowers *page 42*
Primroses *page 66*
Pink pansies *page 198*
Sea life *page 314*
Winter Fair Isle *page 202*

Patti di Cagli
Simply soft *page 96*
Strawberries & cream *page 74*

Sarah Cox
No frills *page 92*

Paula Coyle
Purple berry *page 84*

Janet Crinion
Get well soon *page 326*

Dee Daniell
Feline friend *page 300*

Diane Dowgill
Cornish ware *page 130*

Charmaine Fletcher
Circus act *page 282*
Little black dress *page 118*
Summer mood *page 214*

Gayle Foster (Woolly Mama)
Black poppy *page 18*
Tea roses *page 46*

Debbie Gore
Colourful cables *page 108*

Nicola Haisley
Battenberg slice *page 172*
Fondant fancy *page 338*

Vikki Harding
Peruvian pompom *page 100*

Rosemary Harper
Sunny delight *page 38*

Alison Howard
All buttoned up *page 138*
Chunky lace *page 104*
Devon violets *page 70*
Elegant entrelac *page 160*
Fancy felt *page 176*
Gerbera *page 54*
Ginger spice *page 122*
Pineapple *page 288*
Strawberry fields *page 224*
Striking stripes *page 164*
Turquoise cables *page 126*
With love *page 34*

Sarah Keen
Contemporary cool *page 134*
Stripy sensation *page 144*

Margaret Kelleher
Beaded beauty *page 80*

Caroline Lowbridge
Sheepish look *page 262*

Joyce Meader
Fluffy fish *page 330*

Vanessa Mooncie
Bluebells *page 26*
Butterflies *page 266*
Fruit basket *page 270*
Grapevine on trellis *page 292*
Mermaid *page 304*
Rococo *page 276*
Rosy posy *page 58*
Striped dress *page 310*
Woodland walk *page 240*

Lucy Norris
I Love Tea *page 50*

Tammie Pearce
Country kitchen *page 220*

Rachel Proudman
Funky punk *page 296*

Pam Soanes
Loopy lamb *page 208*

Nicola Styliancu
Octopus *page 334*

Maud Tabron
Glitter ball *page 114*
Tea squares *page 188*

Anita Ursula-Nycs
Cottage garden *page 250*

Emma Varnam
Cross stitch *page 22*
Granny squares *page 194*
Pretty pompom *page 180*
Shell-pattern stripes *page 156*
Wise owl *page 322*

Colleen Webster
Rainbow bright *page 184*

Gina Woodward
Springwatch *page 244*

Sheila Woolrich
Spring morning *page 232*
Cat & Mouse *page 228*

CHARTS
**Gina Alton, Carol Chambers,
Anni Howard, Vanessa Mooncie,
Emma Varnam**

PATTERN CHECKING
**Gina Alton, Carol Chambers,
Sarah Hatton and Jude Roust**

KNITTING & CROCHET
ILLUSTRATIONS
Simon Rodway

Index

To place an order, or to request a catalogue, contact:

GMC Publications Ltd

Castle Place, 166 High Street, Lewes, East Sussex, BN7 1XU

United Kingdom

Tel: +44 (0)1273 488005

Website: www.gmcbooks.com